WRITTEN INTO THE VOID

YALE UNIVERSITY PRESS | NEW HAVEN AND LONDON

PETER EISENMAN

WRITTEN INTO
THE VOID

SELECTED WRITINGS
1990–2004

with an introduction by JEFFREY KIPNIS

Copyright © 2007 by Peter Eisenman.

All rights reserved.

This book may not be reproduced, in whole or in part, including illustrations, in any form (beyond that copying permitted by Sections 107 and 108 of the U.S. Copyright Law and except by reviewers for the public press), without written permission from the publishers.

Designed by Jean Wilcox
Set in Scala, Scala Sans and Solex type by Amy Storm
Printed in China through World Print

Library of Congress Cataloging-in-Publication Data

Eisenman, Peter, 1932–

Written into the void: selected writings, 1990–2004 / Peter Eisenman; with an introduction by Jeffrey Kipnis.

    p.   cm.

Includes bibliographical references and index.

ISBN: 978-0-300-11111-8 (alk. paper)

1. Eisenman, Peter, 1932—Aesthetics. 2. Architecture. I. Title.

NA737.E33A35   2007

720.1—dc22

2006031001

A catalogue record for this book is available from the British Library.

The paper in this book meets the guidelines for permanence and durability of the Committee on Production Guidelines for Book Longevity of the Council on Library Resources.

10 9 8 7 6 5 4 3 2 1

CONTENTS

	Introduction: Act Two by Jeffrey Kipnis	vi
1	Post/El Cards: A Reply to Jacques Derrida	1
2	The Author's Affect: Passion and the Moment of Architecture	6
3	Unfolding Events: Frankfurt Rebstockpark and the Possibility of a New Urbanism	12
4	The Affects of Singularity	19
5	Folding in Time: The Singularity of Rebstock	25
6	Vision's Unfolding: Architecture in the Age of Electronic Media	34
7	Presentness and the Being-Only-Once of Architecture	42
8	Processes of the Interstitial: Notes on Zaera-Polo's Idea of the Machinic	50
9	Separate Tricks	72
10	Written into the Void	79
11	Diagram: An Original Scene of Writing	87
12	Autonomy and the Will to the Critical	95
13	Mies and the Figuring of Absence	100
14	Blurred Zones	108
15	L'ora che è stata	113
16	A Matrix in the Jungle	120
17	Terragni and the Idea of a Critical Text	126
18	Digital Scrambler: From Index to Codex	133
19	The Wicked Critic	151
	Appendix: Letter from Jacques Derrida to Peter Eisenman	160
	Selected Bibliography: Writings of Peter Eisenman, 1990–2004	169
	Sources	173
	Index	175

INTRODUCTION Act Two

Jeffrey Kipnis

INTRODUCTION

It is odd to introduce this second volume of writings by Peter Eisenman, since I suspect that most who have come to it are forewarned and forearmed. If, on the other hand, you have picked it as a first introduction to Eisenman's thought, I fear no preamble can prepare you for what you are about to encounter. To wade through Eisenman's writing is at best a struggle, and these essays include some of his most viscous. Thus, to those at this juncture who do not already know where they are about to go, my advice is to set this volume aside for the moment. Start with *Inside Out*, the first volume of writings, which contains the architect's more influential texts. Those, too, have their difficulties, but, written with prodigious confidence, their arguments are crisper, the propositions more vivid.

The essays in this book constitute Eisenman's second act, in which the protagonist takes a step that will surely seal his fate, which in his case means his place in history. We must wait for a later act to learn whether Eisenman's choice ends in comedy or tragedy, but this act surely reveals his turning point. In synopsis, this drama concerns an architect whose philosophical disposition borders on compulsion like Raskalnikov, Pangloss, and other characters who think too much. In the first act, a young, arrogant architect proposes to transform architecture from an artistic into an intellectual discipline. Though he muses on larger cultural questions, he focuses his philosophical urge outward, onto his effort to discover how to design a critical architecture. His thought deepens from reflections on solid, void, shift, and shear to deep structure, to absence and presence, to de-centering, to such exotic notions as trace and catachresis, yet at each step he produces an immediate demonstration of his latest thinking in a design. And no matter how difficult the design concept he wrestles with, by the time he has finished, he always declares his undertaking accomplished.

In act two, for reasons that are not clear, other than the dark doubts that stain too much time in thought, his mood changes, he turns inward and begins to think less about *how* to do a critical architecture than *why*. The change is marked in his language, where obscure, existential concepts such as *presentness*, *interiority*, and a *third aura* replace the proliferating conceptual design instruments that plot the first act.

One thing is clear: no outside agent, no colleague, critic, or client forces this change. Though he had convinced few, by the beginning of the second act, his scholarly command of the history and literature of the discipline combined with the originality of his early work to earn him broad respect. No one asked of him a deeper validation of his project than he had already offered. The change was of his own volition even if he really had no choice in the matter. But then, such is the case for most protagonists of modern drama.

These essays brood; a certain stridence unseats the confidence of the earlier writings. Under cover of measured reflection, he plunges again and again into ever more mystifying ruminations beset with inconsistency, self-contradiction, recondite jargon, and dubious reasoning that occasionally ventures to the perilous brink of nonsense. A careful reader cannot help but come to wonder not just "of what" Eisenman speaks, but "to whom?"

Of course, there are approachable writings in this volume, and as always with Eisenman stunning aperçus punctuate challenging passages of expert testimony to harass mainstream architectural thought, particularly when it claims a natural or self-evident legitimacy.

Nor do these essays merely reprise the memorable themes of the early writing, but continue to advance these into new territory, even after forty years:

In essence, then, the idea of critical in this text attempts to open up the question of the language of the formal, to reformulate it through the linguistic analogy of the "text," as a tissue of ever changing traces and interpretations . . .
—"Terragni and the Idea of a Critical Text" (2001)

Written four decades after rumors of Eisenman's strange analysis of Terragni's architecture first began to reverberate through the halls of architectural academia, this statement reiterates the two speculations which together distinguish Eisenman's architectural thinking: (1) that architecture is a language, and (2) that when architecture becomes an intellectually and historically self-conscious discipline, it is no longer just a language, *but a mode of writing*. The architect's first act, the early essays, fanfares those two ideas and commences his dogged pursuit of their consequences. To follow that story, we, like the author himself, must ponder these propositions again and again.

However, like the terminology of semiology itself—which, among other limitations, leaves out the phenomenal, the physical, and the affective dimensions of signs—my use of the term *text* also has both positive and negative implications.

If the affirmation of architecture's textuality that begins the passage proclaims his opera's *idée fixe*, then the self-criticism whispered in this counter-theme sets the mood for the second act, as it introduces the three passions that in this set of essays begin to prick the architect—the phenomenal, the physical, and the affective.

To glimpse how his early thought might stand the test of those passions, Eisenman brings the passage to a close with a refrain of the haunting insight that ever burns his Terragni analysis into the psyche of audiences: the aria of the window, the story of the single pane of glass in the Casa del Fascio different from all others. The 300+ pages of the architect's *Giuseppe Terragni: Transformations, Decompositions, Critiques* stand as one of the most incisive formal analyses in all of modern architecture, but the essence of its idea is perfectly distilled in its brief account of one window.

Such limits are indicated by, for example, the movement of one window, the projecting window on the rear façade of the Casa del Fascio, which can be seen as a microcosm of a critical text. This window, which hinges open in a plane parallel to the vertical face of the building, is functionally and visually obscure. It exists both as a textual notation and as an indication of the elusiveness of such a concept to a purely linguistic interpretation. Its significance is accessible only partially through an analysis of the drawings in the context of a linguistic reading, and only partially through a visual and somatic reading. Without an analysis of the drawings, this window can only be read as a "dumb" compositional device. However, . . . when the reading of the drawings is compared to the visual and somatic experiences—a somatic reading, as it were, of the building—additional readings accrue. In plan, the Casa del

Fascio seems to be a square, and the initial casual experience of the building is as a square. However, an examination of the actual drawn dimensions of the plan reveals that the side façades are slightly shorter than the front and rear façades. And when the one window that does not pivot or rotate diagonally —the one window to puncture an exterior façade plane—is opened outward from the rear façade, the building becomes—at least conceptually—a dimensional square. This can be represented—in a lateral sense—only in a drawn plan or section. *But the experience of the open window that causes the building to be an actual square cannot be known from its representation on paper or screen. The window's eccentricity, its positioned view from below, the details of its mechanism, the gap that it leaves when it is activated depend on an experiential view.* [emphasis added]

In retrospect, forty years later, the insignificant metal hinge that regulates the opening of that one window now rises to challenge the dematerialized conceptuality of Eisenman's original argument. In effect, it becomes Terragni's brushstroke, the inescapable material gesture necessary for the artist to render his idea. With its physicality comes the phenomenal —the rivulet of fresh air that flows around the glass barrier into its unique gap—and the affective—the vague feelings that well for a moment when that one open window is seen half consciously by passersby on the street.[1]

Semiotics' insensitivity to the particular physicality of architecture triggers much of the dramatic conflict in these essays, as, for example, in the exchange between Eisenman and Derrida. Yet, the central crisis coalesces in a darker, more exotic space where mind stirs into metaphysics. A secreted portal leads there from almost every essay, and once we find ourselves in it, we encounter a strange menagerie of concepts and formulations. Presumably, the architect conjures these intellectual concoctions to safeguard architecture from some threat or demon, but, then, on the other hand, whence come these demons in the first place? What are they, why do they haunt architecture, specifically?

Of course, in the demystified sobriety of contemporary discourse, demons only refer to one thing: inner demons that plague a mind. That a bit of familiar Freudian psychoanalysis—no more than has already proved instrumental to modern interpretations of *Hamlet*—might bear on these essays is already suggested by a striking curiosity concerning the essay guiding us thus far. "Terragni and the Idea of a Critical Text" was written as an epilogue for the publication of Eisenman's landmark study of the Italian modernist, a relentless exercise in formal analysis that all but erases Giuseppe Terragni as the agent of his own architecture, not to mention as a once-living being. As noted, four decades separate the completion of the original analysis and its eventual publication, a delay that would have awed even the hesitant Dane. Until the belated publication of the Terragni study, the content of the work circulated from student to student not as text but as gossip and rumor— an odd fate for an opus implicated in architecture's accession to the rank of writing. And by the time the architect finally readied the manuscript for publication, he, like Hamlet, could not but join qualms to it.

For the architect who more than any other has foregrounded intellectual agency to have gained foothold through an aggravated assault on agency itself is an intriguing but all too familiar plot. Thus, Eisenman's calculated assassination of pater Terragni cannot be the central crisis of this second act; that crime merely establishes the character flaw of the protagonist. The crisis arises, rather, from a slow dawning wherein the analyst-architect, looking in a mirror, begins to wonder if he may have unconsciously poisoned his beloved architecture. With writing.

And if there were a contest and he had to compete in measuring the shadows with the prisoners who had never moved out of the cave, while his sight was still weak, and before his eyes had become steady . . . would he not be ridiculous? Men would say of him that up he went and down he came without his eyes; and that it was better not even to think of ascending.
—Plato, *Republic VII*, 517

Eisenman's pursuit of architecture as writing was part and parcel of the development of the "linguistic" school by Rossi, Venturi, Jencks and Baird, Graves, and others. Concerned with architectural meaning, these theorists drew upon the model of language to elaborate the discipline into a comprehensive scheme of semantic elements, syntactic formal relationships, and rhetorical devices, patterns, and idioms. The basic idea is easily grasped in Eisenman's oft-repeated assertion that for architecture, a column is not a structural element, but a signifying device. It is a foregone conclusion that a structural system must successfully support a building, whether with classical columns, frames, or *pilotis*. And to be sure, the architect must grasp the basis of the structural problem to begin to work, much as a composer must grasp the basis of the sound production of any instrument for which he writes music. But solving the structural problem is not the work of the architect, which is rather to explore the other effects that a structural system inevitably produces once the load question is settled. Thus, while from an engineering point of view both *piloti* and classical column are load-bearing elements, from the point of view of architecture as cultural discourse, the classical column and the *piloti* are forever joined in a moral debate: while the former celebrates the distinction between ground and sky—with all the metaphysical, theological, and feudal consequences that entails—the latter eradicates it.

For most of its adherents, the language model served architectural discourse by recuperating intrinsic attributes characteristic of every linguistic community such as continuity, tradition, custom, memory, and locality, values that were perceived to have been unduly relegated by modernism's stylistic creed.[2] Eisenman, keen to secure a role for modernism's legacy of intellection and design speculation within the linguistic scheme, deviates from his colleagues on three fronts. Today, the best known of these, of course, stands evident in the eccentric work that emanates from his practice. The other two are found in his writings: (1) he reads the history of architecture as a record of heresy (by certain architects and scholars) retold as orthodoxy, and (2) he theorizes architecture not just as a language, but as writing. While we consider the latter two without reference to the design work, the three are part and parcel. Thus, many of these essays begin with a critique of one of architecture's conventions or traditions, then follow with a project by the architect intended to explore the heterodox implications of that critique.

Heresy

Eisenman is never so vivid in a graduate seminar as when presenting a pivotal moment in architecture not just as a creative leap, but as an act of heresy, from Alberti's synthesis of sacred temple front with the profane triumphant arch to Tony Garnier's apocryphal expulsion from the Ecole des Beaux-Artes for intentionally misplacing a column. Here the term "heresy" is exactly intended; its essential and distinguishing features are that it occurs with the horizons of orthodoxy and avows in principle its higher purpose, but challenging one of its dogmas. From the perspective of Catholicism, for example, neither an aborigine, nor a Jew, nor an atheist is a heretic; they are *heathen* or *infidel*. Nor is a Catholic heretic who abandons the faith or converts to another, but rather *apostate*. To be a heretic, one must be a baptized Catholic who affirms and practices Catholicism, but in such a way as to defy official church dogma. Heresy, therefore, is not merely a synonym for sin, laxity, or misprision. Rather, in its essence it is a purposeful and precise *theoretical* act of resistance that can only be perpetrated by a well-schooled predicant. Prominent Catholic heresies have elevated Mary to the status of Goddess and variously disputed the divinity of Christ, the infallibility of the pope, and the doctrine of transubstantiation. In 1835, Pope Pius X declared "modernism"—then defined as the love of all things modern above all things ancient—as the most insidious heresy then facing the church.

In those terms, Eisenman is Architecture's consummate heretic, a high priest bent on challenging one dogma after another, but never so far as to deny the faith. Though he does not use the concept of heresy per se, its ratiocinations suffuse his texts, informing such key concepts as criticality and interiority. Often, the heretical imperative is associated with the art critic Rosalind Krauss, a recurring figure in the architect's essays. His conviction that orthodoxy in architecture cannot help but serve entrenched power finds a kindred spirit in Krauss's insistence that the visual arts mount a vanguard resistance to the insidious effects of late-capitalism's forces of commodification.

Writing

At first, Eisenman pursued the linguistic model by sidestepping the semantic tactics favored by his colleagues, to explore the "deep structure" of architecture's grammar, following Noam Chomsky's theories of generative-transformative grammars. That effort gave rise to the architect's disposition toward process-based design and to the experiments with architectural syntax launched in his early houses, traits that persist in the work of his studio to this day. Very soon, however, he shifted his attention from grammar to writing. When one recalls that the anthropological concept of "prehistory" refers to the period before writing, then the reasons that Eisenman so stresses the concept of writing for architecture become more apparent. All languages, written or not, produce continuity, tradition, and custom, but only the sustained, detailed record specific to writing gives rise to history, scholarship, intellection, speculation, criticism, and debate, the elements of discourse.

For Eisenman, a body of written discourse about architecture is a necessary but not sufficient condition. Such a body of writing in art history, after all, engendered the *stylistic-periods* model of architectural history that the linguistic model sought radically to revise, if not to replace. To establish the bona fides of an intellectually based speculative project within the linguistic scheme, architectural design itself must be shown to be a kind of writing.

As the architect begins to shift his focus from language to writing, he gravitates toward the texts of Derrida, the name synonymous with the most radical yet compelling reflection on writing offered by contemporary philosophy. Inevitably, Derrida's ideas infect Eisenman's thought. Noting that the structures and processes that semiotics had identified as the basis of all signification were precisely the same as those associated with phonetic writing's relation to speech, Derrida generalizes the concept of writing into "archi-writing." This provides the architect with the intellectual framework within which to theorize architecture as writing. Concomitantly, the philosopher demonstrates that writing, now the very possibility of meaning, also always destabilizes meaning. Hence, the meaning of any text is intrinsically instable, or as Derrida terms it, "undecidable." He shows that, without exception, supplemental assumptions are always necessary to stabilize the meaning of any particular text. Meaning, therefore, can only be achieved at the expense of writing's intrinsically destabilizing nature. Appealing to the inexorable logic of archi-writing, Derrida argues that the assumptions necessary to stabilize a text are themselves intrinsically instable texts requiring their own supplementation ad infinitum. All texts, therefore, form promiscuous chains of significations that can never terminate in any final, transcendent assumption with the power to stabilize the meaning of the resulting tapestry of chains—a situation expressed in his famous aphorism, "There is nothing outside the text."

This work underscored the significance of Eisenman's distinction between architecture as language and architecture as writing, and girded the architect's suspicions that the orthodoxy of architectural discourse unjustifiably suppressed architectural experimentation. He had long argued that architecture was the language most vested in producing stability as meaning, from the stability of a building's structure to the stability of the patterns of everyday life to the stability of familial, social, and political order and hierarchy. In his view, the orthodoxy of architecture served above all to prop up architecture's ability to engender precisely those meanings. Such was the implication of his idea that an architectural column is not a vertical support but a sign of vertical support; we should now say . . . a sign of the stability of that support. With Derrida's work, his criticisms of that orthodoxy deepened.

Finally, Derrida broaches a crucial question: how then does the meaning of a text—the meaning of a philosophical tract, a novel, a conversation, a building, a scene in a movie—seem immediately stable, apparently immune to a dependency on contingent supplementation? How, for example, does speech seem immediately to mean to a speaker what a speaker intends to say? The answer he offers is to posit an irrepressible "metaphysics of presence" wherein every text is always already supplemented by indefensible assumptions that escape critical scrutiny. This metaphysics of presence, then, is an insidious mechanism through which special interests—intellectual, political, historical, or psychological—covertly operate to instill unjustifiable confidence in the meaningfulness of a text. At its limit, the controversial consequence of the *metaphysics of presence* is that meaning as such in any form, discipline, or medium, though always present, nevertheless always arises strictly in the clandestine service of a special interest. Deconstruction names the inflammatory process of ferreting out and critiquing the operations of this confidence game in every discipline and institution with a vested interest in the meaning of a text—from psychoanalysis, philosophy, literature, and criticism to science, history, and law.

For a time, Derrida's thought on archi-writing so approached Eisenman's on architecture as writing that the two seem almost indistinguishable. Yet, in the essays of the first act, the philosopher of deconstruction remains at a distance, a disembodied authority whose message is transmitted more often than not by oblique reference. As we begin the second act, a more corporeal Derrida has approached, but in an extraordinary act of dramaturgy, the becoming flesh of Jacques Derrida—the meeting of the two men, their yearlong collaboration on the Chora L Work[3] garden for Bernard Tschumi's Parc de La Villette, the flowering of a friendship, and the eruption of a brief but poignant clash in a public exchange of letters—occurs *entr'acte*. With "Post/El Cards . . . " the opening essay of act II, Jacques Derrida has come and gone. Yet in that climactic lacuna a fundamental change occurred. From then on, Derrida, once authority, then man, becomes an apparition, a specter of misdeed who haunts the architect.

Eisenman never again invokes his friend to reinforce his own position; rather, he now scripts the philosopher's arguments[4] through a cunning ventriloquy[5] so as to swerve away from them, slowly withdrawing architecture from archi-writing. Architecture remains writing, but gradually becomes writing unlike any other, in its physicality to be sure, but more in its mysteries, a secret writing, available only to a select cognoscenti: those *inside* architecture. Toward the end of this book, for example, one finds the author narrating a wizards' contest staged in the fifteenth century between Luciano Laurana's Ducal Palace in Urbino and Donato Bramante's Santa Maria Della Pace in Rome.[6] If an elect, one can see two architects conjure space, geometry, concept, matter, and being into alternative metaphysical spells; if not, one will see only the dull corners of two courtyards, their differences trifling if perceptible at all. But then, as Eisenman frequently reminds us, architects love to cloak their powers behind the insignificance of corners.

The metamorphosis of Eisenman's thought is well advanced by the publication of such abstruse texts as "Presentness and the Being-Only-Once of Architecture," "Writing Inside," and "Written into the Void." In them, the crisis of the second act, which is to say, the crisis of architecture as writing, reaches a feverous pitch. Jacques Derrida and Rosalind Krauss modulate from kindred scholars to character foils used to circumscribe the predicament of architecture that now compels the author's thought. If Derrida embodies a conceptual project of writing that should entail architecture but cannot cope with architecture's material passions, then Krauss embodies a project of vigilant intellectual resistance in the visual arts that also should entail architecture but cannot, or at least does not, cope with architecture's own history of effects.

In her book *The Optical Unconscious*, Rosalind Krauss discusses a Jackson Pollock painting in relationship to its position in space. She contends that when a Pollock painting is placed in a horizontal position, . . . it is a "savage work." But the moment the canvas is taken off of the floor and moved to a vertical position on the wall, Krauss continues, it becomes "naturalized," reinstitutionalized and reinscribed into the discourse of painting.

> All of this is said with an uncharacteristic innocence about the possible effect of the floor or the wall on this change in perception. She assumes one can lift things up and down, off and on, without any discussion of why the relationship between floor and wall, or, for that matter, between the floor or the wall and the painting, could cause this to happen. . . . Most of those outside of architecture assume that architectural conventions have a thought-to-be naturalness with respect to such things as walls and floors.
> —"Presentness and the Being-Only-Once of Architecture" (1995)

Even for those as astute as Rosalind Krauss, floor and wall are just floor and wall: ("thought-to-be") natural places to throw rugs and hang pictures. Where, then, is the possibility of a savage architecture, when architecture is that place that innately tames the savage? To address that question, Eisenman must retain the criticality that architecture as writing enables, but can no longer risk Derrida's archi-writing, because its lack of discipline threatens to evaporate architecture into thin air.

As he begins to reformulate his approach to architecture as writing, Eisenman revisits architecture's power to domesticate that he notes in Krauss's book. Having long critiqued architecture's orthodoxy for its urge to reinforce that effect, he now considers that perhaps the power itself constitutes the discipline's singularity. Meanwhile, he defers another intriguing question, for who are those inside architecture, or should we ask where are they? For the moment, let us simply note in passing that the two provocations are issued in the same breath: "Most of *those outside of architecture* assume that architectural conventions have a *thought-to-be naturalness* with respect to such things as walls and floors."

However affecting his break with Derrida might have been, on a personal level it was but a waning of briefly shared interests. On the other hand, a palpable disappointment tints Eisenman's choice of Rosalind Krauss to represent "those outside of architecture." The two not only share a long personal friendship and institutional history—Krauss's seminal journal *October* began under the auspices of the Institute for Architecture and Urban Studies founded by Eisenman—but the architect identifies his project in architecture with hers in the visual arts.

Thus, however mild Eisenman's rebuke of Krauss may seem to most readers, it should send a shudder through supporters of her work, for it unsettles a core premise of *The Optical Unconscious*. In that study, Krauss, much like Eisenman, attempts to fend off the effort by art orthodoxy to embrace belatedly the heretical transgressions of such works as Pollock's drip paintings, Warhol's piss paintings, and Twombly's graffiti paintings by treating them ex post facto as if they had always belonged to that orthodoxy's account of high modernism. She positions the works in question as direct, fundamental attacks on a "vertical gestalt," the privileged position of the eye that establishes the domain of form, drawing, the figure, the mark, and the other intellectual and aesthetic values that determine optical consciousness as high art. The work she considers, on the other hand, stakes out the horizontal, a domain "below culture" associated with sex, violence, and excrement, the stuff of the unconscious.

Her argument unfolds through an insightful articulation of the various works of art in their relation to verticality and horizontality. Yet throughout the book, Krauss treats the *vertical* and *horizontal* uncritically, as natural attributes that derive from an erect body's relation to gravity in abstract space.[7] But the context of verticality and horizontality for all of the paintings she discusses is neither nature nor a body in abstract space; it is always an architectural interior, as if the history of painting's orthodoxies and heresies were not joined inextricably to a parallel history of architecture.

Of course, the book treats a specific set of artworks, and Krauss bears no obligation to acknowledge that architecture might churn with the same critical ferment as art. What is suspect, however, is how she takes architecture for granted given that the specific work she discusses depends so strongly upon it, in particular as the scene of transgression. But in her writing, it either ceases to exist, transcending into pure horizontality or verticality, or serves merely as a medium of convenience, as self-evident as it is irrelevant:

By 1955 Twombly had stopped making paintings with the expressionist's loaded brush and had started using the sharp points of pencils to scar and maul and ravage the creamy stuccoed surface of his canvases instead. He had begun, that is, down the attack route which is that of the graffitist, the marauder, the maimer of the blank wall.[8]

To achieve this scene of violence, Krauss here relies on a synonymy of stucco surface and blank wall. Yet, why was it not also a case of violence when an architect before Twombly first schemed to smother the warm, reassuring face of ruddy brick into a wan, featureless oblivion with stucco?

Her indifference to architecture borders on callous when elsewhere she dubs works such as Richard Serra's molten metal *Splashes* as heir to the horizontal transgressions of Pollock's drip painting, given that Serra explicitly pronounced these as works executed "between floor and wall." Less obvious but perhaps more telling is the supportive role architecture might have played for Krauss in the ambition of *The Optical Unconscious* to contest in the arena of the psyche the abiding influence of Clement Greenberg.

In the name of modernism, Greenberg called for autonomy in the visual arts, nominated painting as the prototype of high art among the visual arts, and endowed "flatness" as the teleological conclusion of a history of painting that reached its apotheosis in modernism.[9] All three are part and parcel of the same dogma, one that Krauss's entire oeuvre struggles to discredit. Pollock's drip paintings are a decisive test. Because Greenberg successfully appropriated Pollock's drip paintings to support his doctrine, of necessity Krauss must wrest away custody and exaugurate them to restore their heretical standing. Architecture might have helped her cause, had she let it.

Greenberg derives his conclusions about flatness by isolating the history of painting as an internal movement of formal influences from one painting to the next, adequate in and of itself, a position that resonates with Eisenman's early studies of Terragni. He does not deny that paintings occur in and reflect a larger context, but holds that the specificity of the discipline is to be found entirely in its characteristic practices. But unlike Eisenman, whose formalist readings were largely intended to overcome the reign of aesthetics in architecture, Greenberg's formalism is joined to his quest for an objectivity of taste, a project born in Kant's *Critique of Judgment*. Historians such as Krauss argue that a broader intellectual context is necessary to understand the formal and material evolution of art practices, hence her appeal to Freud, Bataille, Lacan, and other cultural theorists.

In such a broader context, Greenberg's notions of disciplinary autonomy and his theorization of flatness as the apotheosis of autonomous painting are not quite so compatible, particularly if one considers architecture not as passive background but as influential historical process in its own right. Under the influence of formal perspective, the principle that every painting was a "window view" was well established by the Renaissance. By the nineteenth century, artists start to challenge that principle by abandoning strict perspective, loosening color-edge relations, and otherwise compressing the view into the windowpane itself, a process that cannot be separated from the development of clearer, more reflective, and larger glass panes and the concomitant proliferation of and elaboration upon windows in architecture during the same period. As one historian writes,

The way towards the comprehension of a formal approach, linked purely to the plane and renouncing illusionistic effects of depth (as can already be seen in Matisse's *Porte-fenetre* of 1914) has been "flattened"—in the true sense of the word—in part and above all by the motif of the window in the painting of the nineteenth and twentieth century. . . . Just as the representation of perspective in Western painting began with the idea of observing spatial depth through a window, it came to an end with the idea of regarding the figure of the window as subject of an entirely two-dimensional pictorial architecture.[10]

In this view, flatness in painting would be no more autonomous than its counterpart in modern architecture's horizontal windows and glass walls, both of which are in part treated in terms of painting in architecture's discourse. Less a destiny than a signpost in an ongoing process whose motives and ramifications are always as political as formal, flatness grew out of the dialogue between architecture and painting as but another possibility to explore in the relationship between window and picture.

In Krauss's dogged assault on Greenberg, she everywhere challenges his Kantian assumptions such as flatness. One by one, she brings each of these assumptions to its knees by trespassing beyond the limited horizons of art history proper to examine the institutional, economic, and psychological forces that produced them.

In that spirit, if one sets aside Krauss's own metaphysical abstractions and reads *The Optical Unconscious* from the perspective of the co-evolution of painting and architecture, keeping firmly in mind the relationship between painting and window, Krauss's insights amplify extraordinarily. Just beneath the surface of her arguments lies an alternative, a more specific, concrete proposition: that the radical heresy of these artworks is not to abandon verticality for horizontality, but to abandon for the first time in painting the paradigm of the transparent window in favor of the opaque floor or wall. The window arrests time and motion by fixing the gaze, the vehicle par excellence for optical consciousness. The impenetrable wall and floor, on the other hand, make time immediate and set action into motion.

While Krauss uses the psychic domain of the unconscious to retire the vacuous cliché of the existentialist mark that surrounds these works, she is unable to avoid the action of these works entirely—drip, urinate, and scratch—precisely because the unconscious, as Freud argued, can make its presence known only through action. The transgression of Warhol's urine paintings occurs when the canvas is not a horizontal, but a floor. And the "heterogeneity of trash" that Krauss says Pollock "dumped" onto the surface of his 1949 masterwork *Full Fathom Five*—the nails, buttons, tacks, keys, coins, cigarettes, matches— comes into its own as refuse once the canvas becomes the floor. In that sense, one might argue these paintings must be displayed on a wall, because only there do they utterly defeat the window as the existential gestalt of optical consciousness.

According to Eisenman, architecture so insinuates into the horizontal and vertical framework of our nature that it becomes that framework, standing not just *for* the natural but *as* it. So, in the end the goal here is not to indict Rosalind Krauss for indifference to architecture, but rather to call attention to architecture's occult power to seep into critical thinking unnoticed. His attempt to reconceptualize architecture as writing unlike any other now turns on that power.

Insidedness and Presentness

As writing, architecture is always conventional, a mobile, transient, and historically determined scheme of signification, and the early essays articulate the heresies that arise when the orthodoxy of architecture is confronted by a frank analysis of that written conventionality. Now his problem gets much thornier, for how does architecture forge a critical disposition if in its essence it is destined to extinguish criticality itself? The architect does not cut through that dilemma so much as ravel a Gordian knot around it with tortuous formulations so unfathomable that they teeter on madness.

from "Writing Inside"

What, then, is this unique insidedness that is architectural, and why must it be written? Why this necessity of defining architecture as a unique interiority? First, since architecture has a literal insidedness (it will always have 'four walls' and will always enclose and shelter), any other mental construct having inside as an idea will always be in a different relationship to this literal interior than, say, any writing would have to a previously thought internal or external, such as fiction to science writing. Thus, the idea of architecture must first fight its way into architecture in such a way that science writing does not have to do with literary writing: it must literally overcome this literal insidedness. But if it can also be thought that this literal insidedness always contains an architectural idea, then such ideas are already inside and outside of architecture at the same time. But it must be remembered for this architectural idea to exist inside, it also must overcome this unique instrumentality, the fact of architecture's literal being.

from "Presentness and the Being-Only-Once of Architecture"

More than any other term [*presentness*] combines both the idea of time in presence, of the experience of space in the present, while at the same time its suffix *-ness* causes a distance between the object as presence, which is a given in architecture, and the quality of that presence as time, which may be something other than mere presence. This creates the idea of a spacing between presence and the quality of presentness. However, this does not in any way implicate two other characteristics of presentness: that is, its quality of an already given, and its capacity to render that already given as necessarily subversive.

. . .

The importance of presentness as a term for architecture is that it distinguishes [architecture as] a writing from [architecture as] an instrumentality of aesthetics and meaning. Presentness as a writing is the possibility of a subversion of the thought to be convention of type in architecture; that architecture has within it an insidedness which is an already existing possibility for the subversive. Presentness is both the possibility of, if not the need for, architecture to stabilize itself through the reabsorption of the transformation of type brought about by this subversion, and simultaneously the resistance to this reabsorption.

With these excursions to *insidedness* and *presentness*, Eisenman cuts his final tether to Derridian thought. So thoroughly have Derrida's deconstructions of inside/outside relationships and the metaphysics of presence affected the architect's own theories that he cannot but retain them, so he now appropriates and radically rethinks them. He proclaims architecture as that unique writing in which, by dint of the metaphysics of presence, the signification of the natural becomes the natural. On that point Derrida might provisionally concur, en route to its deconstruction. But for Eisenman, the "metaphysics of presence" no longer denotes a suspect, feigned metaphysics as it does for Derrida; from this point forward, the metaphysics of presence peculiar to architecture is for Eisenman an actuality.

Utterly confounding to be sure, but are these twisted monologues merely mad ravings, or are they dramatic tricks used to put into play a plot that some part of Eisenman knows better than openly to dare? The peril for the architect of such a venture into metaphysics is crystal clear. The linguistic movement arose in large part as a response to the discrediting of modern architecture's claim to produce direct functional and social benefit. Though modernism broadly materialized as corporate style, the better future for all it promised did not. The linguistic movement rewrote architecture's manifesto of validation, promising a more familiar, meaningful world rather than a better one. In the first act, Eisenman joined that program with the proviso that architecture must explore more challenging, less familiar meanings. To be sure, he flirted with existential issues throughout the early essays, but the only validation his intentionally difficult, written architecture required at that time was the thought it provoked among those few intellectually prepared and given to read it.

In *one possible interpretation*, he seems in these essays to be attempting to erect an existential infrastructure through which the specific intellectual machinations of a critical practice surreptitiously infiltrate the world without being absorbed into mainstream practice, so that architecture's *insidedness* affects those "outside of architecture." That is why throughout act two *passion, aura, will, affect,* and even *experience* first join then supplant *reading* as bona fide encounters with a critical architecture.

The architect appears to claim that what is unique to architecture as writing is that, by dint of its metaphysics of presence, *all* metaphors of interiority that architecture writes come to assume existential standing as actuality, because the medium of the writing is not ink but building. He seems to suggest that a building is the singular situation where "I am inside" is not only an intellectual fact but an existential truth, one that always feels "literal." From that position, he suggests that all metaphors that relate self to interiority draw upon building as their referent, even such everyday truisms that we each live inside our own bodies and have inner lives. Since architecture as writing insinuates itself into the quotidian expectations of built interiority, it also insinuates itself into all metaphors that refer to that interiority.

Recall that the enchantment of metaphor derives from its power to transfer an attribute from a referent (the "proper term") in which that trait is an actuality to a recipient in which it can only be figurative. So, "scratching at the door, the wind wants in" transfers as figural description the attributes of a dog to the wind. Eisenman takes care, more or less, not to argue naively that interiority is metaphor in every other discipline, but reality in building. In keeping with his commitment to architecture as writing, he suggests something more arcane: Interiority is metaphor in every discipline including architecture, but the "literal insidedness" of lived building inevitably confers actuality upon architecture's interior metaphors. Since it is the metaphor, not the real building, which achieves this strange actuality, much as it is the writing, not the ink, that conveys upon literary metaphors their own special magic, critical architecture need not become the basis of a new mainstream to affect the world.

In this construal of his thought, presentness would denote both the possibility of and the reason for architectural subversion. Standing at any historical moment as the natural, buildings present *a world* as *the world*, and architectural *presentness* names the gap between the two. The gap, however, cannot be the distance between signifier and signified, since the architect asserts that architecture uniquely collapses that latter gap to an absolute minimum. Thus, there is no "real world" to reveal, nor is there another world to which one might make a visionary leap—the naïve error of early modernism. All other or future worlds that might today be imagined already perforce belong to this one, if only as metaphor. But, there is the delusion that this world is a thing rather than a moment in a process. The gap of architectural *presentness*, therefore, is the distance that separates being from becoming.

Though the philosophical minutiae of the argument may elude us—and be warned, there are stranger moments to come—at a more intuitive level, it is easy enough to grasp where it is going and why. Architects at the vanguard of nontraditional design are often charged with academic elitism, the conviction that to serve its own rarified intellectual interests, a small group of architects unduly imposes its experiments on the public. The problem is that in a very real sense, the charge is accurate. But no more so than a similar one leveled at the small group of physicists, mathematicians, painters, filmmakers, writers, composers, and others. All use a highly coded technical argot to communicate difficult concepts and techniques precisely and efficiently as they attempt to expand the knowledge of their respective disciplines through theoretical speculation and experimentation. Only in the case of the other practices, such scholarly elitism is usually less of a charge than an expression of admiration, even gratitude.

The difference between architecture and the others turns on the sense of architecture's imposition, which seems invasive in ways that no other discipline is. We are free to choose whether or not to indulge vanguard speculation in other practices; we cannot escape architecture so easily. We can avoid an experimental film, book, painting, or piece of music, or quantum gravity theories. But we have to use buildings and cope with their idiosyncrasies, and we have to see them whether we want to or not. Because buildings force themselves on us, we believe that an architectural experiment should be intended to serve us by virtue of an improvement in function or appeal, one that might spread widely as a prototype or style.

At a psychological level, we each feel an intense intimacy with buildings, particularly with the house. The house and other buildings appear as central symbolic figures throughout our cultural foundations in our histories, fables, and myths; we design them in our first childhood drawings and haunt them after we depart from life. The House-Tree-Person drawing, a staple of psychological testing developed by John Buck in 1948, formalized the early and deep identification with the house noted by Freud and Jung. In an obvious way, the identification conveys to us the same conservative resistance to change in buildings that it does to the other choices that shape our daily lives, from our haircuts, clothes, and food to the people whose company we prefer.

But more pertinent to Eisenman's thought, the unabated presence of architecture and our profound familiarity with it combine subtly to erase our perception of the significant difference between the building profession and the expert practice of architecture as cultural research and discourse. In his theories, that erasure shows up as his proposal that uniquely in architecture, the distance between the architecture signifier and signified has collapsed to an absolute minimum, beneath awareness. We are aware easily of the difference between experimental film and the familiar representations in entertaining movies, and then between these and reality; likewise, we are aware of the difference between current research in quantum gravity and our familiar understanding of gravity vaguely remembered from high school, and then between these and our lived relation to gravity, which requires no understanding, either Newtonian or Einsteinian, to walk or play catch.

In a sense, the middle term in these relationships acts to buffer us from the self-interested conceits of the small, elite circles of intellectual experimental filmmakers or theoretical physicists. Their work has no immediate bearing on our lives, nor do we ask or expect it to. Because we relate to our buildings not as familiar representations of reality, i.e., as the middle term, but as reality itself, nothing buffers us from the self-interested conceits of the experimental architect. Like such endeavors in other disciplines, the work of such architects is remote with no immediate bearing on our lives, but because they seem to be experimenting on our lives, the remove seems arrogant and irresponsible.

It is at this point that the significance of architectural writing and of the architectural metaphor emerges, because they help the architect accomplish three goals: to demonstrate the necessity of an expert intellectualization and argot to enable architectural research to be conducted at the highest level, to show that despite appearances we are as buffered from the conceits of that research as we are from those in any other discipline, and, most important, to demonstrate how such research is valuable in its own right, without any pretense to prototypical or stylistic generality, the value of architecture's "being only once."

His case for the last of those three goals depends entirely on his account of architectural metaphor. An analogy will help. While most of us can never understand how or why or even what such a counterintuitive idea means, we know from modern cosmology not only that we are not at the center of the universe but that the universe itself has no center. In fact, physicists never say this in their actual work; rather, they write forbidding equations that predict well various measurements of the universe. The equations intrinsically imply the absence of any center as an aftereffect. Nevertheless, because it is a kind of writing, metaphors can and do disseminate from their work to change the way we feel about ourselves, our relation to one another and to the cosmos, without any of us having to pay attention to physics at all. Likewise, most of us will never understand with the discriminating specificity of expert film theorists the how or why of the counterintuitive nondiegetic jump cut, a development within the forbidding theories and techniques that have developed around montage. In it, the film instantly jumps from a scene in the plot to a scene totally unrelated to the previous scene or to the plot. Nevertheless, whether or not we ever actually see the technique in a film, it also spreads from the discipline as metaphor to change our sense of the reality of ourselves and the world, multiplying our points of view and expanding our sense of coincidental simultaneity with events far removed. An important point is that for the work conducted within the horizons of any expert practice, any attempt to take cognizance of these unpredictable cultural effects is of little value and can be counterproductive; the work best proceeds in its own rarified terms.

Along these same lines, Eisenman's argument implies that the rare experiments of speculative architecture disseminate as metaphors from expert practice to affect our sense of ourselves in the world, with one important difference. Because of the unique nature of the architecture metaphor, we, or at least those of us outside of architecture, are virtually unaware of those effects. The new sense of self in the world they produce seems always to have been the natural state of things—the way they, we, and the things around us have always been.

A fascinating generalization of Eisenman's thought might consider that each and every discipline, not just architecture, generates at least two kinds of disseminating metaphors: those, like symbols, of whose figurality we are consciously aware, and those that act beneath consciousness by virtue of a metaphysics of presence specific to that discipline and its material practices. One pitfall of such a generalization, however, is that it exposes a chink in Eisenman's entire conceptual project as regards writing.

In only one discipline, *writing*, in the familiar sense of the term, does metaphor behave as an actuality in the same way as architecture's interiority becomes actual inside a building. That is, only in writing does the term "metaphor" not refer to anything outside itself. In all other uses, the term "metaphor" refers to writing's metaphors in the manner of a concealed simile. Is not what we mean when we refer to an architectural metaphor or a film metaphor an effect that behaves *like* writing's metaphors? To be honest, whenever one reads of architecture as writing in the texts of either act, one always hears "writing" as a metaphor. But as long as the architect kept within the general scheme of poststructural semiotics, we were willing to suspend that feeling as habit. Once Eisenman starts to discuss architecture as a *unique* writing, however, that suspension can no longer be sustained without question.

This is not to say that Eisenman's project has failed in essence, but rather that his thought begins to circumscribe an as yet unthought process that cannot be writing or archi-writing, but some calculus for the production of effects, figural and metaphysical, in each discipline specific to that discipline. While not writing, it produces writing-like effects, but also, while not phenomenology, it produces phenomenological effects, and again, while not aesthetics it produces aesthetic effects.

In any case, returning to our task, let us repeat where we left off: the gap of architectural *presentness* separates being from becoming. To maintain the illusion of being, the orthodoxy of architecture works always to conceal *presentness* and to minimize its effects. Churchill must have intuited as much when in 1941 he declared, "We shape our buildings and afterwards they shape us," as he called for London's bombed House of Commons building to be restored "in all essentials to its old form, convenience and dignity." A critical architecture endeavors to write architecture about the gap between being and becoming, without denying the difference or choosing sides. Critical architecture is neither the ally nor a causal agent of becoming. It recognizes the value of a stable architecture and acknowledges that the forces of history that fuel becoming are too myriad and capricious ever to be harnessed. Critical architecture staves off the ossification of any historical state into empty cliché.

In the exorbitance of Eisenman's delirium *insidednesses* proliferate—counted—there is, for example, another insidedness that architecture somehow has "within it," the "insidedness which is an already existing possibility for the subversive," and still yet another, if one summons "those outside architecture." And it turns out that there are also at least two *presentnesses*. The first, as manifested by Le Corbusier's chapel at Ronchamp, can be reabsorbed by architecture's orthodoxy, but the second, as exemplified by that same architect's monastery at La Tourette, will not.

Though its name changes several times over the course of these essays, *presentness*, especially the second *presentness* that resists reabsorption, guides the second act. Tracking the author's mercurial shifts in terminology can be vexing, but a reliable clue is to stay attentive to the many moments in which a different form of a concept arises, such as another kind of insidedness or index or code. For example, "The corner [at Bramante's Santa Maria della Pace] is the uncovering of an internal possibility of architecture, which, because there is no precedent, acts *as a different form of index*." There are many such moments, they are easy to spot, and it is a good bet that every time you run across one, it is an instance of presentness.

Unabsorbable presentness of the second kind is the soul of critical architecture, the one trait that distinguishes it from all other architectural experiments. If the effort of the latter is to produce new prototypes of value—to discover new functionalities, construction methods, or experiences, to explore new styles or provide any other new instrumentality that the practice as a profession can produce as a commodity—the effort of the former is the opposite. By definition the second *presentness* cannot be about production at all, since it pursues a dislocation of values that so refuses commoditization as to be only-once. Intoxicated by his vision of a new and better world through architecture, Le Corbusier imagined much of his work as new prototypes. He reproduced multiple Villas Savoye in a sketch for a proposed suburb in Argentina, for example. In Eisenman's scheme of things, Villa Savoye achieves its profound influence on architecture and its effects on the world precisely because it failed as a prototype.

The second *presentness*, therefore, cannot be seen as such, it can only be read in certain buildings by certain people, and only exists in a privileged but vulnerable discussion. Recognizing it requires erudition and therefore gives rise to the boundaries that divide those inside architecture from those outside. And, as the basis for a discussion of the values of architecture as such, it gives rise to the possibility of an ethics founded on becoming rather than being. Yet as an architectural metaphor, it too percolates into interiorness as an actuality, though differently from the first, reabsorbed presentness.

From these tormented ecstasies one can just make out the lineaments of a cycle in which *insidedness* writes one moment of a becoming world as material actuality, and an orthodoxy of architecture forms to stabilize that writing as being. Through *presentness* and the heretical bent of a select few, the stranglehold of orthodoxy is loosened, and the process of becoming renews. An unabsorbable residue of *presentness* prevents the cycle ever from completing itself as a final stability, pushing it into a spiral whose historical vector cannot be said to point toward progress, but may fairly be said to point toward increased intricacy. When architecture's *metaphysics of presence* sublimates revealed *presentness* into a new *insidedness*, a turn of the spiral completes.

By its very nature, this cycle cannot be seen, because it operates through metaphor. Nor can it be conclusively demonstrated, since the transubstantiation of metaphor to actuality is metaphysical. But it should at least leave circumstantial evidence.

With a glimpse of that cycle, whether or not it is truly inside Eisenman's thought, this second act is introduced—at least as far as one dare introduce the midst of such a drama. We have met the main characters, outlined the plot, and tracked the protagonist to the threshold of a destiny. Now, each reader must make the tale his or her own, and we all must await the next act.

An Optional Epilogue Wherein a Brief Search for Any Evidence Suggesting the Cycle

Any sound reader will surely understand that as a response to these texts, the alleged sighting of so wondrous a cycle is more a hysterical symptom than an explanation. But for those enticed, let us take one step too many, though nothing in these texts demands it, asks for it, or even permits it. We have already linked Eisenman briefly to another famously tormented soul teetering at the brink of madness. Keeping Eisenman's speculations in mind as we examine the circumstances of *Hamlet*, we might begin to wonder whether the Prince or Architect is quite so mad after all.

I could find myself bounded in a nutshell and count myself a king of infinite space, were it not that I have bad dreams.
–*Hamlet* II.ii

Since Freud first suggested an Oedipal tinge to Hamlet's behavior in his *Interpretation of Dreams*, psychoanalytic readings have come virtually to govern the play, spawning such seminal offspring as Ernst Jones's book-length elaboration of Freud's suggestion in *Hamlet and Oedipus*, Olivier's landmark film adaptation, and Lacan's structuralist correction of Freud in his influential essay "Desire and the Interpretation of Desire in *Hamlet*." Yet, the twentieth century's many psychoanalytic readings of the play are but the latest stage of a protracted evolution. Over the four hundred years since its birth, *Hamlet* has slowly changed from an unheralded tragedy of middling popularity into an archetypal drama of psychological conflict. One key to that transformation has been the attention—theatrical and intellectual—received by the seven soliloquies of Hamlet that structure the play, prompting one overzealous contemporary critic to write, "The soliloquies are in effect the hidden plot of the play because, if one puts them side by side, one notices that the character of Hamlet goes through a development which, in substance, is nothing other than the history of human thinking from the Renaissance to the existentialism of the twentieth century."

Not every critic is so willing to set aside the rigors of historical context to arrive at an interpretation of the play. Studying the adventures of the "To be, or not to be" soliloquy from its original staging to modern productions, the Shakespearean scholar James Hirsh gathers a convincing body of evidence to support his contention that the monologue was not originally written as inner reflection.[11] Revered today as the apotheosis of Hamlet's troubled introspection, the speech has become central to the play's corresponding reputation. Yet, according to Hirsh, Hamlet feigns the soliloquy as a stratagem to press forward his scheme to "catch the conscience of the king," knowing full well that he is overheard by Claudius and Polonius.

To support his thesis, Hirsh notes that the feigned soliloquy occurred frequently in Shakespeare and throughout Elizabethan drama, a version of the eavesdropping scene so popular with audiences at that time. He argues that the writing of the soliloquy in question evidences a distinct style associated with the device that differs from soliloquies with other dramatic purposes, and goes on to list a considerable number of plot and staging anomalies that arise when the soliloquy is not treated as a contrivance. Finally, he outlines events and cultural factors that over the history of the play's performance have contributed to today's misunderstanding of the original intent of the scene. Changes in post-Renaissance culture such as the decline in the popularity of eavesdropping scenes and the emergence of an individualist sense of self in Romanticism reinforced the soliloquy's misinterpretation. Modern literature's fascination with the conflicts that roil in and as our inner lives only redoubled that reinforcement.

Laurence Olivier's film adaptation of the play, widely credited as the first to be wholly conceived in response to Freud, is a particular target for Hirsh:

In the play Hamlet speaks the "To be" passage with three other characters within earshot, one of whom is in full view. In the film version, Hamlet is not merely alone but has fled to the most isolated locale in Elsinore. Once the locale and its implications have been vividly established, filmgoers are shown the back of Hamlet's head, which is then briefly replaced on screen by the startling image of a human brain. It is at this point that we hear the famous words "To be, or not to be" spoken by Olivier in a voice-over as an interior monologue. In two different ways Olivier has thus made literal the post-Renaissance cliché that this speech represents Hamlet's innermost thoughts. A moment later, Hamlet does speak some of the lines, and the remainder of the words alternate between speech and voice-over interior monologue.[12]

Given the ancient correspondence between building and body (and notwithstanding such literary metaphors as the "dark corners of the mind" or "the eyes as windows to the soul") nothing could provide a more suggestive instance of the architecturalization of psychic interiority than Olivier's film treatment of "To be, or not to be." While the voice-over renders the soliloquy as inner thought, the brief nondiegetic cut to a human brain locates that inner-thought inside (metaphorically) Hamlet's brain, which is in turn inside (literally) his skull, confounding interior metaphors as haphazardly as it does equivalencies among self, mind, brain, and body. That an audience in 1948 would so take for granted that a thought actually is "spoken inside" a brain is testimony both to the power of interior metaphors and to their historical mutability, considering how recently had formed the equation between mind and brain necessary to enable the film's device.

In a striking parallel to Hirsh's critique, Ernst van de Wetering and other art historians[13] have raised doubts over the assumption about Rembrandt's self-portraits that prevails among scholar and layperson alike: "Over the years, Rembrandt's self-portraits increasingly became a means for gaining self-knowledge, and in the end took the form of an interior dialogue."[14] Van de Wetering refutes the premise that introspection accurately reflects Rembrandt's original intent. He musters a wide range of evidence to support his dissent, but the cornerstone of his argument is that the experience of the self presumed by such interpretations of the paintings, particularly a self engaged in an "interior dialogue," did not arise until more than one hundred and fifty years after Rembrandt lived.[15]

From our interpretation of Eisenman's thought on the power of certain of architecture's metaphors, the point of interest raised by these studies in self-reference would concern their dependence on metaphors of interiority such as "interior dialogue" or "innermost thoughts." Eisenman suggests that whatever or wherever the interior of one's "inner life" today may be, the sense of that interior would be as mutable as the architecture that informs it.[16]

Hirsh and van de Wetering argue that our modern sense of self is unwittingly retrojected onto premodern representations of self-address, as if the self were natural and remained constant in history. That the modern experience of self finds immediate expression in metaphors of psychic interiority, a presumption that permeates the arguments of both historians, would for Eisenman implicate architectural *presentness*. As would the fact that despite its acute historical awareness, the modern sense of self is experienced as if it were natural, an actuality of being, rather than a becoming that mutates in history. "Most of those outside of architecture assume that architectural conventions have a thought-to-be naturalness with respect to such things as walls and floors."

In our take on it, Eisenman's thought intimates that *interiorness* and *presentness* collaborate to bear on any change of self vis-à-vis interiority. All that remains for us, then, is to find something from architecture's history of vanguard experimentation to suggest architecture's implication in the change of self mapped by Hirsh and van de Wetering, appreciative of the fact that Eisenman never suggests anything like straightforward causality.

In late 1923, a dispute broke out in the pages of the periodical *Paris-Journal* when August Perret attacked Le Corbusier's introduction of the horizontal window. For months, the two carried on an acrimonious debate. At first, it revolved around technical and aesthetic issues such as the use of structure, the management of light, and the formal articulation of massing. Soon, however, the stakes escalate. Perret accuses Le Corbusier's window of violating man himself. Expounding upon the consecrated virtues of the vertical window and its relation to the body, he declares, "The horizontal window is not a window. A window is a man!" The confrontation becomes a classic defense of established orthodoxy, represented by Perret, against the insult of Le Corbusier's heresy. Indeed, in the heat of things Le Corbusier writes to Perret that he gives the impression of "an Olympian God prepared to give utterance."

The architectural theorist Bruno Reichlin has analyzed the record of the debate as it spread beyond the *Paris-Journal* to an ever widening circle of combatants, including other architects, art historians, art theorists, interior designers, and philosophers.[17] Reichlin writes:

Perret rejects the horizontal window because for him it is the symbol of a profound change which calls into question the values heretofore rooted in his culture, especially those rooted in the personal experience of the *interieur*.

His essay cites one after another opinion on the effect on the interior of the general tendency toward more glass and the horizontal window:

"The large window creates too much of a connection between the room and the outside world . . . one ought not go so far as to impair an artistic isolation of the room. . . . We can feel alone in [our room] either with our thoughts or our friends." [C. Gurlitt]

"Seen from outside, the "machine for living" has no face, and inside one would be unable to think, love, suffer. One would not know how to die well there, but it would inspire one to suicide. It has no soul." [Baillie Scott]

Reichlin summarizes the debate with the conclusions that the vertical window revered by Perret protected the "suffused, phantasmagorical half-light of the *interieur*, which attenuates the dense reality of objects . . . form[ing] a protected place of ideological and affective identification." And his assessment of the effect of the horizontal window suggests our cycle:

Through the efforts of Le Corbusier, the subterranean but progressive crumbling of that microcosm, with all the changes in the experience and culture of habitation that it implies, suddenly assumed an architectural, formal and iconographic identity. The strip window ripped open the protective casing of the private man and the outside world poured into the *interieur*.

The allure of larger and more complex expanses of glass began at about the same time that Shakespeare wrote and Rembrandt painted. Robert Smythson's Hardwick Hall of 1597, for example, earned the tag "more glass than wall." Soon after, a pairing of tall but narrow casement windows that often extended as low as the floor came into vogue in France and spread throughout Europe as the French window. But the momentum of architectural transparency was restrained by the limitations of glass-making technology and further braked in both England and France by the friction of a tax. England's window tax, enacted in 1696, remained in force until 1851. Although France did not enact its "doors and windows tax" until 1798, it remained in effect until 1926(!). The technology to produce larger, clearer panes and plates of modern architecture did not begin to develop until the late nineteenth century, with the most dramatic advances occurring between 1905 and 1914, just as Le Corbusier began work.

In terms of our cycle, might not "the subterranean but progressive crumbling of that microcosm" be the manifest effects of presentness produced by architecture's fascination with windows, a fascination arrested long enough by technology and taxes to allow the presentness to be absorbed into a new interiorness expressed in France as its culture of the *interieur*? As the objectivity of the outside world slowly invades the domestic interior over centuries, might not the stirrings of the Renaissance psyche slowly take form as the attenuated phantasms of the Romantic psychic interior? And as the architectural interior becomes even more objective, no longer a retreat from the outside world but an outside world within an outside world, might not the psychic interior eventually too have condensed into the fully formed and independent inner world of Freud and modern psychology? After all, we have seen already a co-evolution of painting and architecture along the same lines and over the same period.

Certainly Eisenman could not ask for a better statement of second presentness than Reichlin's suggestion that the inchoate changes in the culture of the *interieur* "suddenly assumed an architectural, formal and iconographic identity" with Le Corbusier's horizontal window. That window, after its perfect statement in Villa Savoye, continues to exercise a profound effect within the discipline even today though it has yet to be reabsorbed.

If we permit more of these wild speculations, it would seem that the second presentness of Villa Savoye would, unbeknownst to all, including its architect, have marked a completion of a turn of the cycle and the beginning of yet another. In that next cycle, Le Corbusier's unabsorbed horizontal window would no longer be a window as such, but would transubstantiate into one of architecture's unique metaphors as actuality, perhaps, strangely, an architectural metaphor of architecture as metaphor. It would set into motion the formation of a different sense of the interior, perhaps one no longer an inner world as such, but an inner world that is itself experienced in its actuality as self-conscious metaphor, a "written" postmodern psyche that might be isolated as such, analyzed, theorized, and historicized by exotic philosophers such as Lacan or Derrida and architects such as Eisenman. Or used to different ends by scholars such as Hirsh and van de Wetering. Would then the horizontal-window-as-self-conscious-sign have found its second presentness in Venturi's house for his mother or Koolhaas's Villa dall'Ava? Certainly, neither of these has yet to be reabsorbed. Then, one might fairly ask, whom have we become now?

Of course, none of this comes close to the standard of proof or even measured argument. But it is interesting to think about.

Notes

1. Reading this passage, I recall my initial encounter with a "real" Mondrian, the painter who then stood for me as the purest of conceptual painters. To my dismay, the painting confronting me was incongruously palpable, its canvas set forward from the plane of its frame to assert its physicality, its white fields overpainted with

brushstrokes obviously meant to convey impasto, now tattooed with *craquelure*. Duchamp's brusque dismissal of "all those miserable frescoes which no one can even see any more" crossed my mind: "We love them for their cracks."

2. The linguistic schematization of architecture has proven exceptionally powerful as both an analytic and synthetic tool, yielding fresh insight when used to revisit the architectural history while fueling many of the diverse movements that have dominated the discipline in its wake. By providing a subtle means through which to discern the intrinsic continuities that join even the most adventurous of design speculations to the history of the discipline, the linguistic model allowed substantive accomplishments in contemporary architecture to be brought into high relief against mere stylistic novelty. Its operative ethic of invention was also borrowed from linguistics, which notes that for all of language's history of abundant creativity—fiction and nonfiction—to say something new within a particular language, one never needs to invent new grammar (syntax) and rarely needs to invent new words (semantics). Even when one does invent a new word, e.g., "tele-vision," the neologism is almost always formed by recombining existing semantic roots, rather than the coinage of a new sound/word *ab initio*. Such coining does occur, as in the mathematical term "google," though its extension to "googleplex" returned to standard root recombinatorial form. Many new words wheedle their way into a language through misuse, contraction, and common error, as for example "finalize," "mischievous," and "atone."

Of the 16,677 words that constitute the vocabulary of Shakespeare's plays, about 2,000, more than 10 percent, had not been previously recorded. While most use root recombination, others, such as "bump," appear to be inventions based on onomatopoeia or imitation. Many, such as "tortive" and "vastidity," died at birth, but many others, such as "castigate" and "educate," survive intact. In the context of this introduction, one of the most interesting of Shakespeare's coinages is the word "critical," which appeared first in *Midsummer Night's Dream* but more famously in *Othello*'s "I am nothing if not critical." Contemporary etymologists attribute to Derrida the inflection of the term "critical" to the specific sense in which Eisenman uses it to indicate a strategy of analytic reading, citing its occurrences in the philosopher's 1973 writings.

3. Cf. Jeffrey Kipnis and Thomas Leeser, eds., *Chora L Works: Jacques Derrida and Peter Eisenman* (New York: Monacelli Press, 1997).

4. In "L'ora che è stata," for example, we find: "For Derrida, to have presence means to give something form beyond merely its appearance privileged by seeing, i.e., what I see is what I know to be and to be truthful. Thus, for Derrida, presence, and ultimately its metaphysics, is an illusory and uncritical assumption of sight. Derrida would further argue that this ur-presence, this form emanates from a system of concepts, and thus a language, and ultimately a writing which is an irreducible effect of language." The author then goes on to challenge Derrida's assumptions about sight and presence in order to distinguish painting from architecture. Readers well-studied in Derrida will no doubt find this practice exasperating, since the words and ideas the architect puts in the philosopher's mouth rarely offer a rigorous representation of the philosopher's actual position and can deviate markedly from it. While the curious relationship between the thought and lives of Eisenman and Derrida is a fertile topic for study on many levels, it is helpful to remember while reading these texts that the accuracy of the architect's reports of Derrida's thought does not in the end matter to the architect's own conjectures. Eisenman does not seek to derive authority or force from his representation of Derrida's position; like any speculation in dialogue form, the reports are but rhetorical devices to help the architect clarify his own position.

5. I am indebted to the philosopher David Goldblatt for calling my attention to the merit of ventriloquism as an apt model for the complex relationships that take place among voice, speaking, meaning, and writing articulated by contemporary critical discourse. Cf. D. Goldblatt, *Art and Ventriloquism* (New York: Routledge, 2006).

6. See "Digital Scrambler" 2004 pages 133–49.

7. Though Krauss makes extensive use of Freud, Lacan, and others, the principal resource for the arguments in *The Optical Unconscious*, especially those concerning the horizontal and vertical, obtain from the writings of the

French philosopher Georges Bataille, a fact that makes her indifference to architecture all the more noticeable. While Bataille wrote little on art, he paid close attention to orthodox effects of architecture:

> Architecture is the expression of the very soul of societies, just as human physiognomy is the expression of individuals' souls. It is, however, particularly to the physiognomies of official personages (prelates, magistrates, admirals) that this comparison pertains. In fact it is only the ideal soul of society, that which has authority to command and prohibit, that is expressed in architectural compositions properly speaking. Thus great monuments are erected like dikes, opposing the logic and majesty of authority against all disturbing elements: it is in the form of cathedral or palace that Church or State speaks to the multitudes and imposes silence upon them. It is, in fact, obvious that monuments inspire social prudence and often even real fear. The taking of the Bastille is symbolic of this state of things: it is hard to explain this crowd movement other than by the animosity of the people against the monuments that are their real master.

Cf. Denis Hollier, *Against Architecture: The Writings of Georges Bataille*, trans. Betsy Wing (Cambridge: MIT Press, 1990).

8. Rosalind Krauss, *The Optical Unconscious* (Cambridge: MIT Press, 1994).
9. Cf. these excerpts from Greenberg's "Modernist Painting" (1951):

    > The essence of Modernism lies, as I see it, in the use of characteristic methods of a discipline to criticize the discipline itself, not in order to subvert it but in order to entrench it more firmly in its area of competence.

    > It was the stressing of the ineluctable flatness of the surface that remained, however, more fundamental than anything else to the processes by which pictorial art criticized and defined itself under Modernism. For flatness alone was unique and exclusive to pictorial art. The enclosing shape of the picture was a limiting condition, or norm, that was shared with the art of the theater; color was a norm and a means shared not only with the theater, but also with sculpture. Because flatness was the only condition painting shared with no other art, Modernist painting oriented itself to flatness as it did to nothing else.

    > To achieve autonomy, painting has had above all to divest itself of everything it might share with sculpture, and it is in its effort to do this, and not so much . . . to exclude the representational or literary, that painting has made itself abstract.

10. J. A. Schmoll as quoted in B. Reichlin, "'Une petite maison' on Lake Leman: The Perret–Le Corbusier Controversy," *Lotus International*, no. 60 (1989): 59–83.
11. James Hirsh, *Shakespeare and the History of Soliloquies* (Madison, N.J.: Farleigh Dickinson University Press, 2003).
12. James Hirsh, "To Take Arms against a Sea of Anomalies: Laurence Olivier's Film Adaptation of Act Three, Scene One of Hamlet," *EnterText* 1.2 (e-journal): 200–201: http://people.brunel.ac.uk/~acsrrrm/entertext/hamlet/hirsh.pdf.
13. Cf. Ernst van de Wetering, "The Multiple Functions of Rembrandt's Self-Portraits," in *Rembrandt by Himself* (London: National Gallery Publications, 1999).
14. M. Gasser, quoted in translation by van de Wetering (ibid.), 10.
15. According to van de Wetering, the use of the term "self-portrait" did not occur until the nineteenth century. Titles and references to such works until then typically took a form similar to "Portrait of Rembrandt by the Artist."
16. It is interesting to consider how Derrida's approach to these texts would differ from Eisenman's.

    Let us for sake of argument assume Hirsh implies that a single, decisive interpretation of *Hamlet* might reliably be derived from a study of the play's original context, including the author's intent and his audience's expectations. It would not be particularly ingenious to point out that the ambiguity of the writing that enabled the erroneous interpretation to gain such momentum in the first place provides an apt point of departure for counterargument. Had Shakespeare rendered Hamlet's feigned soliloquy more precisely and thus less immune to corruption, might not the play have been more likely to share the fate of its long-forgotten companions? Given the unchecked decline in the popularity of such scenes, surely some of these other plays sank into oblivion at least partly under the weight of all too obvious eavesdropping devices.

In any case it is unlikely that such a discussion would hold interest one way or another for Derrida and his followers. It is common error to attribute to deconstructive reading both a celebration of the intrinsic ambiguity of writing and a challenge to the priority of original intent. Not only were both of these well-established tenets of literary criticism long before the work of deconstructive readings began, but each, in its own way, operates to assert in principle the possibility of a determinable meaning as such. To identify ambiguity asserts in principle the possibility of certainty; likewise and on the same principle, to challenge the priority of an author's intent asserts the possibility of a decidable meaning notwithstanding that intent. Since the principle itself is the quarry of deconstruction, it is far more likely for a deconstructive reading to scrutinize the moments in any argument that seem incontestable than to revel in a text's obvious contingencies.

Thus, short of daring our own deconstruction of Hirsh's *Hamlet*, we might hazard a guess that a likely strategy of such a reading would be to stipulate the historian's contention, but then to scrutinize the structure of the feigned soliloquy. Noticing that a feigned soliloquy is writing (the playwright's) pretending to be writing (the character's, who must script the "soliloquy" to feign it) pretending to be immediate speech, it is clear that the trope multiplies the metaphysics of presence as few others. Not only must the character know that he will be overheard by someone not present, but he must be certain how he will be understood and what the outcome of the stratagem will be. So too must the playwright know a similar array of effects, for, does not every soliloquy in a play amount to a feigned soliloquy for the benefit of the audience? In fact, does not every play reiterate the structure of an elaborately executed feigned soliloquy by its author?

Readers familiar with accomplished deconstructive readings might expect three outcomes of such an excursion into Hirsh reading *Hamlet*: (1) It will operate through strict attention to all of the implicated writings taken together as one continuous text: the soliloquy, the play in its various folios, performances, and other manifestations, Hirsh's writings, and other writings to which he appeals. (2) It will turn out that according to that extended text, the structure of the feigned soliloquy belongs not merely to the curious dramatic device that bears its name, but to the structure of all plays, all criticism, probably even to knowledge itself. (3) We will discover how untenable assumptions necessary to distinguish a feigned soliloquy as such operate to serve a special interest, probably in this case the immediacy and adequacy of speech to itself, given that the study of the relationship between speech and writing launched Derrida's entire enterprise.

The privilege Eisenman claims for architecture's metaphors of interiority further seals the break with Derrida, for the philosopher will not broach the actuality of any metaphor's referent, neither as naïve reality nor as existential authenticity. Derrida strives again and again to demonstrate that the "actuality" of the enabling referent in any metaphor is itself already a metaphor, a version of the argument that "nothing is outside of the text." Derrida might well concur with Eisenman's discussion of architecture's metaphors of interiority, but only to identify yet another instance of the metaphysics of presence, his pejorative catchall for the uncritical operation of untenable suppositions. For Eisenman, from this point forward, the "metaphysics of presence" denotes instead the operations of a genuine metaphysics peculiar to architecture that distinguishes his discipline from the undisciplined and immaterial realm of arch-writing.

17. Reichlin, "Une petite maison," 59–83.

CHAPTER 1

POST/EL CARDS A Reply to
Jacques Derrida

Dear Jacques,

After many months I find the time and the calm distance to reply to your extraordinary letter [see appendix, p. 161]. I was pleased that you would take the time to write a letter of such energy and length, but also disturbed by what I perceived as an implied criticism in your words. I was also quite literally left speechless by your questions, questions that I could not answer personally, questions that, indeed, must be directed to architecture for a reply.

Why was I so stunned, so taken aback? Perhaps, on first thought, because I felt in your criticism a rejection of my work. However, after many rereadings, I no longer feel that same rush of defensiveness but rather a certain exhilaration, a certain sense of an *other* freedom. Why? Because in a way you are right. Perhaps what I do in architecture, in its aspirations and in its fabric, is not what could properly be called deconstruction. But things are not quite so simple: if my work is not something, then it raises questions as to what it is not. In attempting to interrogate what it is not, I will not give answer to all of your questions. Indeed, I do not think that the spirit of your letter was one of inquisition. Rather, your questions seem to outline a provocative framework for thinking about architecture. So I will attempt to follow suit, to elaborate through questions yet another framework, or perhaps a post/work, for architecture.

A question, in one sense, is a frame for an answer, a frame for a discourse that may not be the discourse of the reply. Thus I will use your three numbered questions (only two of which are actually numbered, question 3 beginning instead with the word *finally*) as posts to support me (or perhaps as the cards I might play). Indeed, knowing your fondness for precision and numbers, should I inquire further as to what happened to the missing 3, which is, after all, a reflection of the letter *E*?

How, for example, does one respond to such questions as "Do you believe in God?" or "What do you think of a culture of glass?" or " What about the homeless?" without sounding either evasive or irrelevant? How does one assert that certain urgent problems such as homelessness or poverty are no more questions of architecture than they are of poetry or philosophy without sounding callous? These are indeed human problems, but architecture, poetry, and philosophy are not the domains in which they will be solved. In that sense, such issues are no more relevant than my inquiring about your own domestic, suburban home in relationship to your work. Yet, if I fail to answer, others will ask why. No answer will be interpreted as an answer: as a refusal to answer or an inability to answer or a lack of concern to answer, but never the real answer. The real answer: that to answer is impossible either in the medium of letter or of glass.

Your questions probably require a volume, several volumes, inscribed for you. Perhaps with that you, too, would be led to "ruin and destruction." But if I do not answer some of your questions, it is not through lack of time, interest, or compassion, but rather because the questions perhaps cannot be answered in architecture.

I publish this letter with yours because I think that every architect should witness philosophy against the wall, should have to answer, for themselves, some of your questions. And possibly some day you, too, will problematize architecture in your discourse and thus be forced to answer these same questions. I wonder in passing if the fact of your questions points to problems that architecture poses for something that is now named deconstruction and for the "you" that may now have become the aura of Jacques Derrida. Therefore my response may be less to answer to the specific questions, frames, frame-ups that you have proposed than to place my cards on the table, cards that perhaps cause you some fraction of dis/ease.

Jacques, you ask me about the *supplement* and the *essential* in my work. You crystallize these questions in the term/word/material *glas/s*. You glaze over the fact that your conceptual play with the multifaceted term *glas* is not simply translatable into architectural glass. One understands that the assumption of the identity of the material glass and your ideas of *glas*, in their superficial resemblance of letters, is precisely the concern of literary deconstruction; but this becomes a problem when one turns to the event of building. This difference is important. For though one can conceptualize in the building material glass, it is not necessarily only as you suggest—as an absence of secrecy, as a clarity. While glass is a literal presence in architecture, it also indexes an absence, a void in a solid wall. Thus glass in architecture is traditionally said to be both absence and presence.

Yes, I am preoccupied by absence, but not in terms of this simple presence/absence dialectic, as you might think. For me as an architect, each concept, as well as each object, has all that it is *not* inscribed within it as traces. I am preoccupied with absence, not voids or glass, because architecture, unlike language, is dominated by presence, by the real existence of the signified. Architecture requires one to detach the signified not only from its signifier but also from its condition as presence. For example, a hole in a plane, or a vertical element, must be detached not only from its signifier—a window or a column—but also from its condition of presence—that is, as a sign of the possibility of light and air or of structure—without, at the same time, causing the room to be dark or the building to fall down. This is not the case in language, where you and I can play with *glas* and *post*, *gaze* and *glaze* precisely because of the traditional dialectic of presence and absence.

It is improbable to effect in architecture what you do in language. Opacity is the possibility of the poetic in language. It screens the distance between sign and signifier.

Opacity and density are possible in glass, even in clear glass, which, in your quotation, is "the enemy of secrecy." The textuality of glass in architecture is different from the textuality of *glas*, the letters *g, l, a, s*. Modes of translation from one language to another, from one syntax to another, can do things with the word *glass* that architecture cannot. For that matter, the hinge between Derridean thought and architecture is in neither glass nor ash (gash or ass may be better). It would be naïve to think so, particularly in the face of your work. It is no longer possible to simply accept naïveté in your thought about architecture or in thought in general about architecture. One may have started there. Yet that *there*, which is not the there of my architecture, is difficult because it is dominated by what is already there in architecture: another tradition of sign and signified. Your idea of glass is eminently utilitarian and transparent; whereas there is no transparency in your *glas*, perhaps only *verre* and no truth, no (-)*itas*. Wordplay which produces both opacity and transparency in language has no easy equivalent in architecture. The closest, perhaps, is the classical ideal of virtual space, or the Gestalt of figure-ground. Even so, neither of these concepts moves architecture from its belief in the theory of origins to something *other*. Only when the thought-to-be essential relationship of architecture to function is undermined, that is, when the traditional dialectical, hierarchical, and supplemental relationship of form to function is displaced, can the condition of presence, which problematizes any possible displacement of architecture, be addressed. It is not that there is no possibility of deconstruction in architecture, but it cannot simply take issue with what you have called the metaphysics of presence. In my view, your deconstruction of the presence/absence dialectic is inadequate for architecture precisely because architecture is not a two-term, but a three-term system. In architecture, there is another condition, which I call *presentness*, that is neither absence nor presence, form nor function, neither the particular use of a sign nor the crude existence of reality, but rather an excessive condition between sign and the Heideggerian notion of being: the formation and ordering of the discursive event that is architecture. As long as there is a strong bond between form and function, sign and being, the excess that contains the possibility of presentness will be repressed. The need to overcome presence, the need to supplement an architecture that will always be and look like architecture, the need to break apart the strong bond between form and function is what my architecture addresses. In its displacement of the traditional role of function it does not deny that architecture must function, but rather suggests that architecture may also function without necessarily symbolizing that function, that the presentness of architecture is irreducible to the presence of its functions or its signs.

All of these issues lead into our differences on the question of aura. You want no aura, or the deconstruction of aura, and I want this aura that is the aura of the third—this excess that is presentness. My architecture asks, Can there be an *other* in the condition of aura in architecture, an aura that both is secret and contains its own secret, the mark of its absent openness? This may involve the difference between the thing as word and the thing as object, between language and architecture. Unlike language, which is understandable through the gaze alone, in architecture there is no such thing as the sign of a column or a window without the actual presence of a column or a window. Both the gaze and the body are implicated by the interiority of architecture. This interiority, this necessity to enclose, is not found in language or even in painting or sculpture. Thus, you may be right that architecture strives for an aura, one having nothing to do with text, or good or bad, or truth or God, but, nevertheless, with something that needs to be explained. Presentness is the possibility of another aura in architecture, one not in the sign or in being, but in a third condition. Neither nostalgic for meaning or presence nor dependent on them, this third, nondialectical condition of space exists only in an excess that is more, or less, than the traditional, hierarchical, Vitruvian preconditions of form: structure, function, and beauty. This excess is not based on the tradition of plenitude. This condition of aura is perhaps something that also remains unproblematized in your work, despite your protestations to the contrary. I believe that by virtue of architecture's unique relationship to presence, to what I call presentness, it will always be a domain of aura. After all, aura is presence of absence, the possibility of a presentness of something else. It is this *else* that my architecture attempts to reveal.

I say this because when I read your work on Valerio Adami, I am fascinated by your discourse, yet when I look at his painting, I find it lacking: it lacks the aura possible in marking a surface with lines, paint, color, texture, etc. I feel the same way about psychoanalysts who put symbolic and ritualistic drawings and paintings in frames on the walls of their offices and think of them (because they are framed) as art. While these works may have psychological content and intent, they are, for me, illustrated psychology, not art, because they do not establish a critical relationship to traditional art. They are not analytic or critical in the terms of their own medium, either painting or drawing. They do not take into account the history and specificity of painting. No matter how important your thoughts on Adami are, he remains uninteresting to me as an artist because of this very lack of aura. Now you probably believe that this painterly aura I speak of is one of secrecy and distance, a traditional aura of an original work ripe for deconstruction. But I am not talking about this kind of Benjaminian aura—the aura of metaphysical fullness—but rather of an *other* aura evolving from the remainder of the here and now after its deconstruction: presentness, not the presence, of the work. Traditional architecture collapses presentness into presence and has always viewed their separation as dangerous. In my view, the most virulent translation of undecidability in architecture rests on this point.

My architecture holds that architecture could write something else, something other than its own traditional texts of function, structure, meaning, and aesthetics. So, as you have observed, it always has strived, implicitly, for this other aura. Now, it is one thing to speak theoretically about these matters and it is another thing to act on them. You see, Jacques, when you leave your own realm, when you attempt to be consistent, whatever that might mean in architecture, it is precisely then that you do not understand the implications for deconstruction in architecture—when deconstruction leaves your hands. For me to toe the party line is useless; for in the end, Jacques, you would be more unhappy with an architecture that illustrates deconstruction than with my work, wherein the buildings themselves become, in a way, useless—lose their traditional significance of function and appropriate an other aura, one of excess, of presentness, and not presence. No amount of talking about absence, or of wordplay between *presence* and *present* can create such an aura that distances architecture in building from the past and future of building.

In the end, my architecture cannot be what it should be, but only what it can be. Only when you add one more reading of my work alongside your reading of it in pictures and texts—that is, a reading in the event of a building—only there will you see the play between presence and presentness, only then will you know whether I have been faithful.

Yet, I remain yours faithfully,
Peter Eisenman

CHAPTER 2

THE AUTHOR'S AFFECT PASSION AND
THE MOMENT OF
ARCHITECTURE

Throughout its history, architectural theory has concerned itself with the definition of Architecture. Up to now, my own writing also has revolved around this theme. Recently, however, stimulated in part by the topic of the Anyone conference, I have begun to think that we should take up the question, What is an architect? I would like to discuss my initial efforts to map out this question and to suggest some of its terms and conditions.

Passion and Aura

I had not intended to read, or better still reread, Maurice Blanchot's book *When the Time Comes* before this conference. However, I am pleased that I remembered this book in time. If I had not read it I would not have been reminded to what extent the role *passion* plays in the definition of the author that I want to propose for architecture. Elsewhere I have tried to identify a condition in architecture that resists interpretation, a condition I have referred to as an aura or a "presentness." I believe this thought to rest between object presence and language; it never involves the subject or the author. After reading *When the Time Comes* I believe this aura can also be thought in terms of the author, but not the author as traditionally defined in architecture. Rather, it is an *other* author as redefined by Blanchot, that is, as a construct of self and language. What brings a different dimension to Blanchot's author is the fact that between the terms *self* and *language* he inserts a third term, an excess he terms *passion*.

In *When the Time Comes* the author is the self, and the two central female characters play out the other two terms: Claudia is language and Judith is passion. That there are three characters is not incidental because this *other* author could not have been played out in two. Claudia is the most articulate and the most frightened by passion; she also sings, but in a language foreign to the author. Judith speaks in yet a third language. Blanchot's author does not know the other languages, but his self understands them. The *other* author knows the self and language, figured by Claudia, and resents his relationship to the third condition of passion or excess, figured by Judith. The passion Blanchot describes is the pure excess of an instant, a moment in time. This moment, which I will call an *excessive present*, becomes both the instant and the instance of passion. It is also a passion detached from subject or object. This moment comes between the self and language and introduces passion between them.

Now what does this mean for architecture and for its author/architect? Before attempting to answer this question I should say that the definition of this *other* author I want to propose does not depend on the correctness of my interpretation of Blanchot. Rather, this definition depends on the introduction of the implications of an extension of the idea of passion as an *affect* of the author/architect in a moment of time.

There is a passion that can be detached from both subject and object to become a moment between the two. Indeed, both subject and object are constructed in this moment, in this excess of time. Considered in this way, passion becomes structural as opposed to individual and expressionistic. Since it is structural it can be used to conceive thought— another collective which stands outside the opposition of the many and the one. The structure of passion relates the moment to architecture and the collective to the any of *anyone*. Thus the passion of the moment does not depend on the discourse of the subject or the object

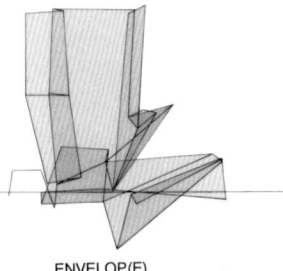

ENVELOP(E)

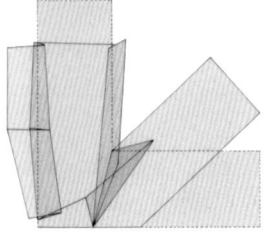

INFOLDING

TYPOLOGICAL EL

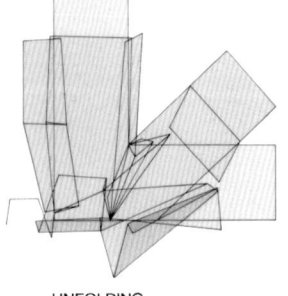

UNFOLDING

2.1a–d Alteka Corporation Project, Tokyo, Japan, 1991. Conceptual Diagrams (elevations).

or on the philosophy of the one or the many but rather on passion structured as an instant in time.

The difference between architecture and writing is typically configured as between the thing and the sign. Things and signs participate in systems of deferral, and these systems both contain a moment of excess, an excess that is also a deferral of that moment. Here lies the most crucial difference between these systems, for the difference between systems of things and systems of signs resides in the difference between the moment of the reception of a word and the moment of the reception of a column. The respective auras of architecture and writing are loaded in that moment.

Within: The Eye and the Body

The architectural aura involves the eye and the body differently than does a written text. That difference rests upon the fact that the body and the eye are always within architecture in a way that is not the case for writing. It is this condition of *within* that determines the aura of architecture, its interiority and its presence, as different from the aura of writing. The eye and the body have always been implicated in the aura of architecture because architecture was traditionally defined by a monocular vision that made the subject the center of three-dimensional perspectival space. While architectural modernism displaced perspective with the axonometric through the flattening out and layering of space, it did nothing to decenter the subject. Architectural modernism never considered the possibility of the eye within because its view of vision was constantly deployed in support of rationality and standardization, that is, from an abstraction without.

In the affect of architecture, there is always the body because architecture deals with a condition of interiority. This affect will be defined here not as an object that can be contained or understood so much as the *affect* of a moment of experience, which is not an experience of an active or transitive nature but rather one which is intransitive or passive. It is a moment of experience that does not involve an interactive relationship between the self and language, nor between the self and the unconscious, but between the self and the gaze of this passion, the affect of passion. This idea of affect is no longer to be understood as a merely bodily or romantic passion but as a thought affect.

Visuality and the Gaze

Thus in architecture, while affect is complicit with reason and not with structure, so too is the eye. But the idea of the gaze introduces a possible way of seeing which, while it provides a structure, is not complicit with reason. For ultimately it is the idea of the gaze that will define this moment of passion for architecture.

The question of the gaze is something that has been discussed by many authors, but rarely has it appeared in architectural discourse. The gaze as a concept is as different from sight as vision is from visuality. Vision and sight deal with the objectifiable and quantifiable aspects of the relationship of the eye to space and time. Visuality and the gaze deal with the social and historical aspects, in a sense the before and after of vision. But the gaze also deals with the question of writing and reading. It also involves the question of affect or aura, which we have seen is an issue that is both critically important for architecture and also differentiates architecture from writing and painting.

The idea of the gaze concerns the idea of the looking back of another subject or, in the case of architecture, the looking back of an object. This looking back does two things. It changes the relationship of subject to object in architecture by decentering the subject, and thus critically limits the validity of classical organizations of perspectival space such as axes, symmetry, etc. This looking back can become the gaze of a passive excess when the moment deals with a condition of deferral in the present. Such a notion of looking back, of deferral, would require a more fragmentary conception of space, fragmentary not only in terms of place but also in terms of a notion of deferral in time. It is through the gaze that passion and affect become structural. The idea of the gaze of the other, which is outside ourselves, also suggests our own finiteness, the continuity of time before and after ourselves. This relates to another idea of the collective. It changes the idea of thinking about the moment because it becomes part of the zeitgeist; passion and affect become part of the collective responsibility.

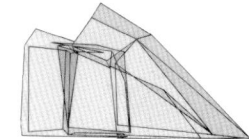

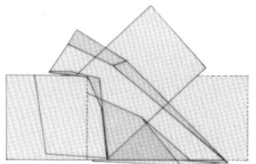

Individuality and the Gesture

The traditional dialogue in architecture has always been constituted in terms internal to language—between form and content, rather than between the self and language. When the architect appears in history it is usually as a romantic Howard Roark figure; the possibility of the architect as author has never been addressed. This is because the dominant culture of architecture, particularly modern architecture, and its complicity with technology and rationality rarely introduced ideas of the self or affect into its theoretical formulations. Instead, the idea of the self was abstracted into the collective notion of the zeitgeist. Mies van der Rohe, for example, said that architecture is the will of an epoch translated into space. Here the self—the modernist author—was removed from a narrative and discursive function to one that merely interpreted, as if with a Ouija board, this spirit of the age. This marked the becoming autonomous of the author, the removal of the hand of the architect. There are those who oppose this notion of the autonomous author; they question the right to interpret the will of the epoch and ask why such interpretations always have a specific aesthetic. These are important questions. But it is possible to look at the zeitgeist in a different way, and thus a way of thinking affect in architecture.

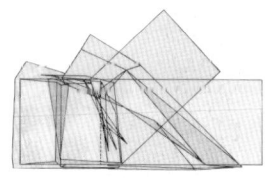

2.2a–d Alteka, Corporation Project, Tokyo, Japan, 1991. Conceptual Diagrams (plans).

While the zeitgeist always includes a condition of time present, it also implies an idea of the collective. The collective is usually defined by the opposition between the one and the many, between the indulgences of the individual avant-garde and the idea of collective responsibility. Thus while the zeitgeist often results from a summation of individual avant-gardist gestures, this same zeitgeist will always deny the effect of the individual.

The character of the individual gesture can be summarized in Blanchot's idea of passion. This differs from the traditional concept of passion in architecture, which is linked to romantic or expressive emotions. In architecture there is an absence of the idea of passion as a theoretical construct. Equally, when passion is thought in architecture it is never detached from a subject or an object, nor is it ever thought as a passion of the moment, that is, as linked with time.

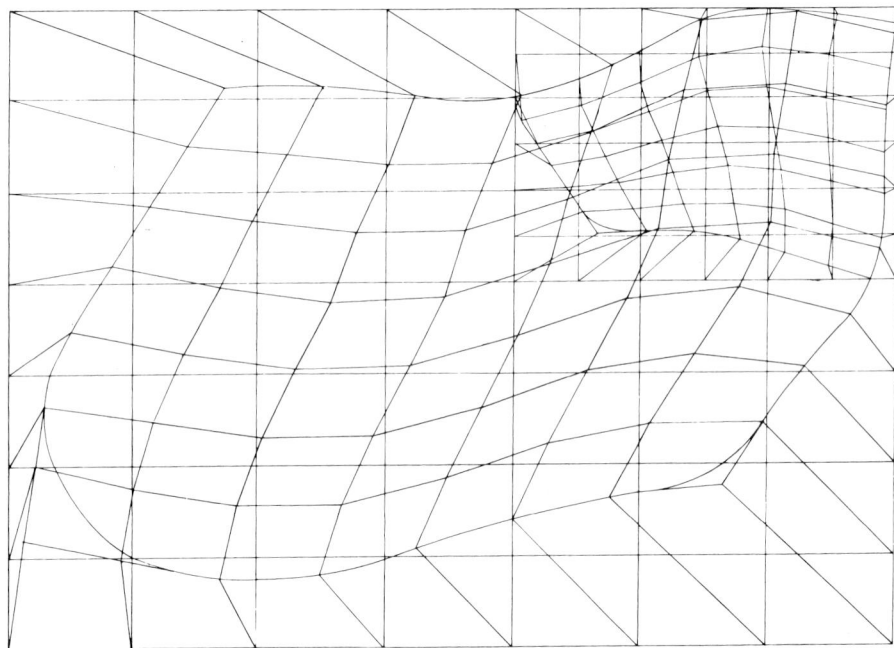

2.3 Rebstockpark Competition, Frankfurt, Germany, 1991. Folded net.

A Moment Deferred

Blanchot says at the end of *When the Time Comes,* "And yet even though the circle is already drawing me along, and even if I had to write this eternally, I would write it in order to obliterate eternity, because eternity never allows for the single moment, this moment of passion, in order to obliterate the always and capture the moment." This introduces the idea of the deferred moment into the concept of the author/architect.

A moment of the gaze of the other can be this moment of passion in which the author sees the self and, as in Blanchot, realizes that language alone can never in itself be the moment of passion, nor can it contain that gaze. For architecture this revelation is critical. For while architecture is different from writing in the way it contains—we are always in one sense inside architecture—it may realize a moment of passion through a deferral of that moment, by suggesting that this passion is no longer in the object or in the subject. In order to experience a moment in architecture it has to be inscribed, but the writing of the moment can never be the moment itself. In other words, language would always be deferred from this end, the end that comes after language.

So it is necessary to write architecture, realizing that language alone can never capture the possibility of that moment of passion. Writing will in some sense always be a deferral of that moment. So it is both necessary for the self to attempt that moment through the writing of architecture and to know that the self alone can never reach that moment through writing.

Thus the moment, this condition of affect, passion, and excess, requires and proposes another kind of self, another kind of author writing within the context of a moment in time, writing within the context of the gaze of the other. This writing is not merely the record of the

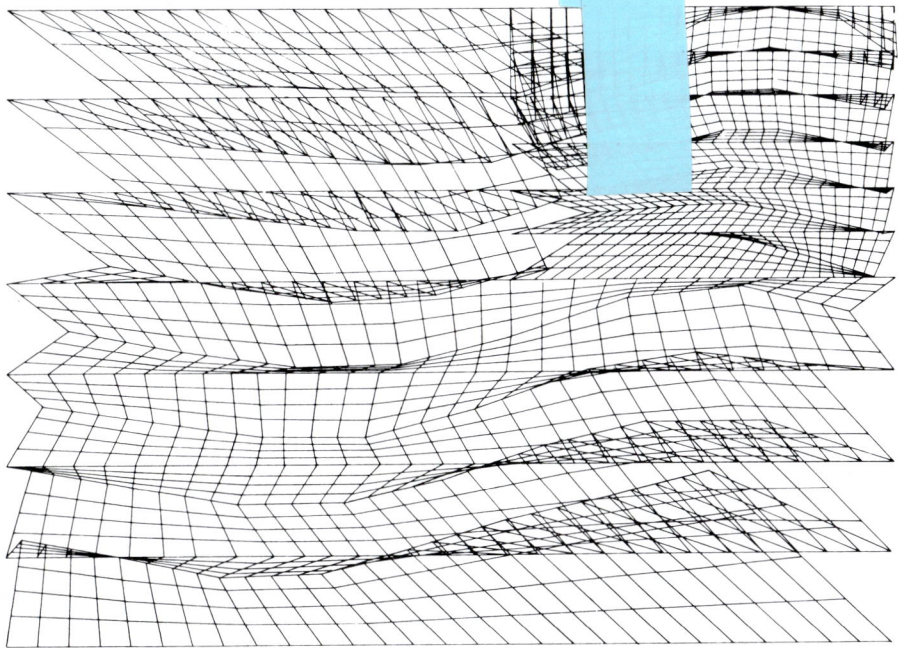

2.4 Rebstockpark Competition, Frankfurt, Germany, 1991. Transformation of the net.

experience of objects. Rather it is an *affect*, an intransitive and passive condition *of* events which has no real time and real place, but rather the affect of time and place. This then suggests the possibility of an *other* kind of architectural writing by an almost involuntary, passive author who is not in control but only sets the framework to be out-of-control.

The idea of this other author/architect is not merely the question of control or out-of-control because these terms deal only with the self and language. Rather, it is a question of this third condition—the moment of passion. Thus it is not possible to set out as an author to effect this moment of passion—the aura of the excessive present—for it is constituted neither in the language of the subject nor in the language of the object, but in this third condition. One can only write, in a sense, both to defer the possibilities of the third condition and to make it possible. Therefore, there is no rational analogue, no prescription for, and no containment of this excess. This excessive present, which is different from object presence, comes from the possibility of the gaze and the body redefining space in a moment in time. For me it is the self as an *other* author, as this excess which offers another way to locate presentness in architecture. If there is such a moment as presentness in architecture, perhaps it can be outlined by self, language, and now passion.

This mapping excursion is of necessity preliminary and far from well defined. Yet it begins to point in directions that previously were uncharted in architecture. What seems clear is the effect on my recent work of this reconsideration of the author. As always the work precedes this discourse, but in fact becomes clarified in light of these notes. Without the work these notes would have little relevance.

CHAPTER 3

UNFOLDING EVENTS Frankfurt Rebstockpark and the Possibility of a New Urbanism

The entry of Germany on the scene of philosophy implicates the entire German spirit which, according to Nietzsche, presents little that is deep but full of foldings and unfolding.
—Gilles Deleuze, *Le Pli*

The German soul is above all manifold [*Vielfaltig*] . . . its disorder possesses much of the fascination of the mysterious; the German is acquainted with the hidden path of chaos . . . the German himself is not, he is becoming, he is developing.
—Friedrich Nietzsche, *Beyond Good and Evil*

In all of the design arts, we are experiencing a paradigm shift from the mechanical to the electronic; from an age of interpretation to an age of mediation. Mechanical reproduction, the photograph, is not the same as electronic reproduction, the facsimile. The former is the essence of reproduction because change can occur from the original; the latter, because there is no change from the original, that is, no interpretation, has no essence at all. While in both cases the value of an original is thrown into question, mediated reproduction proposes a different value system precisely because there is no interpretation. Contemporary media undermine the essence and aura of the original, indeed the very nature of reality. Media environments, such as advertising, or synthetic realities such as Disney World, have now become so potent that they form a new reality. Whereas architecture formerly served as a baseline for reality—bricks and mortar, house and home, structure, and foundation—were the metaphors that anchored our reality. What constitutes this reality today is not so clear.

Traditionally, architecture was place-bound, linked to a condition of experience. Today, mediated environments challenge the givens of classical time, the time of experience. For example, on a Sunday afternoon anywhere in the world, whether it be at the Prado in Madrid or the Metropolitan Museum in New York, there are literally hordes of people passing in front of artworks, hardly stopping to see, at best perhaps merely photographing their experience. They not only have no time for the original but even less for the experience of the original. Because of media the time of experience has changed; the sound bite—infinitesimal, discontinuous, autonomous—has conditioned our new time.

Architecture can no longer be bound by the static conditions of space and place, here and there. In a mediated world, there are no longer places in the sense that we used to know them. Architecture must now deal with the problem of the event. Today, rock concerts might be considered the only form of architectural event. People go to rock concerts not to listen, because you cannot hear the music, but in fact to become part of the environment. There is a new type of environment being projected, composed of light, sound, movement. But this kind of event structure is not architecture standing against media, but architecture being consumed by it. Media deals neither with physical facts nor with interpretation but rather with the autonomous condition of electronic reproduction. The rock concert with amplified sound and strobe lighting attempts to deny physical presence. This architecture cannot do. However, architecture can propose an alternative, some other kind of event, one in which a displacement of the static environment is not merely an electronic one-liner but rather one in which the interpretation of the environment is problematized, where the event comes between sign and object.

Traditional architectural theory largely ignores the idea of the event. Rather, it assumes that there are two static conditions of object: figure and ground. These in turn give rise to two dialectical modes of building. One mode concerns figure-ground contextualism, which assumes a reversible and interactive relationship between the solid building blocks and the voids between them. A typical example of contextualism would say that there exists in any historical context, the latent structures capable of forming a present-day urbanism. The other mode concerns the point block or linear slab isolated on a tabula rasa ground. Here there is no relationship between old and new or between figure and ground. Rather the ground is seen as a clear, neutral datum, projecting its autonomy into the future. In each case, the two terms *figure-object* and *ground* are both determinant and all-encompassing; they are thought to explain the totality of urbanism. But as in most disciplines such all-encompassing totalities have come into question; they are no longer thought to explain the true complexity of phenomena. This is certainly true of urbanism.

Germany, and specifically Frankfurt, seems always to clearly trace changes in Western urbanism. In the late eighteenth and early nineteenth centuries, the typical perimeter housing and commercial block of German cities defined both the street space and the interior court space as positive. These spaces seemed literally to have been carved out of a solid block of the urban condition. In the mid–nineteenth century, with the development of the grand boulevards and allées, a new kind of spatial structure appeared in German cities. The streets were still positive spaces but were lined with ribbon buildings, so that the rear yards became leftover space. This idea led to the development of the German *Siedlung*, where, since there were no streets adjacent to the buildings, the backs and fronts were now the same. Now all of the open space was in a sense left over; the "ground" became a wasteland. The object buildings seemed detached, floating on a ground that was no longer active.

Nowhere was this *Siedlung* urbanism more prevalent than in the developing ring around the urban center of Frankfurt. While Ernst May's prewar housing was revolutionary, its cor-

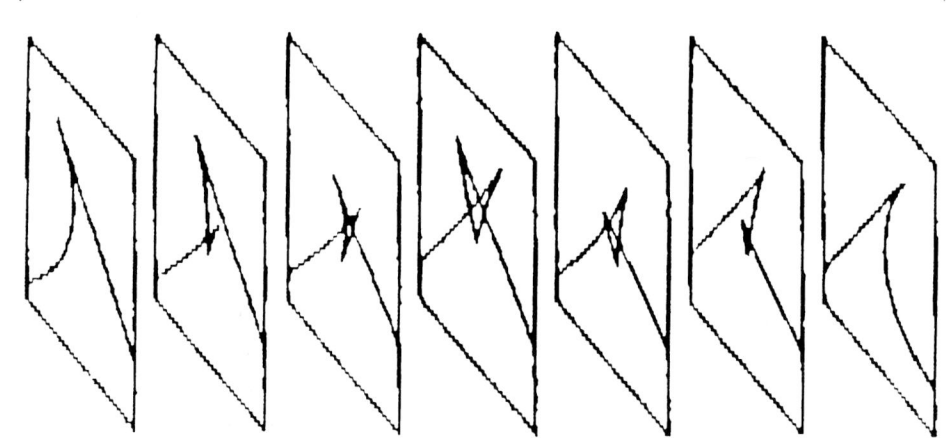

3.1 Seven sectional drawings represent the "butterfly cusp," a three-dimensional diagram of a catastrophic event which occurs in the fourth dimension, as conceptualized by René Thom. According to Thom, a catastrophe begins with a stable condition, moves through the radical moment of change, and then returns to a stable condition. Isolated in their original sequence, these figures are the residual inscriptions of a condition that is impossible to represent in a single frame of time or space. These ideas of "event" and "catastrophe" circumscribe the project for Rebstockpark and formalize, as indices of a mathematical process, the urban context of Frankfurt.

UNFOLDING EVENTS

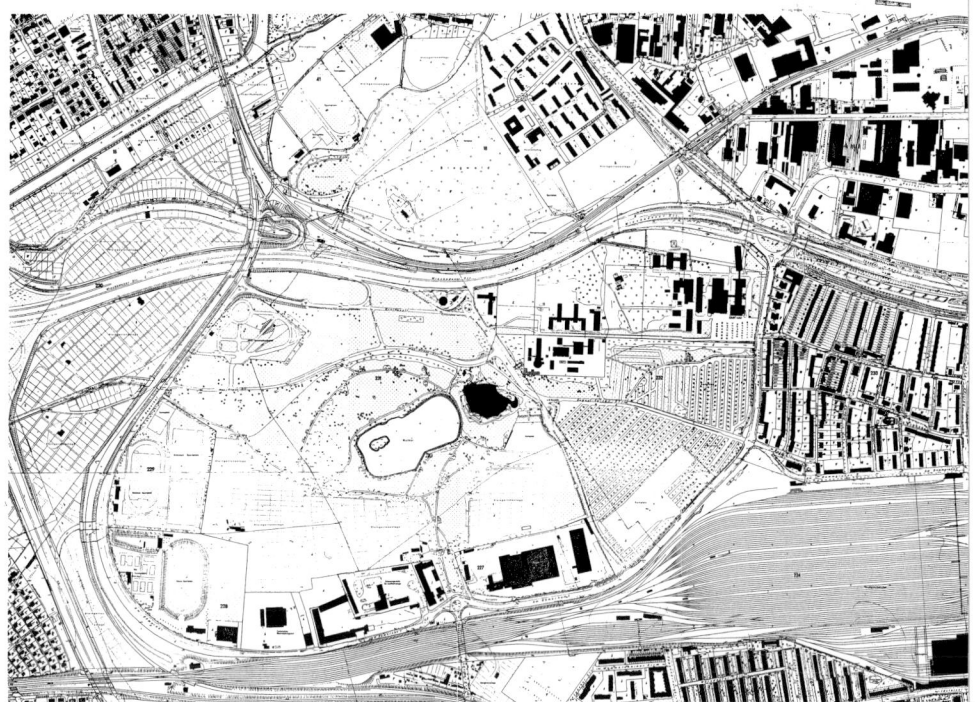

3.2 Rebstockpark has been marked throughout its history with artifacts of one intervention after another. As indicated by its name, at one time the park was a vineyard, during World War II it was an airfield for the Luftwaffe, and it has since been formally defined by the Autobahn to the north, athletic fields to the west, warehouses to the south, a lake in the center, and a public swimming pool. Only the site in the northeast quadrant has been set aside for new development.

rosive effect on the urban fabric is now everywhere to be seen. In the postwar era, with the expansion of the autobahn and air travel, a new, more complex task faced urban development. No longer was the simple *Siedlung* or the figure-ground perimeter block adequate to contain the new complex urban realities; the city no longer totally defined the possible context of an urbanism. Yet the form of the perimeter block of the historic urban centers became the basic unit of an urban theory known as contextualism, the vogue of postmodern urbanism. But its nostalgia and kitsch sentimentalism never took into account the manifold realities of contemporary life.

What is needed is the possibility of reading object-figure-ground from another frame of reference. This new reading might reveal other conditions which may have always been immanent or repressed in the urban fabric. This reframing would perhaps allow for the possibility of new urban structures and for existing structures to be seen in such a way that they too become redefined. In such a displacement, the new, rather than being understood as fundamentally different from the old, is seen instead as being merely slightly out of focus in relation to what exists. This out-of-focus condition, then, has the possibility of blurring or displacing the whole, that is, both old and new. One such displacement possibility can be found in the form of the fold.

It was G. W. Leibniz who first conceived of matter as explosive. He turned his back on Cartesian rationalism and argued that in the labyrinth of the continuous, the smallest element is not the point but the fold. From Leibniz, one can turn to the ideas of two contemporary thinkers concerning the fold: Gilles Deleuze and René Thom. In the idea of the fold, form

UNFOLDING EVENTS

3.3 Rebstockpark competition model, 1991. View of housing blocks looking west. Perimeter block and *Siedlung* typologies are transformed by the spatial operation of "folding" and the temporal construct of "the event" into a new typologous relationship where solid and void figures assume their shapes in deference to the morphology of the fold.

is seen as continuous but also as articulating a possible new relationship between vertical and horizontal, figure and ground, breaking up the existing Cartesian order of space.

Deleuze says the first condition for Leibniz's event is the idea of extension. Extension is the philosophical movement outward along a plane rather than downward in depth. Deleuze argues that in mathematical studies of variation, the notion of the object is changed; no longer is it defined by an essential form. He calls this idea of the new object an object/event, an *objectile*—a modern conception of a technological object. This new object for Deleuze is no longer concerned with the framing of space, but rather a temporal modulation that implies a continual variation of matter. The continual variation is characterized through the agency of the fold. For Deleuze, the idea of the fold was first defined culturally in the baroque. He differentiates between the Gothic, which privileges the elements of construction, frame, and enclosure, and the baroque, which emphasizes matter, where the mass overflows its boundaries because it cannot be contained by the frame, which eventually disappears. Deleuze states that the fold/unfold are the constants today in the idea of an object/event.

The linking of fold and event also influences work in other disciplines, specifically the mathematics of Thom. In his catastrophe theory Thom says that there are seven elementary events or transformations. These transformations do not allow any classical symmetry and thus the possibility of a static object, because there is no privileged plan of projection. Instead of such a plan there is a neutral surface formed from a variable curvature or a fold. This variable curvature is the inflection of a pure event. For Thom, the structure of the event of change is already in the object but cannot be seen, only modeled (by the neutral surface of the catastrophe fold). Thus, while a tiny grain of sand can trigger a landslide, the conditions leading up to the moment of movement are already seen to be in place in the structure. Thom's seven catastrophes were proposed to explain precisely this phenomenon.

In one sense catastrophe theory can also explain abrupt changes in the state or form of such control as figure to ground, urban to rural, commercial to housing, by means of a complex fold that remains unseen. This type of folding is more complex than origami, which is linear and sequential and thus ultimately involves a frame. This quality of the unseen in the folding structures of our site deals with the fact that the folded object neither stands out from the old nor looks like the old, but is somewhere in between the old and something new. Such an in-between or third figure may be likened to the *passe-partout*, which is the matte between the frame and the figure in a painting. However, the idea of a *passe-partout* is always another framing, a reframing in a certain way. It can never be neutral; it always will be more or less than what is there. The fold in this sense is neither figure nor ground but contains aspects of both. Architecture could then interpret the fold, which is essentially planar, in three-dimensional volumes. These folds would not be merely an extrusion from a plan as in traditional architecture, but rather something which affects both plan and section. The neutral surface of the catastrophe fold is already between figure

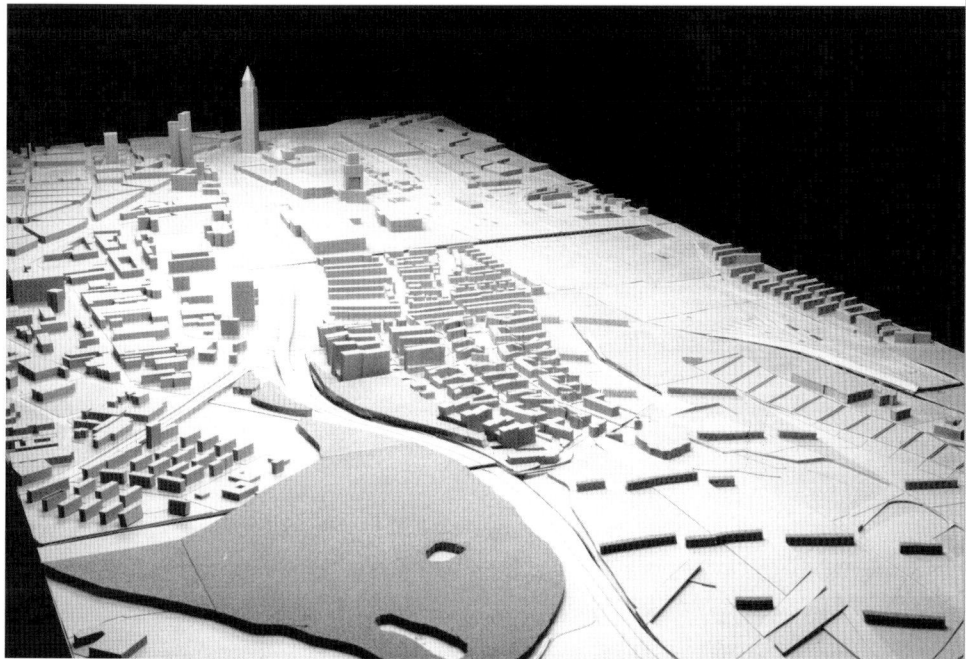

3.4 Rebstockpark competition model looking east toward the Messe and downtown Frankfurt.

and ground, between plan and section, yet it is homogeneous; it is not merely the appearance of a third; it is a third in its own being.

By introducing the concept of the fold as a nondialectic third condition, one which is between figure and ground, yet reconstitutes the nature of both, it is possible to refocus or reframe what already exists in any site, and, specifically, conditions latent in Rebstockpark. This reframing changes what exists from that which was repressed by former systems of authority (such as figure and ground) to a potential for new interpretations of existing organizations. Through the concept of the fold, it is possible to refocus what already exists in Frankfurt.

The fold then becomes the site of all the repressed immanent conditions of existing urbanism which, at a certain point, like the drop of sand which causes the landslide, has the potential to reframe existing urbanism, not to destroy it but to set it off in a new direction. The idea of the fold gives the traditional idea of edge a dimension. Rather than being seen as an abrupt line, it now has a volumetric dimension which provides both mediation and a reframing of conditions such as old and new, transport and arrival, commerce and housing. The fold, then, can be used not merely as a formal device, but rather as a way of projecting new social organizations into an existing urban environment.

Thus as we near the end of one era and are about to enter a new one, there is an opportunity to reassess the entire idea of a static urbanism, one which deals only with objects rather than events. In a media age static objects are no longer as meaningful as timeful events, where the temporal dimension of the present becomes an important aspect of the past and the future.

CHAPTER 4

THE AFFECTS OF SINGULARITY

There are two English words, *affect* and *effect*, that sound alike but mean quite different things. *Effect* is something produced by an agent or cause. In architecture it is the relationship between some object and its function or meaning; it is an idea that has dominated Western architecture for the past two hundred years. Since the French Revolution, architecture, in its political, social, and economical sense, has dealt with effect. If it is good it is effective: if it is good it serves more people. The clearest example of effect is the utilitarian creed of modern architecture: form follows function. This argued that a socially viable program, properly elaborated, would provide good architecture. *Affect*, on the other hand, has nothing necessarily to do with good. *Affect* is the conscious subjective aspect of an emotion considered apart from bodily changes. Affect in architecture is simply the sensate response to a physical environment.

Effect can be contrasted with the word *affect* in many different contexts. This is particularly true when it comes to mediated environments. For example, when I lecture in a foreign country, everyone listens with headphones to a technical translation of my words. This experience is different from the here and now of a physical place: the earphones diminish the affect of my live voice; its emotion, animation, and spirit. At the same time the translator desperately tries to tell the audience what I mean. And what I mean is precisely what is at issue. The audience feels it must understand what I say—it must have an effective response to my presence. But I want them to feel my presence, my affect. Like the audience at my lecture, people all over the world are walking around wearing headphones and listening to rock music, losing the affect of being in space. The loss of the individual response to unmediated stimuli is one consequence of the phenomenon.

The same loss of affect appears when we watch television. For example, for sporting events there is something called instant replay, which allows you to watch the play over again in slow motion. Now there is also instant replay in the actual arenas because people are so attuned to watching the play in slow motion they can no longer see the actual event because of its speed; they begin to cheer only after they have seen the instant replay. This is because we have all become junkies of simulated reality rather than junkies of the reality of the event itself. For example, after the kickoff in a recent Super Bowl of American football, the players all ran and tackled, but the referee blew his whistle and said, "No play." What was wrong? The television cameras were not ready, so they had to go back and kick off again. The question arises: "Is this real or is it a mediated event?" And the effect of this nonhuman mediation is very real; it has become another kind of affect in itself.

The same thing happened at a wedding a year ago. As the bride was coming down the aisle (they were filming for home video use), suddenly the producer said, "Cut, okay, go back. We need this again." And so the bride stops, walks back, and comes down the aisle again. This continued through the whole service: the exchanging of rings, the "I do's," and the kiss. The question, again, was whether there was ever a real event because it looked rather like a rehearsal for a videotape. Perhaps the only time the real wedding would be seen would be on the edited videotape, in which case the edited videotape would become the reality. In a similar sense, just this year, in a beauty contest being taped for airing later, they had to shoot two different endings with two different contestants making acceptance speeches and pretending to be happy about winning. This was done because the judging had not taken place. Again the affective reality of the event lay in the videotape.

Another agency that contributes to this loss of affect seeping into our homes is the "1984"-like creature called CNN, which is everywhere on the globe bringing us "instant" news. I remember one night at home before dinner two years ago when I was suddenly watching the bombardment of Baghdad. This action was interspersed with soft drink and travel commercials. I remember the grotesque paradox of watching people being annihilated live, as if for television, only to be interrupted by "normal" life: buy a car, have a beer. Sitting in front of the CNN television news, one is practically anesthetized to an affect. Does one believe the commercials or the live bombing? Is it possible to know what is real in such a situation and, therefore, is it possible to have any affective response to such a juxtaposition? That is not to say that simulation is not a form of reality. It would be ingenuous to say that what is on television is not real, that it is some form of child's nightmare, a Grimm's fairy tale brought up to date. But if this is the case, that we are uncertain today what reality is, then it is also difficult to understand what architecture is, because architecture has traditionally been seen as the home of reality.

This is addressed by Walter Benjamin in his essay "Art in the Age of Mechanical Reproduction." Benjamin says that a photograph is clearly an original, although a different kind of original from that which, let us say, is crafted by hand. In one sense the art or the craft product, such as a handmade piece of furniture or a handmade book, is different from a book that is made on a mechanical press or a piece of bentwood furniture—which are reproduced many times. But in another sense they are both original, the craft product being individual and the bentwood furniture multiple.

Now, there is a difference between repetition in mechanical reproduction and repetition in electronic reproduction: this is the difference between a photograph and a telefax.

The photograph is mechanically produced; it is a product of repetition. It is not a unique, handmade artifact; that is, it is not an object of art as craft. The mechanical paradigm dealt with the shift in value from the individual hand, as in the hand of a painter as an original maker, to the value of the hand as intermediary, as in the developer of raw film; from the creation of an individual to the meditation of the multiple. The photograph can be manipulated by an individual to have more contrast, more texture, more tone. Thus, there remains within the mechanical repetition of a photograph a unique, individual quality; it remains a particular object even within the idea of the multiple. And within the process, the individual subject is still able to effect as well as affect.

In electronic repetition, that is, the telefax, there is less human intervention, a less value-added dimension by the individual. Further, the condition of the original is thrown into question. Whereas one can agree that there is an original negative plate for a photograph and that this plate can be reproduced, there is no negative plate in a telefax. The original may be on a disk in a computer; it is no longer an object but rather a series of electronic impulses stored in a matrix. Even the disk original is often modified by corrections, and thus a unique individual original is hardly ever kept. And in fact now, with telefax, the original may not even be sent so as not to confuse its reception with the reception of the telefax.

The nature of both repetition and originality changes from mechanical reproduction to electronic reproduction. The change in the nature of originality effects a definition of singularity. Thus, it is difficult to know what reality is, the reality as the former notion of reality, as the scientific, the organic, the anthropocentric notion of reality that existed in the mechanical paradigm. But if it is said only by virtue of the relationship of media to reality that reality is no longer homogeneous but rather heterogeneous, then there are possibilities for conceptualizing architecture.

Within the mechanical paradigm the subject's relationship to the object was clearly understood since the mechanical paradigm evolved from the classical anthropocentric, organicist paradigm. There was a continuity; that is, with every change there was a homogeneity within each paradigm. The individual knew how to react to the object, even though the individual became clearly displaced from his or her centric position. It can be argued that architecture, even though it deals with the same physical individual with the same functional needs and the same need for an affective response to a physical space, no longer produces the same affect because of the shift of the human subject's relationship to the paradigm, that is, the shift from the mechanical to the electronic.

From the beginning of the mechanical paradigm, that is, from the beginning of the fifteenth century, architecture was considered strong media. There is no question that architecture was the sine qua non of the mechanical paradigm in that it was the embodiment of the material resistance to natural forces. In its sheltering and enclosing function it provided not only a metaphorical image but an actual physical image of statistics; architecture stood against natural forces. Architecture, in order to shelter and enclose, was therefore not only actually but metaphorically a symbol of a mechanical paradigm.

For example, in the late Middle Ages, in the Gothic cathedrals and even in the early Renaissance wall churches, the symbolic evocation of a town was in the church, was articulated in the body of the church itself—in the façades, the side chapels, the carvings, etc. The discourse of the mass was the discourse of the structure, organization, and decoration of the Gothic church. Now obviously this all changed in the fifteenth century, with the change from theocentrism to anthropocentrism.

Another important change occurred in the eighteenth century, when new functions and new political institutions began after the French Revolution. With the rise of the social and economic state, there was a new demand for architecture to make apparent these institutions through new forms. New building types, for example, the library, the prison, the hospital, the public school, and social housing, were introduced into architecture. Because of this, architecture of necessity became more effective; there was a primary relationship between the object of architecture and the physical program, rather than with the mediating or symbolic functions. As a result, architecture began to lose its condition as strong media. While it housed and provided for the functions of society, it began to symbolize these functions less. The more the effective nature of the mechanism became important, the less the affective nature of both the medium and the message; the social and political type replaced the metaphorical or the affective type. As public recognition of these building types became more important, little distinction was made between the type and the unique instance of the type in the individual building. As architecture became more of a public, collective concern, it naturally began to deal with the question of repetition and standardization.

Throughout the nineteenth century, there is a development of architecture for a mass society parallel to the development of the new political state. It is not without interest that the modern political state of the late eighteenth and the early nineteenth centuries corresponded to the rise of social and economic institutions and to the beginning of the change of architecture from strong media to weak media. While strong media as architecture was about affect, strong media today, in terms of commercial television and journalism, is basically concerned with effect: how quickly, compactly, and distinctly can the message be gotten across?

But crucial to this argument is the fact that the mediated behavior of today does not come from any personal or individual form of behavior; it is collective behavior. Media not only sets out to destroy the possibility of individual affect in order to be affective itself, but also must substitute effect for affect. Media assumes that an affective message must be an effective one, and this influence alone has entirely altered our concept of affect as well as of individual behavior. For example, media cannot tolerate the possibility of mistake, the misgotten message, error and untruth, all of which are part of the possibility of affect.

Architecture not only does not deal with affect but no longer deals with effect as well as strong media. How, then, does architecture stand in the face of media, and specifically with the loss of the affecting aspect of individual expression? A possible way of returning architecture to the realm of affect may be not through the idea of the individual or the expressive, or through any kind of standardization or repetition of a norm, but, in fact, through an idea of singularity.

Architecture—now operating as weak media—needs to regain the possibility of an affective discourse. The term *singularity* begins to explore the possibility of a discourse which brings to the electronic paradigm what particularity, individuality, personal expression were to the mechanical paradigm. That is a general context for exploring the possibility of an architecture of affect. It begins to suggest a contemporary notion of how architecture which is seen as singular can operate as weak media in an affective way within the electronic paradigm.

One way to approach the question of affect in architecture is by looking at the difference between singularity and individual expression and answering the questions, "Why is individual expression no longer valid?" and "Why is singularity not merely a form of expressionism?" The difference is at the heart of the idea of singularity. Singularity, as the Japanese critic Kojin Karatani suggests, is the difference between "I" the individual subject and the "I" which belongs to the general category of everybody. It is precisely the difference between a "this I" and all "I"s that must be distinguished. The attachment of the "this" to the "I" does not mean that "this I," the "me," is special. Rather, the reverse: it is taking the ego, the individual subjectivity, the persona, out of the "me," which is in "this I." This begins to distinguish the idea of singularity from the idea of particularity and individuality. Even though I know that I am like everyone else, I am not anyone else. What is at stake here is the "this" in "this I" and not the "I" as consciousness. It is the qualification of "I," the naming of the "this I," that is important in this context. What is the this of "this I"? This applies equally for Karatani from the subject to the object thing and to "this thing." Karatani says that "thisness" of the subject and object, "this I" or "this thing," has nothing to do with its formal or physical features and characteristics. The "this-ness" of a "this I" or a "this dog" is a singularity, it distinguishes it from particularity. So it is the "ness" of this — the "this-ness" — that is the condition of singularity as opposed to the "I." Singularity does not mean that a thing is unique. As opposed to particularity and individuality, which are seen as unique in relationship to generality, singularity is a condition that is no longer able to belong to the realm of generality. The singularity of a thing is inseparable from the act of calling it by a proper noun. Thus the nomination of "this thing" also begins to separate singularity from particularity.

CHAPTER 5

FOLDING IN TIME The Singularity of Rebstock

Modern urbanism, which marked a radical change in urban form, was articulated in three different building types: the high-rise or point block; the *piloti* or the horizontally extruded slab; and the *Siedlung*. While all three played a dominant role in the development of the city in the twentieth century it was the *Siedlung* form which dominated German urbanism in the first half of the century. Nowhere was this evocation more prominent than in the area in and around the city of Frankfurt.

With the advent of the idea of mass production, multiplicity, and repetition on the one hand and the need for health and hygiene on the other, coupled with the emerging need for mass housing, a new housing industry and with it a new technology of standardization was born. These new ideas of repetition and standardization brought about a need to rethink urban form typology and in particular the perimeter block, which had been the staple of German housing in the previous centuries. The problem with the perimeter block was twofold: first, it conformed to an outdated urban pattern of streets which made each repetition unique rather than standard; second, the perimeter block was enclosing and therefore not metaphorically open to the new concerns for health and hygiene.

The *Siedlung* form brought a new attitude to urban structure. In the eighteenth century, urban building was considered traditionally as ground with the void spaces as figure. This changed in the late nineteenth century, when the grand boulevards and avenues cut through not only the existing fabric, but also into the open land surrounding the cities, where no urban pattern existed. Now the thoroughfares became the ground to figural building which defined its edges. The *Siedlung* changed this again, and the ground became a neutral datum, while the buildings, which were still seen as figural, had no relationship to any existing pattern. However, the *Siedlung* was not a true figure in the sense of a perimeter block or a freestanding villa. It was a new linear type form that could be extended infinitely in one direction. However, unlike the horizontal extrusions of Le Corbusier at Algiers and Nemours, it eschewed pattern for its autonomous condition of form. This autonomy brought a new principle to building typology. The *Siedlung*, unlike any other previous building type, had no back or front. In a sense it was all front since the apartments were entered on both sides of what was a conceptual line; a line which had no hierarchy and no regard for the traditional ideas of place and the public and private realm. In one sense the *Siedlung* form with its denial of former patterns of land ownership and privilege was an ideal incarnation for the social ideas of the time. In the world of the *Siedlung*, everyone and everywhere was equal. Whether of spatial modulation or individual identity, difference was homogenized in favor of an implacable idea.

Quite naturally such a totalizing idealization would be eventually problematized. This was the case in the immediate postwar years, when the devastation of the European city required an urgent solution. While the problem of the mass remained the same, the solution was of necessity to be different. No longer were the cool rationality and autonomy of the *Siedlung* form thought to be sufficient to provide for the possibility of a restored urban fabric. In fact, the desolation of the *Siedlung* was seen to be as much of a problem to the urban context as was the bombing. In the flight from the grim reality of postwar Germany, the *Siedlung* was abandoned and the picturesque nostalgia of the perimeter block returned as an evocation of the past, now projected into the future present.

The argument proposed here is that the idea inherent in the *Siedlung* type was not wrong but rather was poorly or inadequately conceptualized, particularly in relationship to the changing ideas of the individual and mechanical repetition. Therefore, it will be argued that it is not a return to the structures of the past that is the solution to urban form today, but is perhaps a reconsideration of the *Siedlung* type with respect to ideas of the individual and repetition which may provide a possible context for a solution. This reconsideration of the *Siedlung* is the basis for the urban strategy deployed in the Rebstock project.

Basically, this reconsideration deals with two aspects of twentieth-century urbanism: space and time on the one hand and repetition and the individual on the other. What the *Siedlung* did was to treat the idea of the individual unit within a new idea of the multiple; that is, the repetitive unit was treated as if it were the same as the individual unit in the figuration of the perimeter block. In doing so it caused the individual unit to lose its specific identity. Whereas the unit in the perimeter block retained its individuality because of the overall specific character and figuration of the block, in the *Siedlung* the block lost its identity and so did the individual unit.

This change in the idea of the individual unit in the *Siedlung* can also be seen in the change in the role of individual expression. With the individual unit this change lies partly in the nature of the conception of its repetition. In this context, repetition not only involves space but also time. It will be argued here that the idea of repetition has been greatly altered

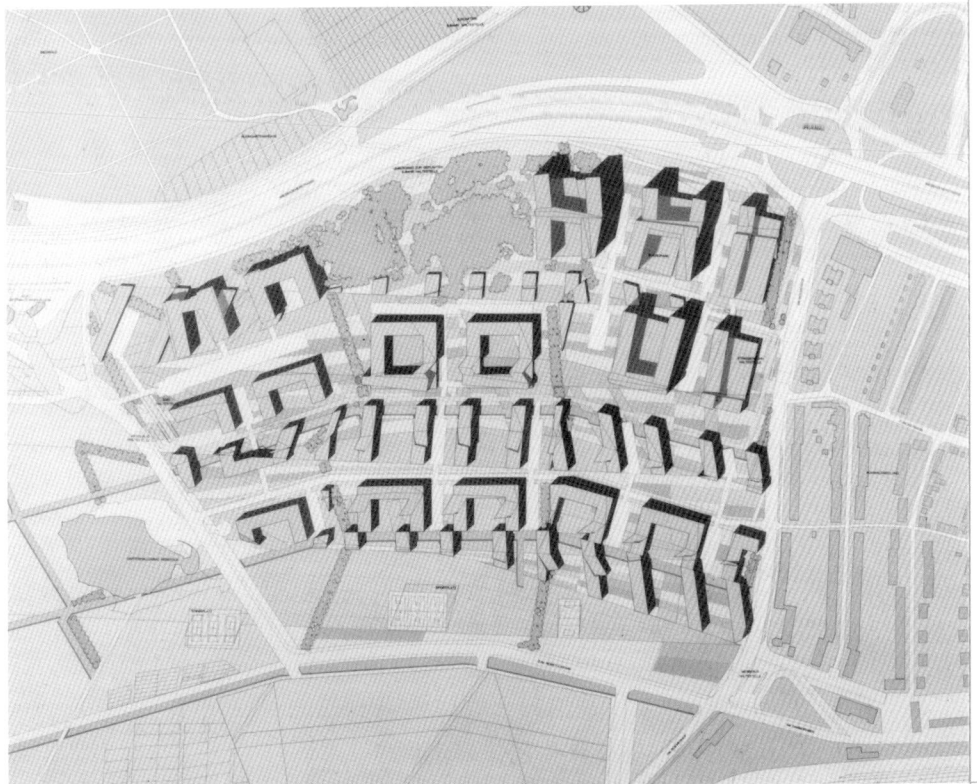

5.1 Rebstockpark Competition, Frankfurt, Germany, 1991. Site plan.

by the shift from what can be called the mechanical paradigm to the present era of the electronic paradigm. The idea of repetition has changed because the idea of time has changed. Formerly, time in the mechanical paradigm was narrative, linear and sequential.

Now, because of media, time has lost its immediacy. Time can be speeded up or slowed down, replayed or fast-forwarded. The consequence of this change of the condition of time in the electronic media also clearly faces us with the loss of individual expression and response to an *immediate* or present action. This loss cannot be replaced by merely reinstating the old forms of individual expression, because media has brought about a permanent change in the nature of multiplicity and repetition. This difference became important as early as the late nineteenth century. The change is addressed by Walter Benjamin in his essay "Art in the Age of Mechanical Reproduction," in which he states that a photograph is clearly an original, although a different kind of original from that which, let us say, is crafted by hand. In one sense the art or the craft product, such as a handmade piece of furniture or a handmade book, is different from a book that is made on a mechanical press or a piece of bentwood furniture which is reproduced many times. In another sense they are both original; the craft product being individual and the bentwood furniture multiple. Now there is a difference between the multiple or repetition in mechanical reproduction and repetition in electronic reproduction: this is the difference between a photograph and a telefax.

The photograph is produced mechanically. It is a product of a repetition not a unique handmade artifact—that is, it is not an object of art as craft. The mechanical paradigm dealt with the shift in value from the individual hand (the hand of a painter as an original maker) to the value of the hand as intermediary (as in the developer of raw film); from the creation of an individual to the mediation of the multiple. The photograph can be manipulated by an individual to have more contrast, more texture, more tone. Thus, within the mechanical repetition of a photograph there remains a unique, individual quality; it remains a particular object, even within the idea of the multiple.

In electronic repetition, that is, the telefax, there is less human intervention, a less value-added dimension by the individual. Furthermore, the condition of the original is thrown into question. Whereas one can agree that there is an original negative plate for a photograph and that this plate can be reproduced, there is no negative plate in a telefax. The original that may be on a disk in a computer is no longer an object but rather a series of electronic impulses stored in a matrix. Even the disk original is often modified by corrections, and thus a unique original is rarely kept. And in fact now, with telefax, the original may not even ever be sent so as to not confuse its reception with the reception of the telefax. The question remains, how does one make an urbanism in this new media time, a simultaneous time of narration and repetition? For this answer it is possible to introduce two interconnected concepts: the idea of the fold and the idea of singularity—concepts which are both active in the Rebstock project.

For Gilles Deleuze, the fold opens up a new conception of space and time. He argues in *Le Pli* that "Leibniz turned his back on Cartesian rationalism, on the notion of effective space and argued that in the labyrinth of the continuous the smallest element is not the point but the fold." If this idea is taken into architecture it produces the following argument.

Traditionally, architecture is conceptualized as Cartesian space, as a series of point grids. Planning envelopes are volumes of Cartesian space which seem to be neutral. Of course these volumes of Cartesian space, these Platonic solids that contain the stylisms and images of not only classical but also modern and postmodern space, are really nothing more than a condition of ideology taken for neutral or natural. Thus, it may be possible to take the notion of the fold—the crossing or an extension from a point—as an *other* kind of neutrality. Deleuze goes on to argue that Leibniz's notion of this extension is the notion of the event: "Extension is the philosophical movement outward along a plane rather than downward in depth." He argues that in mathematical studies of variation, the notion of object is change. This new object for Deleuze is no longer concerned with the framing of space, but rather a temporal modulation that implies a continual variation of matter. The continual variation is characterized through the agency of the fold: "No longer is an object defined by an essential form." He calls this idea of an object an "object event."

The idea of event is critical to the discussion of singularity. Event proposes a different kind of time which is outside of narrative time or dialectical time. This other time, this outside of time, begins to condition the idea of event as well as the idea of singularity. The latter attempts to restore that quality of individuality lost in the *Siedlung*, without resorting to the static nineteenth-century idea of individuality. Singularity can be defined as different from either the individual, the specific, or the particular. Whereas the particular can always be defined in relation to the general, singularity cannot. Singularity is always other, always different. Singularity is an individuality no longer able to belong to the realm of multiple as formerly defined. For singularity does not mean that a thing is simply unique. Singularity refers to the possibility in a repetition or a multiple for one copy to be different from another copy. The difference lies not so much in form, in size, or in shape as in the distinction of a *this* thing from any other like thing. Singularity resides in this "otherness" of the *time* of such a *this* thing; not so much in its form or space.

Place and time when no longer defined by the grid but rather by the fold will still exist, but not as place and time in its former context, that is, as static, figural space. This other definition of time and place will involve both the simulacrum of time and place as well as the former reality of time and place. Narrative time is consequently altered. From here to there in space involves real time; only in mediated time, that is, the time of film or video, can time be speeded up or collapsed. Today the architecture of the event must deal with both times: its former time and future time of before and after and the media time, the time of the present which must contain the before and the after.

Events correspond to what Deleuze calls a heterogeneous series, which is organized into a system which is neither stable nor unstable; in other words, not in a dialectical either/or relationship but rather endowed with what can be called a potential energy. Potential energy is the energy of the event. Potential energy lies in the pre-present. An event is that which is previous to the present and which also lingers after. It includes the time of nothingness which is prior to and after the present of the event.

These events can never realize the old linear time of a stasis that inhabited those places, because today these very places are overwhelmed with a new mediated time of repetition—

with speeding up and slowing down; with "instant replays" that do not replicate narrative time. Therefore, any condition of place has to be more concerned with this "other" notion of the particular and the specific which acknowledges this time of repetition. Image must be replaced by mapping, and individuality reconceptualized in the idea of singularity. This raises the possibility of reading the *Siedlung* in another frame of reference, one different from the traditional figure-ground.

The *Siedlung* form assumed a ground datum as both neutral and ideal. It was a ground that was infinitely extendable and repeatable—there was no specificity of context and thus no realizable edge or boundary, because the ground was neutral. Singularity is not something that emerges from a ground or from a figure form. It is the quality of unfolding in time that allows the possibility of singularity. Thus the fold can never be a neutral datum; it will always be a moment if not a specific object or place in time. As such, it can be an unstable or nonstatic being in time as well as place. The fold in this sense is neither a frame nor a figure as ground, but contains elements of both. Thus the ground of the Rebstock project (fig. 5.2) must be distinguished from a ground as origin, or a ground as in figure-ground. The ground of Rebstock is no longer a datum or a base condition but rather is, in fact, something which already contains a condition of singularity; that is, a groundlessness which can be said to be inherent in the notion of ground. It is a groundless ground. This groundless ground as realized at Rebstock is in the possibility of the fold. The folded ground of Rebstock inhabits a netherworld of a time between the organic and the crystal; between surface and depth. The mediating device between the organism and the crystal is the idea of the membrane, and in the case of Rebstock it is the folded surface. The fold is

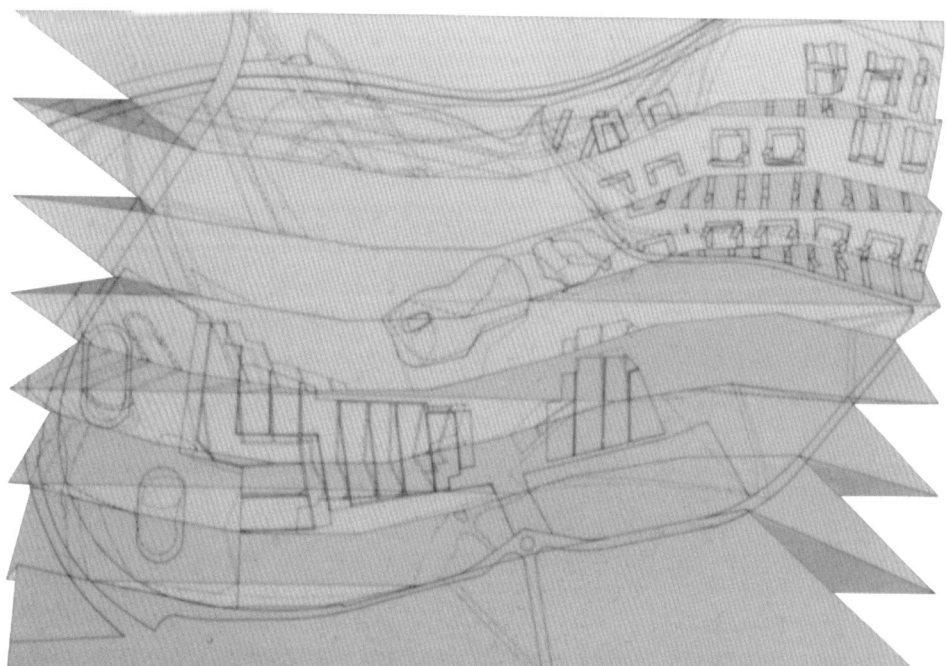

5.2 Rebstockpark Competition. Concept drawings.

an aspect of singularity. The fold is never the same, either in space or time. It is a physical condition of difference, of a "thisness" rather than an "objectness." A folded surface maps relationships without recourse to size or distance; it is conceptualized in the difference between a topological and a Euclidean surface. A topological surface is a condition of mapping without the necessary definition of distance. And without the definition of distance there is another kind of time, one of a nomadic relationship of points. These points are no longer fixed by X, Y, and Z coordinates; they may be called X, Y, and Z, but they no longer have a fixed, spatial place. In this sense they are without place, they are placeless on the topological ground. Thus, Rebstock uses the fold as an attempt to produce conditions of a singularity of place and time using the *Siedlung*. Here the topological event, the dissolution of figure and ground into a continuum, resides physically in the fold; no longer in the point or the grid. The ground surface as a membrane which becomes a topological event/structure is also simultaneously the building form. This topological event/structure which has a before and after as well as its own present is distinguished from pure media which has only a present. It is the time of art beyond media. If media time is concerned with time in the present—the time of the simulated event—then the time of singularity contains the time before and after within the present of the event itself.

The thought-to-be neutrality of the Cartesian grid or the Platonic solid was seen as a value—a place where order and rationality could begin to create specificity. The crossing

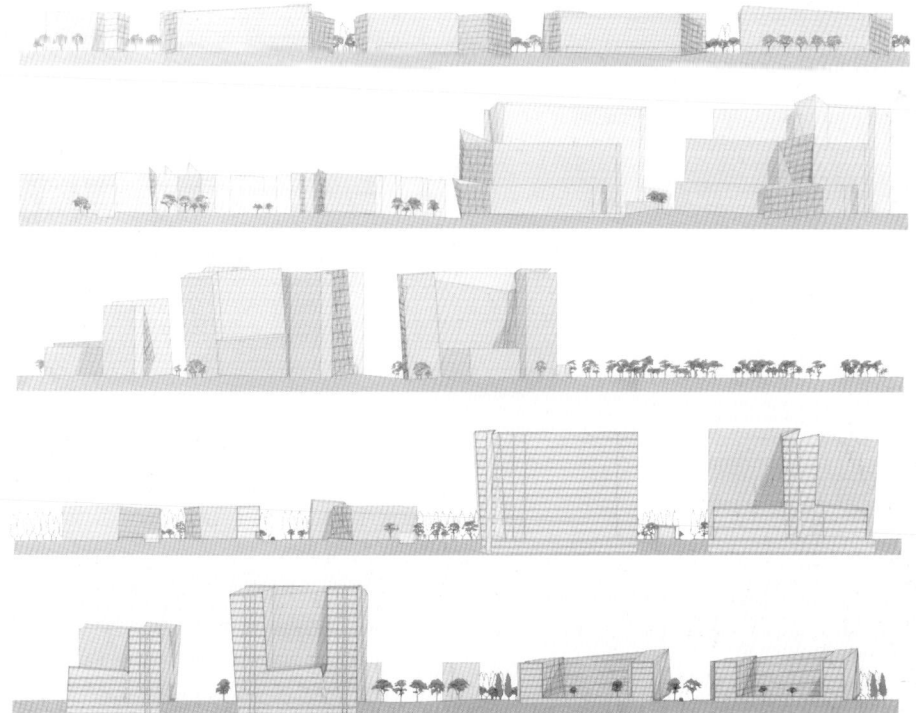

5.3 Rebstockpark Competition Elevations and sections.

of the *cardo* and *decumanus*, the earliest articulation of gridded urban space, was if nothing else a specific symbolic point. The fold is a different kind of symbol; it is no longer about image or iconic representation, but rather about index and mapping its own being, a mapping of its thisness in time as an event or a spectacle. As the sublime was to the time of the classical, so too is the spectacle to the time of the fold. Thus, where the specificity of the grid referred to place, the singularity of the fold refers to time. In the movement from grid to fold place no longer remains the dominant spatial condition. In the fold there is a specificity of location but as a singularity not bound by traditional coordinates of space and time.

The use of the fold in Rebstock might reveal other conditions which may always have been immanent or repressed in the urban fabric of Frankfurt: conditions of singularity seen in terms of the ebb and flow of time which could reframe existing structures. The idea of the fold as a time event is neither a call for a radical intervention into the Rebstock area nor a return to the nostalgia of context as a tabula rasa. Rather, it is to see something which extends an existing context into time, producing in this extension the possibility of singularity. Due to the omnipresent simulacra of the electronic paradigm, a time-bound place has lost its placeness. It has moved to a kind of placeless, timeless condition. The fold attempts not to return place and time to what they were formerly, but to bring them into the fold.

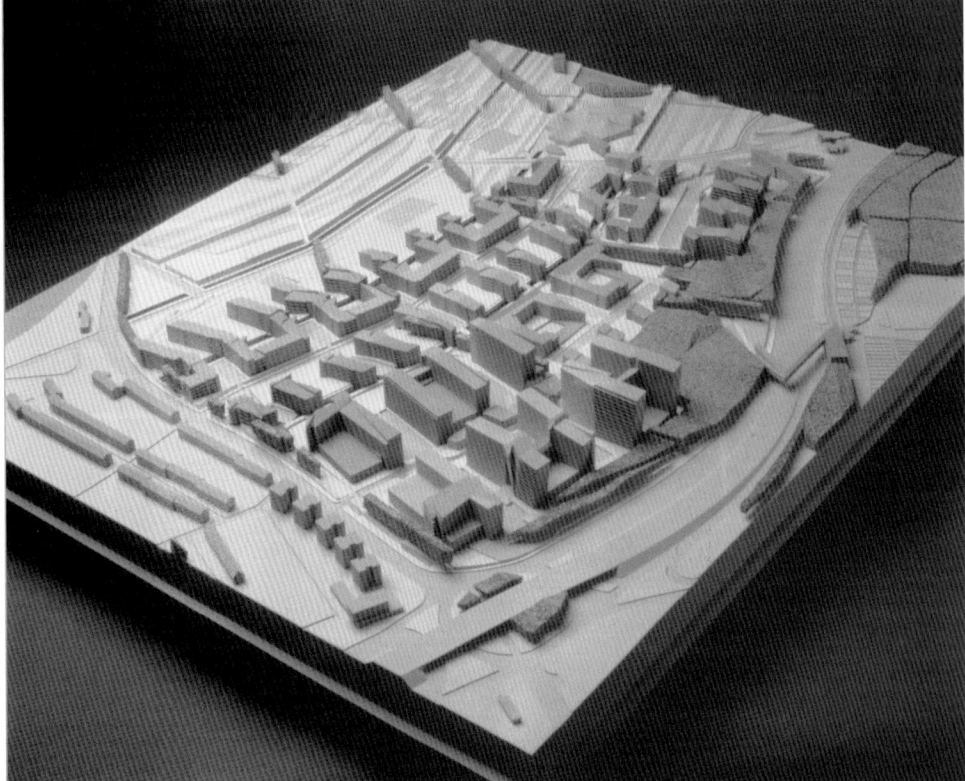

5.4–5.6 Rebstockpark Competition. Views of site model.

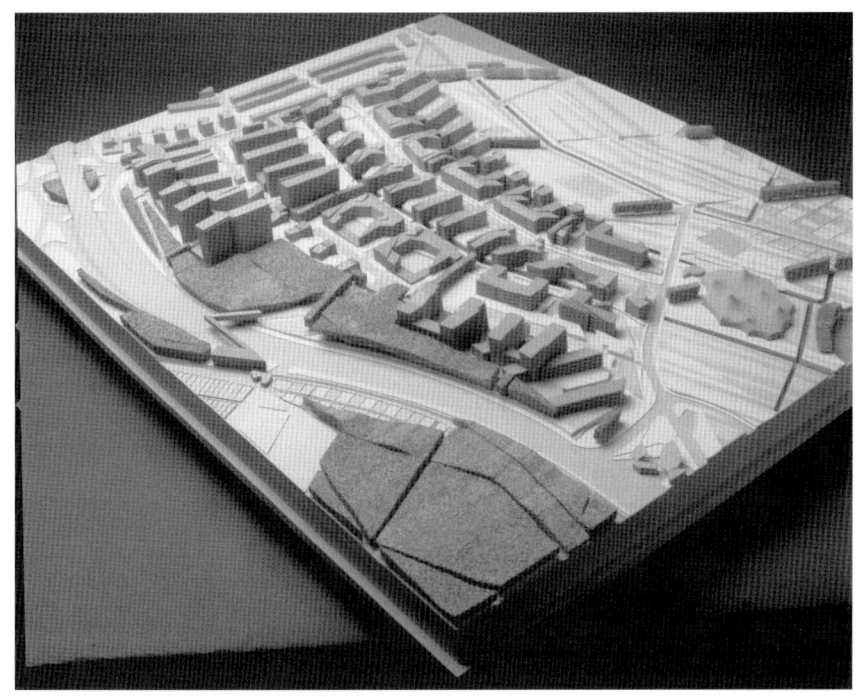

CHAPTER 6

VISION'S UNFOLDING Architecture in the Age of Electronic Media

During the fifty years since the Second World War, a paradigm shift has taken place that should have profoundly affected architecture: This was the shift from the mechanical paradigm to the electronic one. This change can be simply understood by comparing the impact of the role of the human subject on such primary modes of reproduction as the photograph and the fax; the photograph within the mechanical paradigm, the fax within the electronic one.

In photographic reproduction the subject still maintains a controlled interaction with the object. A photograph can be developed with more or less contrast, texture, or clarity. The photograph can be said to remain in the control of human vision. The human subject thus retains its function as interpreter, as discursive function. With the fax, the subject is no longer called upon to interpret, for reproduction takes place without any control or adjustment. The fax also challenges the concept of originality. While in a photograph the original reproduction still retains a privileged value, in facsimile transmission the original remains intact but with no differentiating value since it is no longer sent. The mutual devaluation of both original and copy is not the only transformation affected by the electronic paradigm. The entire nature of what we have come to know as the reality of our world has been called into question by the invasion of media into everyday life. For reality always demanded that our vision be interpretive.

How have these developments affected architecture? Since architecture has traditionally housed value as well as face, one would imagine that architecture would have been greatly transformed. But this is not the case, for architecture seems little changed at all. This in itself ought to warrant investigation, since architecture has traditionally been a bastion of what is considered to be the real. Metaphors such as house and home, bricks and mortar, foundations and shelter attest to architecture's role in defining what we consider to be real. Clearly, a change in the everyday concepts of reality should have had some effect on architecture. It did not because the mechanical paradigm was the sine qua non of architecture; architecture was the visible manifestation of the overcoming of natural forces such as gravity and weather by mechanical means. Architecture not only overcame gravity, it was also the monument to that overcoming; it interpreted the value society placed on its vision.

The electronic paradigm directs a powerful challenge to architecture because it defines reality in terms of media and simulation, it values appearance over existence, what can be seen over what is. Not the seen as we formerly knew it, but rather a seeing that can no longer interpret. Media introduce fundamental ambiguities into how and what we see. Architecture has resisted this question because, since the importation and absorption of perspective by architectural space in the fifteenth century, architecture has been dominated by the mechanics of vision. Thus architecture assumes sight to be preeminent and also in some way natural to its own processes, not a thing to be questioned. It is precisely this traditional concept of sight that the electronic paradigm questions.

Sight is traditionally understood in terms of vision. When I use the term *vision* I mean that particular characteristic of sight which attaches seeing to thinking, the eye to the mind. In architecture, vision refers to a particular category of perception linked to monocular perspectival vision. The monocular vision of the subject in architecture allows for all projections of space to be resolved on a single planimetric surface. It is therefore not surprising that perspective, with its ability to define and reproduce the perception of depth on a two-dimensional surface, should find architecture a waiting and wanting vehicle. Nor is it surprising that architecture soon began to conform itself to this monocular, rationalizing vision—in its own body. Whatever the style, space was constituted as an understandable construct, organized around spatial elements such as axes, places, symmetries, etc. Perspective is even more virulent in architecture than in painting because of the imperious demands of the eye *and* the body to orient itself in architectural space through processes of rational perspectival ordering. It was thus not without cause that Brunelleschi's invention of *one-point* perspective should correspond to a time when there was a paradigm shift from the theological and theocentric to the anthropomorphic and anthropocentric views of the world. Perspective became the vehicle by which anthropocentric vision crystalized itself in the architecture that followed this shift.

Brunelleschi's projection system, however, was deeper in its effect than all subsequent stylistic change because it confirmed vision as the dominant discourse in architecture from the sixteenth century to the present. Thus, despite repeated changes in style from the Renaissance through postmodernism and despite many attempts to the contrary, the seeing human subject—monocular and anthropocentric—remains the primary discursive term of architecture.

The tradition of planimetric projection in architecture persisted unchallenged because it allowed the projection and hence the understanding of a three-dimensional space in two dimensions. In other disciplines—perhaps since Leibniz and certainly since Sartre—there has been a consistent attempt to demonstrate the problematic qualities inherent in vision, but in architecture the sight/mind construct has persisted as the dominant discourse.

In an essay titled "Scopic Regimes of Modernity," Martin Jay notes that "Baroque visual experience has a strongly tactile or haptic quality, which prevents it from turning into the absolute ocular centrism of its Cartesian perspectivalist rival." Norman Bryson, in his article "The Gaze in the Expanded Field," introduces the idea of the gaze (*le regard*) as the looking back of the other. He discusses the gaze in terms of Sartre's intruder in *Being and Nothingness* and in terms of Jacques Lacan's concept of a darkness that cuts across the space of sight. Lacan also introduces the idea of a space looking back, which he likens to a disturbance of the visual field of reason.

From time to time architecture has attempted to overcome its rationalizing vision. If one takes, for example, the church of San Vitale in Ravenna, one can explain the solitary column almost blocking the entry or the incomplete groin vaulting as an attempt to signal a change from a pagan to a Christian architecture. G. B. Piranesi created similar effects with his architectural projections. Piranesi diffracted the monocular subject by creating perspectival visions with multiple vanishing points so that there was no way of correlating what was seen into a unified whole. Equally, cubism attempted to deflect the relationship between a monocular subject and the object. The subject could no longer put the painting into some meaningful structure through the use of perspective. Cubism used a non-monocular perspectival condition: it flattened objects to the edges, it upturned objects, it undermined the stability of the picture plane. Architecture attempted similar dislocations through constructivism and its own, albeit normalizing, version of cubism—the International Style. But this work only *looked* cubistic and modern; the subject remained rooted in a profound anthropocentric stability, comfortably upright and in place on a flat, tabular ground. There was no shift in the relationship between the subject and the object. While the object looked different, it failed to displace the viewing subject. Though the buildings were sometimes conceptualized by axonometric or isometric projection rather than by perspective, no consistent deflection of the subject was carried out. Yet modernist sculpture did in many cases effectuate such a displacement of the subject. These dislocations were fundamental to minimalism: the early work of Robert Morris, Michael Heizer, and Robert Smithson. This historical project, however, was never taken up in architecture. The question now begs to be asked: Why did architecture resist developments that were taking place in other disciplines? And further, why has the issue of vision never been properly problematized in architecture?

It might be said that architecture never adequately thought the problem of vision because it remained within the concept of the subject and the four walls. Architecture, unlike any other discipline, concretized vision. The hierarchy inherent in all architectural space begins as a structure for the mind's eye. It is perhaps the idea of interiority as a hierarchy between inside and outside that causes architecture to conceptualize itself ever more comfortably and conservatively in vision. The interiority of architecture more than any other discourse defined a hierarchy of vision articulated by inside and outside. The fact that one is actually both inside and outside of architecture, unlike painting or music, required vision to conceptualize itself in this way. As long as architecture refuses to take up the problem of vision, it will remain within a Renaissance or classical view of its discourse.

Now what would it mean for architecture to take up the problem of vision? Vision can be defined as essentially a way of organizing space and elements in space. It is a way of looking *at* and defining a relationship between a subject and an object. Traditional architecture is structured so that any position occupied by a subject provides the means for understanding that position in relation to a particular spatial typology, such as a rotunda, a transept crossing, an axis, an entry. Any number of these typological conditions deploy architecture as a screen for looking-at.

The idea of a "looking-back" begins to displace the anthropocentric subject. Looking back does not require the object to become a subject, that is, to anthropomorphize the object. Looking back concerns the possibility of detaching the subject from the rationalization of space. In other words, to allow the subject to have a vision of space that no longer can be put together in the normalizing, classicizing, or traditional construct of vision; an other space, where the space "looks back" at the subject. A possible first step in conceptualizing this "other" space, would be to detach what one sees from what one knows—the eye from the mind. A second step would be to inscribe space in such a way as to endow it with the possibility of looking back at the subject. All architecture can be said to be already inscribed. Windows, doors, beams, and columns are a kind of inscription.

Suppose for a moment that architecture could be conceptualized as a Moebius strip, with an unbroken continuity between interior and exterior. What would this mean for vision? Gilles Deleuze has proposed just such a possible continuity with his idea of the fold.

For Deleuze, folded space articulates a new relationship between vertical and horizontal, figure and ground, inside and out—all structures articulated by traditional vision. Unlike the space of classical vision, the idea of folded space denies framing in favor of a temporal modulation. The fold no longer privileges planimetric projection; instead there is a variable curvature. Deleuze's idea of folding is more radical than origami, because it contains no narrative, linear sequence; rather, in terms of traditional vision, it contains a quality of the unseen.

Folding changes the traditional space of vision. That is, it can be considered to be *e*ffective; it functions, it shelters, it is meaningful, it frames, it is aesthetic. Folding also constitutes a move from *e*ffective to *a*ffective space. Folding is not another subject expressionism, a promiscuity, but rather unfolds in space alongside of its functioning and its meaning in space—it has what might be called an excessive condition or *a*ffect. Folding is a type of affective space which concerns those aspects that are not associated with the *e*ffective, that are more than reason, meaning, and function.

In order to change the relationship of perspectival projection to three-dimensional space it is necessary to change the relationship between project drawing and real space. This would mean that one would no longer be able to draw with any level of meaningfulness the space that is being projected. For example, when it is no longer possible to draw a line that stands for some scale relationship to another line in space, it has nothing to do with reason, of the connection of the mind to the eye. The deflection from that line in space means that there no longer exists a one-to-one scale correspondence.

My folded projects are a primitive beginning. In them the subject understands that he or she can no longer conceptualize experience in space in the same way he or she did in the gridded space. They attempt to provide this dislocation of the subject from effective space, an idea of presentness. Once the environment becomes affective, inscribed with another logic or an ur-logic, one which is no longer translatable into the vision of the mind, then reason becomes detached from vision. While we can still understand space in terms of its function, structure, and aesthetic—we are still within the "four walls"—somehow reason becomes detached from the affective condition of the environment itself. This begins to produce an environment that "looks back"—that is, the environment seems to have an order that we can perceive even though it does not seem to mean anything. It does not seek to be understood in the traditional way of architecture yet it possesses some sense of "aura," an ur-logic which is the sense of something outside of our vision. Yet one that is not another subjective expression. Folding is only one of perhaps many strategies for dislocating vision—dislocating the hierarchy of interior and exterior that preempts vision.

The Alteka Tower project begins simultaneously with an "el" shape drawn in both plan and section (fig. 6.1). Here, a change in the relationship of perspectival projection to three-dimensional space changes the relationship between project drawing and real space. In this sense, these drawings would have little relationship to the space that is being projected. For example, it is no longer possible to draw a line that stands for some scale relationship to another line in the space of the project; thus the drawn lines no longer have anything to do with reason, the connection of the mind to the eye. The drawn lines are folded with

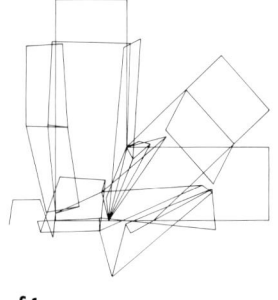

6.1

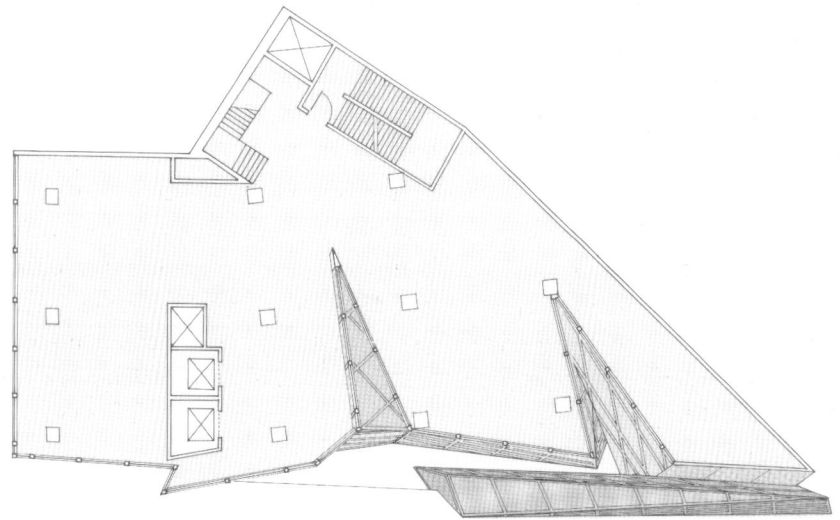

6.2 Alteka Tower, Tokyo, Japan, 1991, Second-floor plan.

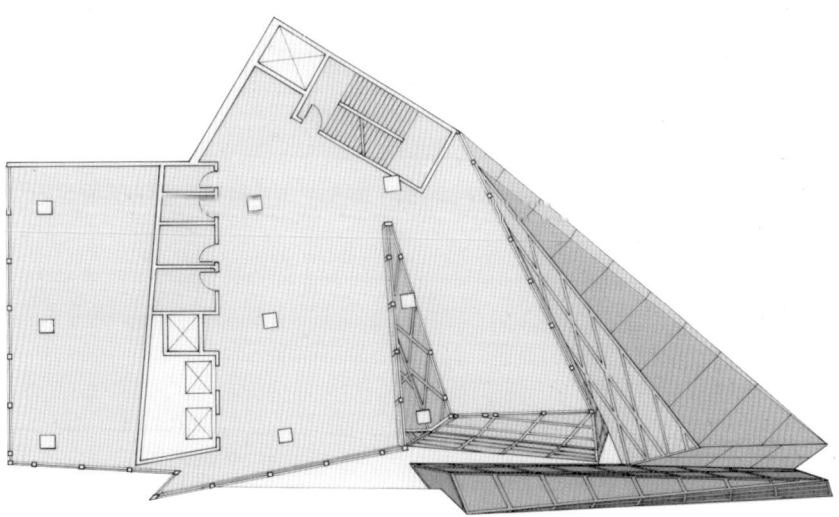

6.3 Alteka Tower, Tokyo, Japan, 1991. Third-floor plan.

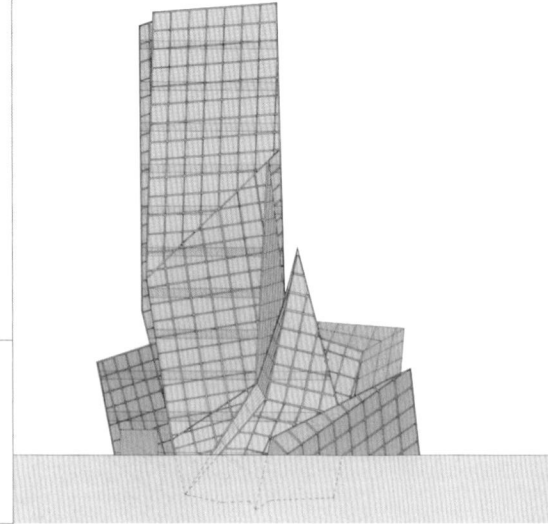
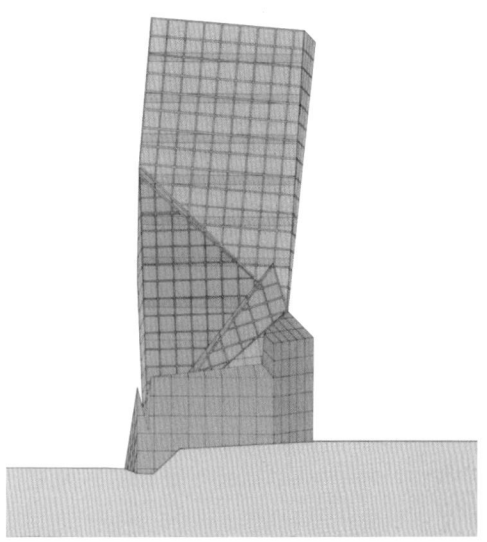

6.4 Alteka Tower, Tokyo. South elevation.

6.5 Alteka Tower, Tokyo. East elevation.

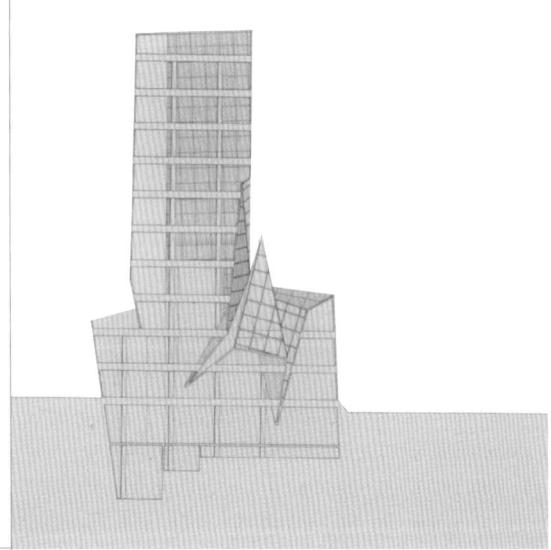

6.6 Alteka Tower, Tokyo. Section.

some ur-logic according to sections of a fold in René Thom's catastrophe theory. These folded plans and sections in turn create an object, which is cut into from the ground floor to the top.

When the environment is inscribed or folded in such a way, the individual no longer remains the discursive function; the individual is no longer required to understand or interpret space. Questions such as What does the space mean? are no longer relevant. It is not just that the environment is detached from vision, but that it also presents its own vision, a vision that looks back at the individual. The inscription is no longer concerned with aesthetics or with meaning but with some other order. It is only necessary to perceive the fact that this other order exists; this perception alone dislocates the knowing subject.

The fold presents the possibility of an alternative to the gridded space of the Cartesian order. The fold produces a dislocation of the dialectical distinction between figure and ground; in the process it animates what Deleuze calls a smooth space. Smooth space presents the possibility of overcoming or exceeding the grid. The grid remains in place and the four walls will always exist, but they are in fact overtaken by the folding of space. Here there is no longer one planimetric view which is then extruded to provide a sectional space. Instead it is no longer possible to relate a vision of space in a two-dimensional drawing to the three-dimensional reality of a folded space. Drawing no longer has any scale value relationship to the three-dimensional environment. This dislocation of the two-dimensional drawing from the three-dimensional reality also begins to dislocate vision, inscribed by this ur-logic. There are no longer grid datum planes for the upright individual.

Alteka is not merely a surface architecture or a surface folding. Rather, the folds create an affective space, a dimension in the space that dislocates the discursive function of the human subject and thus vision, and at the same moment creates a condition of time, of an event in which there is the possibility of the environment looking back at the subject, the possibility of the *gaze*.

The gaze, according to Maurice Blanchot, is that possibility of seeing which remains covered up by vision. The gaze opens the possibility of seeing what Blanchot calls the light lying within darkness. It is not the light of the dialectic of light/dark but the light of an otherness, which lies hidden within presence. It is the capacity to see this otherness which is repressed by vision. The looking back, the gaze, exposes architecture to another light, one which could not have been seen before.

Architecture will continue to stand up, to deal with gravity, to have four walls. But these four walls no longer need to be expressive of the mechanical paradigm. Rather they could deal with the possibility of these other discourses, the other affective senses of sound, of touch, and of that light lying within the darkness.

CHAPTER 7

PRESENTNESS AND THE BEING-ONLY-ONCE OF ARCHITECTURE

In her book *The Optical Unconscious*, Rosalind Krauss discusses a Jackson Pollock painting in relationship to its position in space. She contends that when a Pollock painting is placed in a horizontal position, that is, on the floor as it was painted, it is a "savage work." But the moment the canvas is taken off of the floor and moved to a vertical position on the wall, Krauss continues, it becomes "naturalized," reinstitutionalized and reinscribed into the discourse of painting.

All of this is said with an uncharacteristic innocence about the possible effect of the floor or the wall on this change in perception. She assumes that one can lift things up and down, off and on, without any discussion of why the relationship between floor and wall, or, for that matter, between the floor or the wall and the painting, could cause this to happen. What is clear in Krauss's argument is that the contexts provided by architecture, in this case the floor and the wall, do affect how the subject conceptualizes a painting. Yet the issue of how or why such an effect is possible is not discussed. Such an omission is by no means unique to Krauss's argument. Most of those outside of architecture assume that architectural conventions have a thought-to-be naturalness with respect to such things as walls and floors. Jacques Derrida even points out that we must be wary of the idea that architecture "is destined for habitation," that the concept of architecture is "a heritage which comprehends us even before we could submit it to thought." Walter Benjamin also attempts to explain this idea of "destined for habitation" in a different way. He says, "[In] architecture, habit determines to a large extent even optical reception. Architecture cannot be understood by optical means alone, that is, by contemplation. It is mastered gradually by habit." Thus in one sense the wall is already seen in any specific context by habit. This could be responsible for the naturalizing of the Pollock painting, since it is known that all paintings by force of habit are hung on walls and not on floors. Clearly, the question of habit and the habitual is already predetermined when dwellings are called places of habitation as opposed to, say, places of occupation. But this assumption of habit alone, it will be argued here, is not enough to account for the naturalizing effect of the wall on the Pollock painting. Nor can the ideas of an a priori destiny or naturalness, the assumption that "this is the way things are," be the only cause of this effect. Clearly something else must be at work. And it is this something else that makes architecture a problematic discourse.

The very conditions that bring about this idea of an a priori destiny or a thought-to-be naturalness of architecture, and thus what makes architecture problematic, lie initially in the fact that architecture is alone of all the discourses in its particular linking of its iconicity with its instrumentality, its meaning with its objecthood. A wall in architecture is not merely holding something up, it also symbolizes that act of holding up. Architecture, Derrida says, "cannot be without meaning." One cannot have the wall without the sign of the wall and vice versa; architecture will always implicate the wall. When Vitruvius, in his famous dicta on architecture, used the term *firmitas*, he did not mean that buildings should stand up (since all buildings of necessity must stand up) but rather that they should look like they stand up. It has been argued that in all disciplines instrumentality in some way affects iconicity; for example, the form of a book, its pagination, type, and binding all affect our reading of the text, but not all texts are necessarily in book form. Yet in architecture there will always be the presence of walls, walls that are both icon and instrument. It is this unique linkage that becomes problematic, because in order to "deconstruct" the meaning of architecture, one must attempt to separate the presence of the wall from the meaning of the wall—what in fact cannot be separated. Thus, unlike any other discourse, architecture both resists and requires the deconstructive impulse. This resistance alone should be of interest to deconstructive thought.

In addition to the strong connection between iconicity and instrumentality, architecture also has a unique relationship to what Derrida refers to in *The Truth in Painting* as the "once only" of a work of art. The condition of this "once only" at work in architecture is not the same as it is in painting or in photography. Derrida poses the issue of the "being-only-once" of a work of art as the fault line of deconstruction in its relationship to painting and photography. He cites Walter Benjamin and says, "As soon as the technique of reproduction reaches the stage of photography a break line and also a new front traverses the whole space of art. The presumed uniqueness of production, the 'being-only-once' of the exemplar and the value of authenticity, is practically deconstructed." Therefore it could be argued that the work of deconstruction has as one of its objects the notion of the displacement of the original, the prior condition of either a painting or a photograph.

In terms of photography, the "being-only-once" formerly devolved upon the issue of the original photographic plate in relation to the serial print. The plate is manipulated in development to produce a serial work which bears the mark of the hand of the author as well as that of the process. For example, a photograph can be developed with more or less grain, more or less contrast, and more or less light and intensity. Under these circumstances, the value of the photographic object relies on both the quality of the original plate and the quality of the reproduction as well as the limited seriality of the reproduction. The number one-of-ten is of more value to a collector than the number two-of-ten. There is a prior value given to the closeness of the copy in time to the plate, which in this case is the being-only-once. The use of the plate and the collection of the plate—whether plates are destroyed or not—define the problematic of originality in the era of mechanical reproduction.

When one moves from the mechanical paradigm to the electronic paradigm another issue enters in. Conditions are no longer the same for the photograph (it should be noted that for the sake of this argument the question of replication in photography only and not in painting is at issue). The possibility of an electronically reproduced photograph becomes interesting in this context as it represents the ultimate deconstruction of the original. Now, instead of a plate, a physical negative, there are only electronic impulses, ones and zeroes —impulses of light. The object no longer contains being, but exists only as contiguous electronic impulses; there is no longer a being-only-once. This erasure of the being-only-once that is proposed by the digitized photograph has several consequences. At one and the same time it turns the mediation that was present in the photograph from a condition of self-similarity to selfsameness. For it is possible to digitize a photograph in such a way as to reproduce it so that even an expert cannot tell if it was the first instance or the second. In digitized reproduction the selfsame characteristic is so strong that it is impossible to discern the difference even with a so-called expert mediating eye. In other words, all of the potential subjective characteristics of the being-only-once are erased. But equally, the converse is true.

Formerly, one was able to trust a photograph for documentary evidence. For example, if one wanted to buy a Rembrandt, verifying that the Rembrandt was authenticated by a signature, this could be done through a photograph. Therefore, a selfsame photograph would become the most objective record one could have. But the digitized photograph—the new selfsame record—is now most open to mediation and thus to being manipulated. It is possible to change a photograph of an original painting, an original that did not have a Rembrandt signature, by putting in such a signature without anyone being able to detect that the photograph had been doctored. It would thus appear that the evidence originally there was in fact not. In the digitizing process two things happen. First, there is a collapse of the idea of the being-only-once as the idea of the original or the authentic, and second, the role of the hand of the author, which formerly was a distinguishing characteristic between an objectifying and a subjectifying process, also becomes blurred. These two processes become, as it were, superposed over one another; time and space as the limits of difference are erased. In fact, it can be argued that they deconstruct one another because there is no longer the possibility that the photograph can be relied on for objective truth. But equally the digitized photograph bears no trace of its process, and thus it is no longer possible to tell if there was any authorial mediation. In fact, the digitized photograph becomes simultaneously subject to the most mediation and to the least mediation.

This produces a condition whereby the mediation of the author is seen within a different spectrum. It either takes place, on the one end, as the traditional art object, with its value in presence, or, at the other, as the nihilistic gesture of the erasure of the object and the authorial trace. This spectrum of discourse, it can be argued, is possible only in print media—that is, where the possibility of repetition and replication is at issue. This is not the case with architecture.

The discourse of replication, and thus the question of the original, would seem not to be at issue in built architecture. That a building is always a unique instance would be the argument of conventional wisdom. But before this can be assumed, one must first put aside the unique relationship that built work has to its drawing (which in its more general consequences is a broader issue that will not be discussed here). Oftentimes the drawing of architecture is more of an original than the work of architecture: as when Palladio redraws all of his buildings as they were designed to be, rather than as they were built; or when Daniel Libeskind in his Micromegas project draws an architecture that is not intended to be built; or when G. B. Piranesi draws, in his Carceri series, architectures that could never be built. In each of these examples the drawing of architecture becomes an original instance, and thus questions the simplistic view of building as an example of a being-only-once. But it is not the instance of building that is intended here as the reference for this unique being-only-once of architecture. While in one sense the built work in its site and programmatic specificity is always a unique instance, this is again an overly determined answer, one that does not speak to a condition which can be considered unique in architecture.

Derrida himself comes closer to defining this unique condition when he says that architecture is more like the idea of an event, which "reinvents architecture in a series of 'only onces' which are always unique in their repetition." This idea overlays replication with the idea of the unique, that architecture can be replicated, and that this replication is always unique. This quality of the unique is brought about by the fact that architecture always demands presence. While it is possible to challenge the idea of the presence of an object with regard to works of photography, and clearly to works of other written, mediated discourses on tape or on film, it is not as simple to challenge in architecture.

While deconstruction seems to take into consideration the idea that architecture, unlike painting and photography, is a highly conventionalized system, and while it may be possible to loosen architecture's relationship to its instrumentality, that is, to loosen the relationship between form and function, it is impossible to deny architecture's metaphysics of presence. Even in a condition of virtual reality, architecture is conventionalized as the metaphysics of presence; within virtual reality, architecture is still imagined as a physical body. It is this metaphysics of presence which dominates any discussion of architecture. Therefore, in order to propose a deconstruction of architecture it is necessary to propose something that can overcome this dominance of presence.

It will be argued here that this unique conventionality of architecture, which links its iconicity and instrumentality, already contains the capacity to open up and separate its condition of presence from its meaning. This opening up creates a possibility for another condition of being-only-once. That is, once the separation of the thought-to-be natural and normative conditions of architecture is proposed, there is the possibility of another being-only-once, which can be seen as the opposite of the deconstruction of the being-only-once in painting. And it is the deconstruction of this natural relationship that puts into place another being-only-once that is unique to architecture. This condition can be properly called *presentness*.

Presentness can be defined in several different ways. First, the term should not be confused with Michael Fried's use of a term with the same name. According to Krauss, presentness for Fried is a "reinscribing of modernism within a historic metaphysic." For Fried, presentness was a moment which collapsed time into the inexorable present, where there was no difference between thinking and experience. For Derrida, experience is something outside of, or different from, this time frame. The event for Derrida, that is, the time frame of the moment, requires the "writing of a space," a mode of spacing which distinguishes the space of the event from the time of the event. My use of the term *presentness* also begins from an idea of spacing, a spacing which is required in the loosening of the relationship of the architectural object from its thought-to-be natural condition of instrumentality. Thus in one sense, *presentness*, as I conceive it, is precisely the opposite of the Fried definition. As Krauss points out, the central concept of the phenomenology of self-presence requires an undivided unity of a temporal present, that is, between the object and the sign. Precisely because this relationship is so predetermined in architecture, the term *presentness* offers a means to loosen the inexorable relationship of the architectural object from its thought-to-be natural condition of instrumentality.

If *presentness* is such an occupied term, why the insistence on its use? More than any other term it combines both the idea of time in presence, of the experience of space in the present, while at the same time its suffix *-ness* causes a distance between the object as presence, which is a given in architecture, and the quality of that presence as time, which may be something other than mere presence. This creates the idea of a spacing between presence and the quality of presentness. However, this does not in any way implicate two other characteristics of presentness: that is, its quality of an already given and its capacity to render that already given as necessarily subversive. These latter two characteristics, unique to architecture, also distinguish *presentness* from Derrida's use of the term *maintenant*, which in many respects may be seen as similar. *Maintenant*, while implicating both time and space in its idea of maintaining, does not demand the quality of subversion as a prior condition to any transformation, which it is argued here is a necessary condition of architecture. It is precisely the subversion of the type and the norm, of the thought-to-be natural relationship between icon and instrument that creates architecture's being-only-once. As long as the instrumentality of architecture is seen to be its form and its function—whether that function is its site, program, or structure, and its form is its aesthetic, style, or iconography—and as long as this thought-to-be natural condition is seen as a two-term system, it represses the possibility of presentness.

The importance of presentness as a term for architecture is that it distinguishes a writing from an instrumentality of aesthetics and meaning. Presentness as a writing is the possibility of a subversion of the thought-to-be convention of type in architecture; that architecture has within it an insidedness which is an already existing possibility for the subversive. Presentness is both the possibility of, if not the need for, architecture to stabilize itself through the reabsorption of the transformation of type brought about by this subversion, and simultaneously the resistance to this reabsorption. This insidedness as a writing is both a trace of this already given and the possibility to experience this trace in space. Trace is the possibility of the subversion of a primordial type, which itself is constantly being over time, to become at any given time in the history of architecture, the then-existing convention of type. To achieve this subversion, architecture must always overcome the normative typological and social gestures that, at any given time, attempt to maintain its status quo. Architecture only continues and maintains itself precisely because of this subversive impulse to produce its being-only-once. For example, in Michelangelo's Laurentian Library there is a subversion of the type form of the then-existing library type. Because to this day this subversion has not been absorbed into the library type, that is, the library type has not transformed itself to include the subversion of the more general type manifest in the specific instance of presentness in the Laurentian Library, it still retains the same affective charge, the presentness of its being-only-once, that it had in the sixteenth century. Thus while part of this idea of presentness obviously deals with the condition of the new and the time of the new, it also deals with the time of duration, that is, with the subversion of presence as trace. Clearly, when Michelangelo subverted the type-form of the library in his Laurentian project, it was a subversion also of the existing style of architecture, and in that sense it was also new. The fact that today one experiences this duration of presentness (and this is a condition of experience and not so much of drawing) means that the subversion has been a continuous one that has not been absorbed into the conventional instrumentality of architecture.

This idea of presentness as a being-only-once unique to architecture, that is, as a sub-

7.1 Le Corbusier, Chapel at Ronchamp, France.

7.2 Le Corbusier, La Tourette Monastery at Arbresle, France.

version of type, can also be seen if one takes two late projects by Le Corbusier, the chapel at Ronchamp (fig. 7.1) and the monastery at La Tourette (fig. 7.2), both of which contained at the time of their building a presentness. It could be argued that Ronchamp contained only a presentness of the new, that is, that it was theatrical and performative. While it affected experience because of its newness, it did nothing to displace the instrumentality of type in the notion of the church. It is precisely the theatricality of the gestures of Ronchamp that has been reabsorbed in architecture, so that today the presentness of Ronchamp is no longer what it was. However, at La Tourette, a monastery, presentness was brought about by the subversion of both type-form and icon. There was a new idea of what it was to be a monastery. At La Tourette this condition of presentness remains in place today because the dislocation of the type has not been reabsorbed in the conventional idea of the monastery type. It still remains a displacement, a subversion of the condition of the type that had formally existed. This same idea could also be argued in my own work, for example, in the Wexner Center (fig. 7.3) in Columbus, Ohio, and in the convention center (fig. 7.4) in the same city. The Wexner Center is an example of presentness precisely because it subverts the instrumentality and iconicity of the museum, whereas the Columbus Convention Center is more theatrical and does not involve the subversion of type (in fact, it involves the maintenance of type) and therefore will be less articulate in the future as a condition of presentness.

If architecture is a unique condition of discourse in which the sign and the signified are more closely linked than in any other discourse, presentness is a way of opening up what is repressed in the assumed to be natural instrumentality of form and function, or of meaning

7.3 Eisenman Architects, Wexner Center for the Visual Arts, Columbus, Ohio.

and function. Presentness requires the constant subversion of this instrumentality in order to write an architecture as a trace of presence within presence. This becomes particularly critical within the terms of an electronic paradigm, where the former boundaries that maintained any discourse are blurred. As in contemporary physics and biology, where the hegemony of cause and effect has been undermined, so too the cause and effect of architecture, form and function, presence and absence, could be opened up by a condition of presentness.

Architecture can neither merely return to a dialectic of the metaphysics of presence nor return to a nihilism which denies presence. Presentness is an alternative term that does not force a choice between these two. It could be argued that, since presentness is an already-given of architecture, it has always been potentially active in the problematic of architecture, but because of the bond between icon and instrument has tended to be repressed by them. It could further be argued that the simultaneous resistance and requirement of an architecture to the idea of a being-only-once would allow deconstruction to think its discourse through architecture in a way that it could not in other modes of being. This would allow one to say that architecture, in its resistance to deconstruction, also requires deconstruction, and that architecture provides a space different from the space of language, literature, or painting, which could be an effective means for deconstruction to rethink itself today.

7.4 Eisenman Architects, Greater Columbus Convention Center, Columbus, Ohio.

CHAPTER 8

PROCESSES OF THE INTERSTITIAL Notes on Zaera-Polo's Idea of the Machinic

In his essay "The Making of the Machine: Powerless Control as a Critical Strategy," Alejandro Zaera-Polo suggests that my resistance to what he calls "the space of power" is produced not by subjective opposition but rather through the replacement of the subject by an instrumental, or what he calls a *machinic*, process. Zaera-Polo goes on to say that my major discovery is to have located the space of a machinic performance. In this sense, he calls me the first truly machinic architect. Zaera-Polo's use of *machinic* in this context is taken from Gilles Deleuze and Félix Guattari's initial use of the term in *A Thousand Plateaus*.[1] This essay will examine Deleuze and Guattari's model of the machinic in order to investigate whether Zaera-Polo's assessment has any validity or whether it is only a useful approximation, a heuristic device to explain another similar, yet somewhat different process. Clearly Zaera-Polo's idea of my process as an attempt to resist the traditional terms of design, which are seen to be compliant with the space of power, is a reasonable beginning. While most resistance attacks the compliant forms of the object, it will be argued that my work challenges both the object and its processes and, in so doing, questions its basis in *forming*. Central to such a possible machinic process is a shift from forming to what can be called *spacing*, in an attempt to produce an architectural object that is no longer complicit with its previous terms of embodiment or with the form/matter dialectic. While the machinic deals with the idea of *becoming* as a state of the object, as will be seen below, this becoming does not differentiate between forming and spacing; both would be understood as equivalent processes of becoming. Yet it is precisely this shift from forming to spacing that will be seen to be crucial in the context of an architecture, where space as opposed to form has often remained untheorized. Again, Zaera-Polo in a second article, "Eisenman's Machine of Infinite Resistance," proposes that architectural space could be theorized in a way similar to the process proposed by Deleuze and Guattari in their idea of the machinic. Such a possible theorization can only be partly accounted for in both Deleuze and Guattari's and Zaera-Polo's description of the machinic.

Architecture, according to most traditional descriptions of it, embodied meaning and was legitimized by function. This meant that architecture, in addition to its being in form, also had to look like its function. Thus in architecture, the firmness of the Vitruvian triad, commodity, firmness, and delight, was not so much about a literal structure or firmness as it was about a structure that had to embody the idea of firmness; it had to look like it stood up. Instead of merely having an object that stood up, the act of standing was always necessarily represented in that standing up. Thus when something looked like structure, its being was legitimized by this "looking like" and not necessarily by the structure itself. This embedded relationship of image to icon has always been thought to be a natural condition of architecture. Thus one aspect of the nature of embodiment in architecture is the a priori, "already given" linkage of iconicity and instrumentality.

In this context, the design process, as it has been known, produced something called architecture that always looked like something which was characterized by a genre; either something looked rational or it looked expressionistic. Recently the signature, as another category of representation, another *look like*, differentiated individual as opposed to generic representation. In either case, the architectural object was always seen as a result of authorial

PROCESSES OF THE INTERSTITIAL

8.1 Eisenman Architects and Silvia Kolbowski, "Like the difference between Autumn/Winter '94/95 and Spring/Summer '95," Comme des Garçon, New York, 1995. Montage

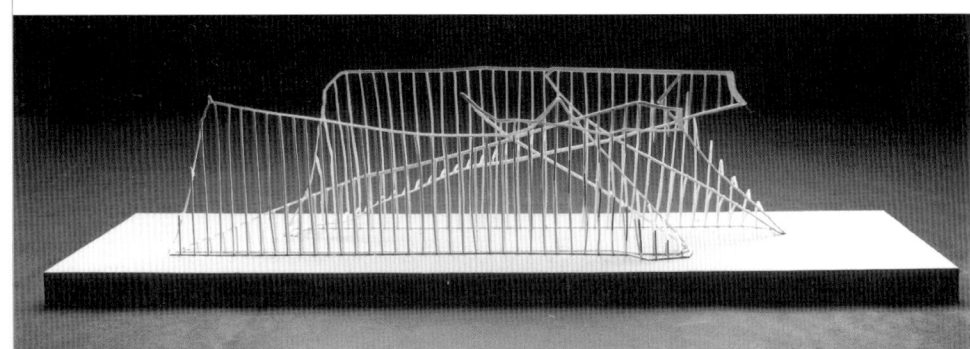

8.2 Study model.

8.3 Installation.

PROCESSES OF THE INTERSTITIAL

intervention and expression. However, it is possible to propose a process that has as a necessary precondition the displacement of authorial expression from the production of the object, the idea being that a traditional authorial role can use only traditional methods, which in turn can produce only objects legitimized within a traditional discourse. Such an *other* process, which is different from, and in fact at odds with, these traditional design methods, has three concerns. The first is to deny architecture's traditional modes of legitimation by function and meaning without denying their necessary presence in the object. The second is to suggest a process which, while it undercuts the legitimation of these modes of functioning, can also extract an *other* condition of the object which will still contain function, meaning, and an aesthetic. It is not merely the idea of extraction that is critical to this process, but rather the recognition that architecture is different from other disciplines, since cutting architecture from its previous modes of legitimation in function, meaning, and aesthetics does not mean that architecture will not have these functions. The third concern is to define in this new context of the object the differences that such a process necessarily produces in what will be called here the *tropic* conditions of architectural space. Just as there is no literature without its literary tropes, such as metaphor and metonymy, and there is no painting without its pictorial tropes, such as flatness and edge stress, there can be no architecture without its formal tropes, such as shear and compression. However, the change from forming to spacing will be seen to have important consequences in figuring architectural tropes and in particular with their traditional basis in formal, figure/ground relationships.

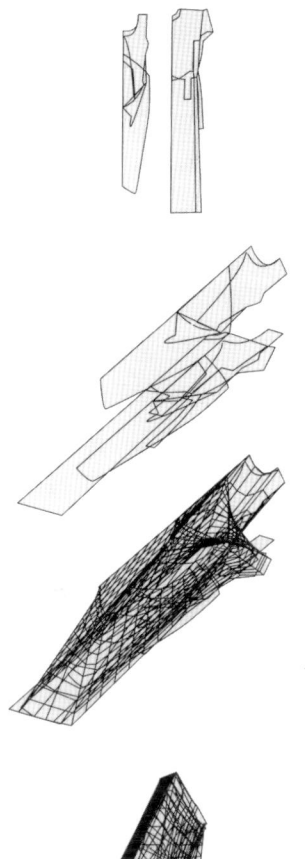

Traditionally, processes of architectural design have used what can be called on/off procedures, of choosing between two alternatives, solid/void, figure/ground, etc., rather than operating where the two conditions are possibly embedded within one another. The traditional ways of deciding which alternative to choose were based upon a condition of architecture as already embodying significance, that is, by a container or enclosure which by its very naming and function had meaning and use. This container also always looked like architecture, that is, it looked like it functioned and stood up. As has been said above, architecture uniquely contains an iconicity embedded in its instrumentality. Therefore, architecture was seen to contain an embodied sign system, that is, it was already within a regimen of signifiers and it conformed to that regimen of signifiers. Further, such an idea of architecture was legitimized by these signifiers as they represented or looked like certain desired meanings, functions, or aesthetic preferences.

8.4 Comme des Garçon, New York, 1995.

The machinic process, on the other hand, begins with the idea that architecture does not necessarily either contain or legitimize an already given or embodied sign system. The machinic would propose an architecture that does not conform to an already embodied condition, that does not have a preexistent condition of meaning in relation to its function, or an already given system of signification in the dialectical or metaphysical sense. For such a process to be possible, there also must be means for evaluating its results. How does one know, for example, when one has arrived at a condition that is cut off from its previous forms of legitimation? And since such a detached condition does not exist a priori, how does one know that such a cutting represents, in a subjective assessment, the best within a set

PROCESSES OF THE INTERSTITIAL

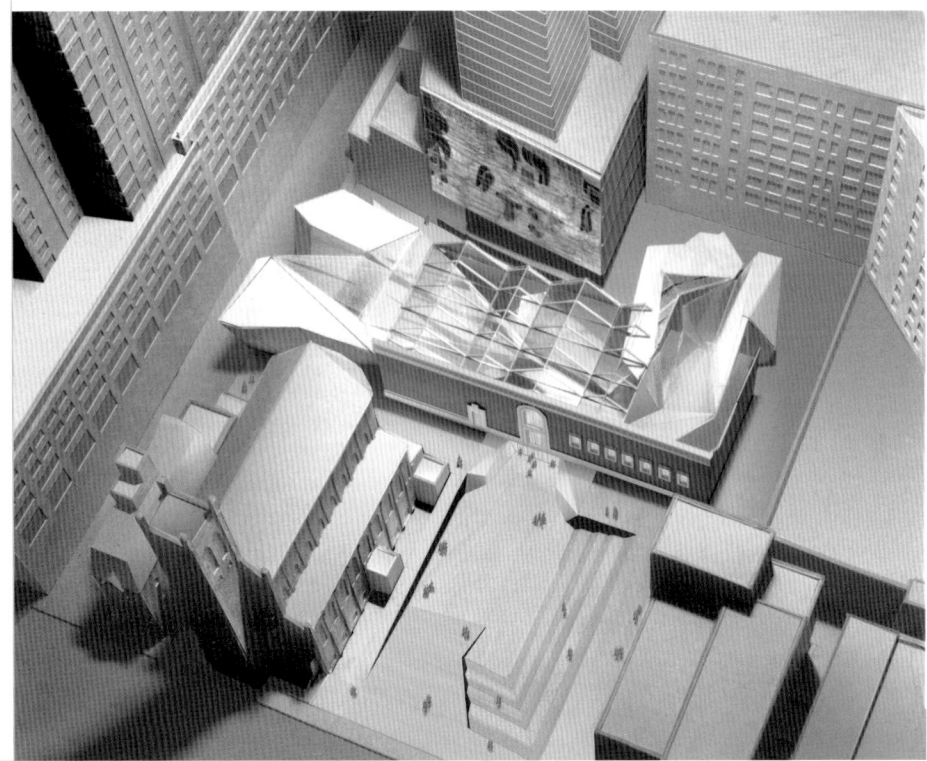

8.5 Eisenman Architects, The Jewish Museum of San Francisco, 1996. Aerial view of model.

8.6 The Jewish Museum of San Francisco. Interior view, computer rendering.

of circumstances? And of what value is the "best" in a set of circumstances, since it cannot be judged by traditional modes of legitimation—of the best aesthetically, functionally, formally, or significantly—since these are the very traditions which the process is trying to displace?

While the value systems for assessing the existing process known here as *forming*—such as the classical value system of aesthetics; the classical system of signs and signified; conditions of use, public vs. private, etc., that have traditionally demanded certain conditions of signing—are already in place, there are no value systems in place for a process called *spacing*. While there is no model of invention for such unknown conditions, the machinic process proposes that in its own internal consistency there are operative processes for such a valuation. For example, in the traditional forming process, while presences such as enclosing walls, floors, and roofs are given an initial value, in that they are designed and theorized first, the functioning spaces are usually seen as resulting from this initial forming. Such spaces have traditionally remained untheorized in that it is assumed that the forming process exists a priori to them. In this context, the forming process also placed a

8.7 Eisenman Architects, Bibliothèque de L'Huei, Geneva, Switzerland, 1997. Site plan.

priority on knowing and thus signaling, for example, where a front door is or the clarity of the internal circulation, and thus upon an architecture as providing a level of information. The suggestion in a machinic process is not so much a condition of providing a clarity of information, a yes/no set of answers, or a condition of form versus space, presence versus absence, but a process whereby the idea of spacing will be revealed to lie within the forming, where presence lies within absence, and so on. While a process similar to the machinic promises initially to extract one of these conditions out of the other and thereby produce necessarily different tropic conditions, it will be seen below that it cannot, a priori, achieve this; that to produce a spacing, which in turn will condition what will be proposed as the necessary resultant differences in the *tropic* conditions of architecture, requires something in addition to a machinic process.

It is difficult to define *machinic* because it is not a common word in English. A machine has machinic processes, so the word is not only adjectival, as it names a working; it is between an adjective and a verb. In a footnote in his book *A User's Guide to Capitalism and Schizophrenia*, Brian Massumi writes, "Deleuze and Guattari's frequent use of the terms *machine* and *machinic* (as in *desiring machine*) are often misinterpreted as a metaphor between the body as organism and the machine as technological apparatus. Deleuze and Guattari, however, make a basic distinction between the *machinic* and the *mechanical*."[2] This distinction between machinic and mechanical, according to Massumi, is that both the

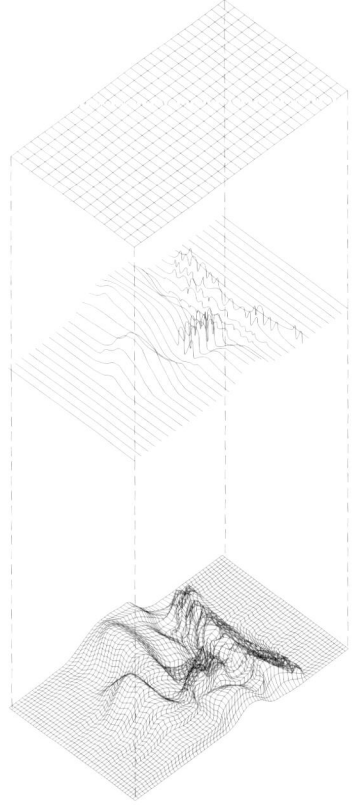
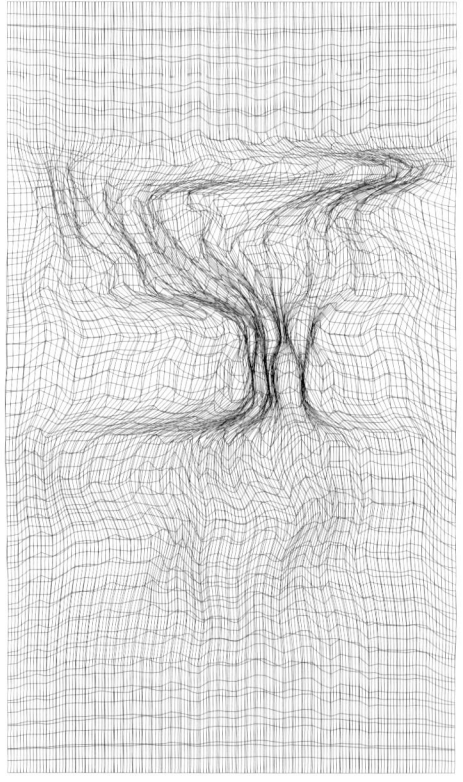

8.8–8.9 Bibliothèque de L'Huei, Geneva, Switzerland, 1997. Concept diagrams.

organic and the mechanical belong to the *molar*,[3] while the machinic belongs to something more complex. The mechanical refers to a structural interrelating of discrete parts working harmoniously together to perform work. The organic is the same organizational model applied to a living body. The machinic, on the other hand, refers to a more aleatory, arbitrary, even chaotic activity.

In his article "On Machines," Guattari talks about what machinic activity is and how it differs from the mechanical and the organic. He says that the essence of the machine, that is, the idea of the machine in the machinic, is not mechanical; it is "linked to procedures which deterritorialize its elements, functions and relations of alterity [otherness]."[4] *Deterritorialize*, in this context, could be construed to be the same as the term *delegitimize*. Second, Guattari says that machinic systems are not in themselves technological. "In the history of philosophy," he writes, "the problem of the machine has generally been regarded secondary to a more general system—that of *technè* and technique. I would propose a reversal of this point of view to the extent that the problem of technique would now only be a subsidiary part of a much wider machine problematic."[5] In other words, the machine opens outward to a "machinic environment" rather than inward toward technique.

In the context of an architecture, Deleuze and Guattari's idea of the machinic can be taken to mean something which functions out of its own immanence or interiority, that is, internally, by contagion rather than by comparison, subordinate neither to the laws of resemblance nor utility. Architecture, if it is anything, has always been subordinated and legitimated by laws of resemblance and utility in such dicta as form follows function. If form follows function, then form already has meaning, and when form follows function, form is already subordinated to the laws of resemblance and utility. While form is subordinated in both of these contexts, it has always had a priority over space. What Deleuze and Guattari are saying is that machinic processes do not subordinate values, but rather are a special type of production. Living bodies and technological apparatuses are machinic when they are *becoming*; organic or mechanical when they are functioning in a state of stable equilibrium. For architecture to be machinic would mean that it would not be subordinated to the laws of resemblance or utility and would not produce conceptually stable form objects but rather give a priority to conditions of space always in a state of becoming. Clearly, the idea of architecture as a state of becoming already defies its traditional idea of stability and stasis. But what is an architecture of becoming?

Guattari says, "Rather than having an opposition between *being* and the machine [that is, between being and becoming] or being and the subject, this new notion of the machine now involves *being* differentiating itself qualitatively and emerging onto an ontological plurality, which is the very extension of the creativity of machinic vectors."[6] Thus in architecture such a process might be iterative, might have directions and energy, and might deal with forces and flows which could be multiple, reversible, and deformative rather than linear and transformative. Guattari continues, "Rather than having a *being* as a common trait which would inhabit the whole of machinic, social, human and cosmic beings, we have, instead, a machine that develops *universes of reference*—ontological heterogeneous universes, which are marked by historic turning points, a factor of irreversibility and singularity."[7]

PROCESSES OF THE INTERSTITIAL

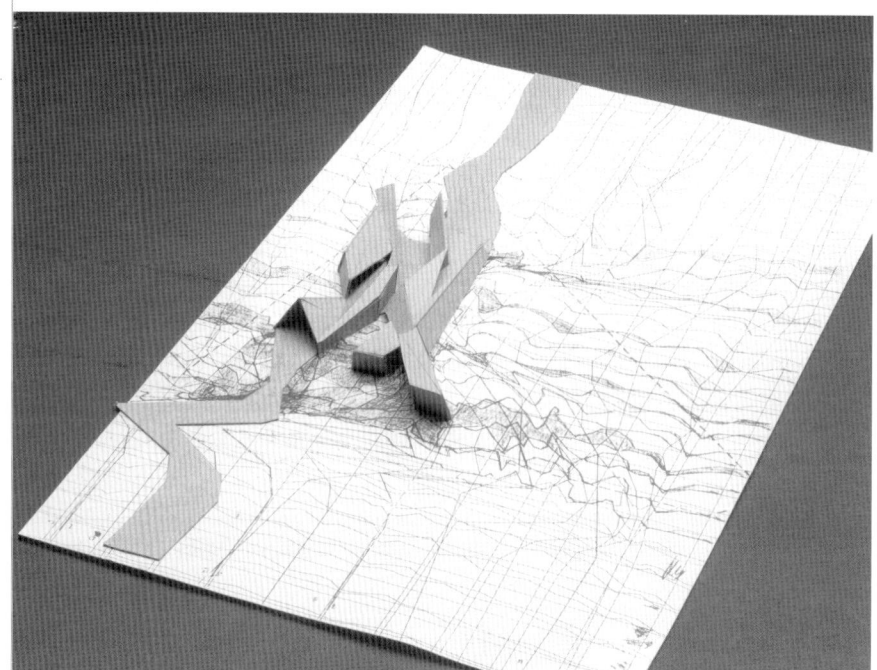

8.10 – 8.11 Bibliothèque de L'Huei, Geneva, Switzerland, 1997. Study models on site diagrams.

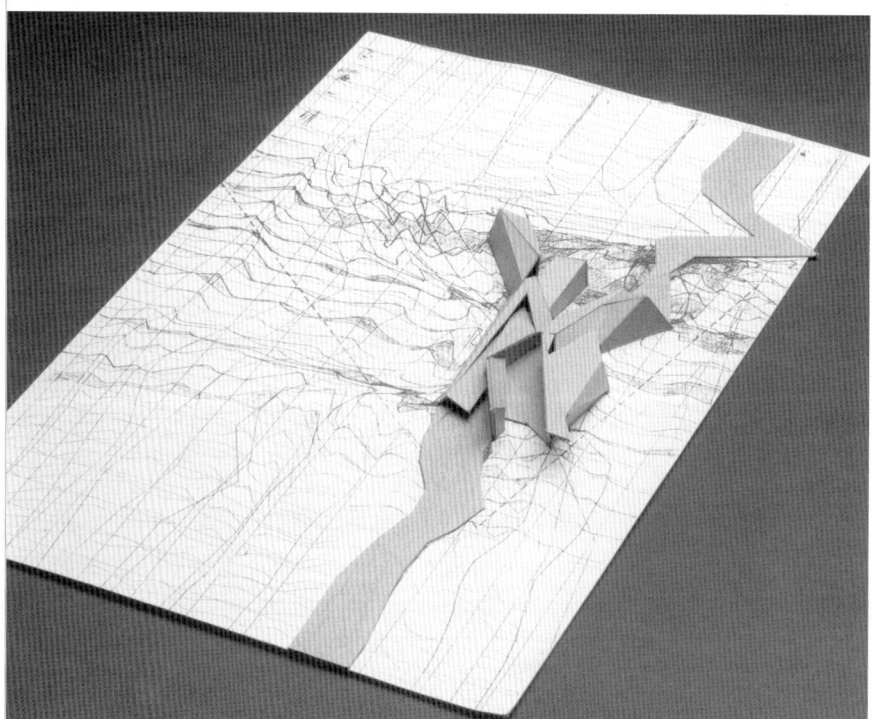

PROCESSES OF THE INTERSTITIAL

The [illegible] uggestion in Guattari's idea is that while the machinic is a process that can be re[illegible] initely, it never produces the same condition of becoming; that is, in its repetition [illegible] ys a singular instance of becoming.[8]

The f[illegible] f any architectural process has very little relationship, at first glance, to a process t[illegible] be described as machinic. Yet such a first step could be a necessary part of any atte[illegible] stance both authorial expression and authorial aesthetic and from any resultant o[illegible] ally this first step, after a specification of a program, is the production of a diagram or *parti*. This diagram usually contains several factors: one, an organization of functions; two, an organization of the functions by type; three, an organization of the first two by site considerations. Often site is defined by several factors, not simply the actual physical conditions of the site but also its past and present histories—buildings, roads, contingent contexts—all of which are figured into the site diagram. Often this site diagram interacts with the diagrams of function and type in an iterative process that produces a melding of all three. This diagram or *parti* will always contain what is the best entrance point, the clearest idea of circulation, as legitimizing conditions for its existence. This three-part organization is usually as far as most traditional processes go, in that the form of a two-dimensional plan container is given by them. This container is usually extruded into a three-dimensional volume with an aesthetic, materiality, and profile. The form of the container is clearly predetermined by its function as shelter and enclosure and because of this has its own meaning, whether intentional or not.

It is only after such a hypothetical container is produced that the process can enter into what might be called a machinic phase. For at this point it is possible to undercut these traditional modes of legitimation produced in the container and image described above. This does not mean there will be no function or no image, but rather that these will no longer be used to legitimize the container. Therefore, the machinic must propose a way to include function and image without having the container be seen as a result of their intervention.

This second phase is probably the most difficult and perhaps the closest to the machinic. It requires the choice of an outside agent, another diagram, almost a deus ex machina, which contains processes which when superposed with the first diagram will produce a blurring of the form/function and meaning/aesthetic relationships that seem to have produced the first diagram. Such a second diagram may or may not be immanent in either the first diagram or in the formal interiority of architecture, but must contain a process which has the capacity to modify the first diagram.

Diagrams of soliton waves, neural functioning, DNA structures, liquid crystals, and others from outside architecture have been used in such a second diagram. Equally, geometric processes such as sine waves, fractals, and morphing have also functioned in a second diagram. The question as to the nature of the second diagram is crucial. Do the processes of that diagram need to be immanent in the program, site, or architecture of the first? While on first thought it would seem that there should be some immanence, it is precisely such an immanence which could be said to resituate architecture in the same attitude of legitimation from which such a diagram is trying to escape. Perhaps it is precisely

PROCESSES OF THE INTERSTITIAL

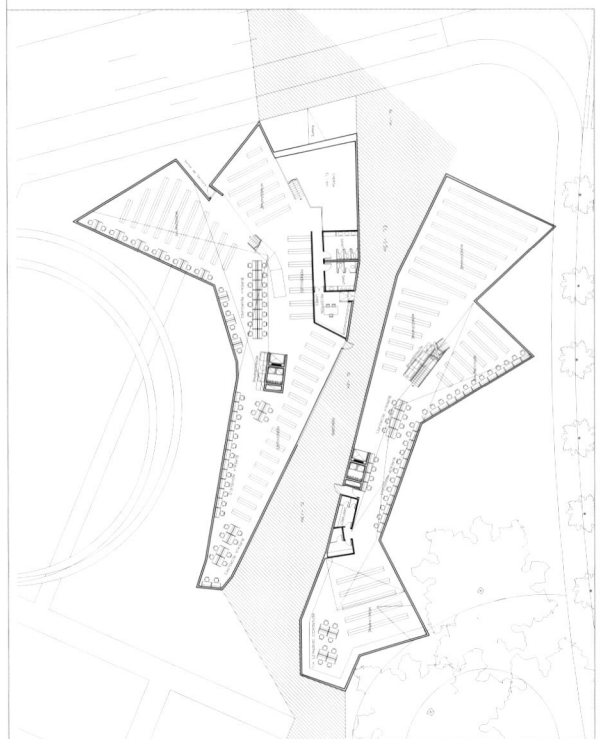

8.12 Bibliothèque de L'Huei. Ground-floor plan.

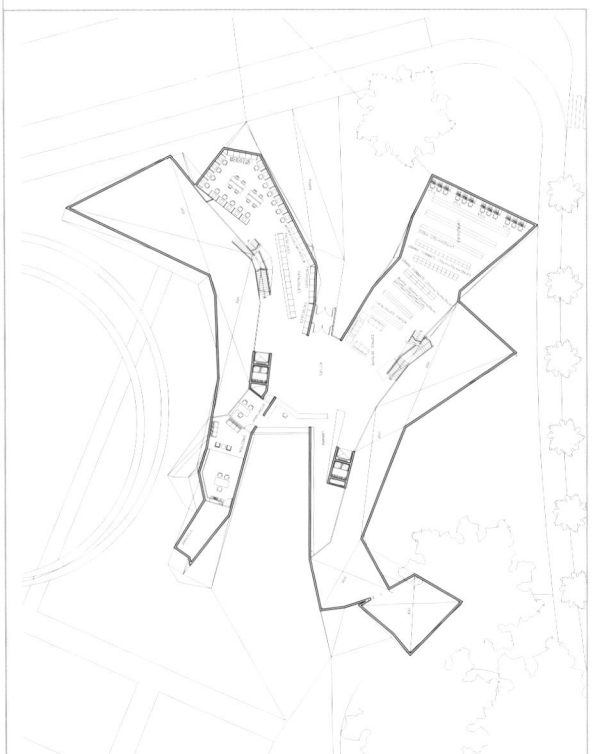

8.13 First-floor plan.

the seemingly arbitrary nature of the second diagram which would help open up and reveal the new possibilities which previous modes of legitimation have obscured.

It is precisely the potentially arbitrary nature of the second diagram which introduces the machinic into what might appear to be an organic or mechanical process. It is here that another of Deleuze's ideas becomes useful. This involves his idea of extraction, which he defines in relation to his ideas of the extraction of the figural from the figurative. Deleuze says that the figurative is associated with the illustrative and the narrative character of things. In this context the illustrative is representational and therefore embodied; the figurative also embodies an idea of narrative meaning. For Deleuze, the figurative is not a universal condition but a convention which derived from the Renaissance system of perspective and what came to be thought of as a natural relationship of subject to object. Thus he says modernism's attempted escape in cubism, de Stijl, and constructivism was only a symptom of the problem. Another way to overthrow the memory of the figurative, which was probably even suppressed by the abstractionist moderns, is through the purely figural. He suggests that this may be possible through a process of blurring. It is important to understand the difference between a literal and a conceptual blurring: one occurs in two dimensions; the other occurs in three. This, it will be seen, is another important difference between architecture and painting.

When talking about blurring as a process, Deleuze says, "What concerns us here is an absolute proximity, a coprecision, a line that is a shared contour of the field that functions as a background and the figure that functions as a form on a single plane. This is why there needs to be a certain blurriness of the contour between the background and the figure. . . . The blur is obtained in two ways: by destroying a clarity of the figure with another clarity that by its very mechanical precision is opposed to the legibility of one over the other [two clarities equal a blur] and the other is a blurring that is obtained by a wiping, where the distinction between the two becomes blurred."[9]

But the process of blurring is of necessity different for architecture than it is for painting. This can be seen in the difference between a contour in painting and a profile in architecture. A contour in painting is merely a membrane, a line between a figure and a ground, while a profile is a three-dimensional, formed container. When architecture is drawn it is always drawn as a formed profile. Heinrich Wolfflin says, for example, that the difference between the Renaissance and the baroque lies in its profile. In the Renaissance it was a hard-edged profile and in the baroque it was a blurred profile. Equally, a profile presents different conceptual problems than a contour. Contour in painting is on the same plane as both its figure and the ground. In architecture the profile is not on the same plane; it is always elevated and separate from its ground. Therefore the architectural profile and the contour in painting cannot be blurred in the same way. While different conditions of blurring of contour, such as deep space, shallow space, illusionistic space, stretched space, are possible in painting, in architecture, where there is a literal shelter, there is no such possibility. What is possible is a blurring of the diagram, where not only the profile but the entire organization is blurred conceptually so that it is no longer seen as merely fulfilling a function of embodying its interior form. Rather the blurring of the two diagrams produces an extraction

PROCESSES OF THE INTERSTITIAL

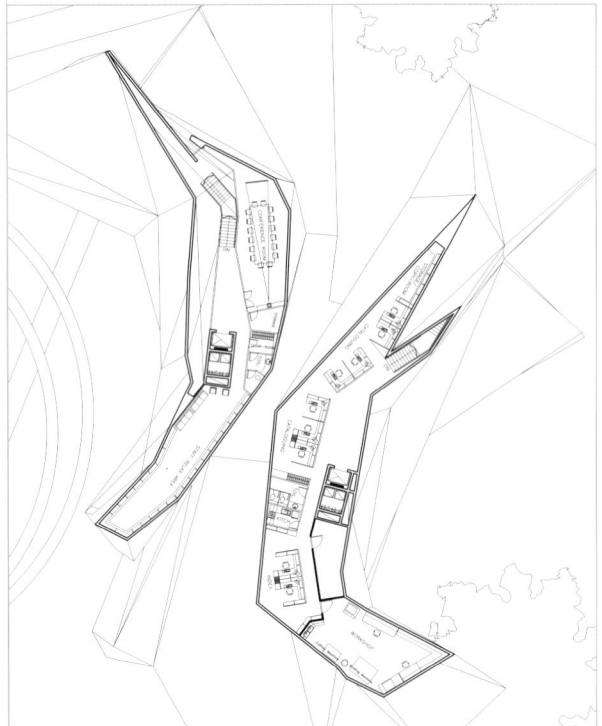

8.14 Bibliothèque de L'Huei. Second-floor plan.

8.15 Aerial view of model.

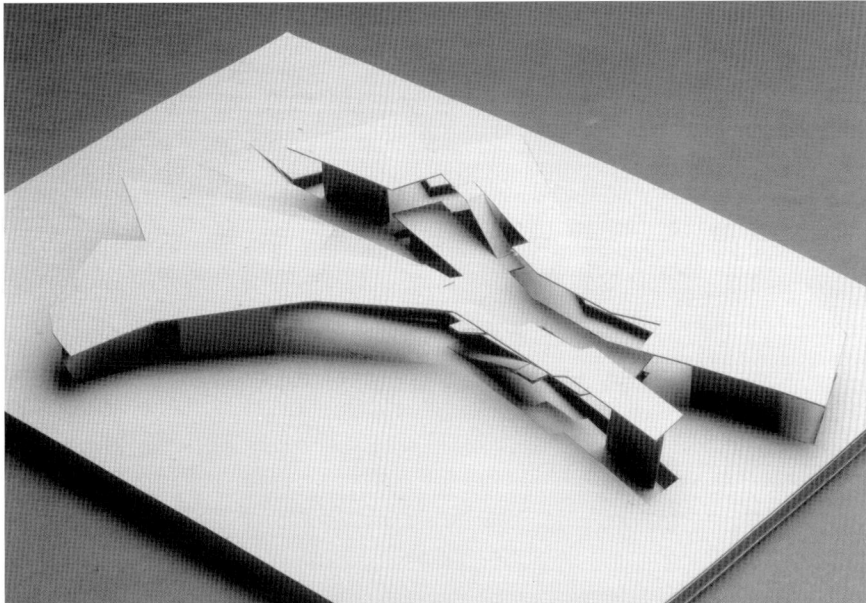

8.16 – 8.17 Bibliothèque de L'Huei. Study models.

of both from their previous functions. This brings the process to a condition of form, which in many senses is close to Deleuze's idea of the figural.

While it has been useful in this context to examine what is meant by the machinic, and while the term is helpful in modeling a process in architecture that is capable of first cutting and then extracting the object from its embodied conditions cited above, there is a suggestion

PROCESSES OF THE INTERSTITIAL

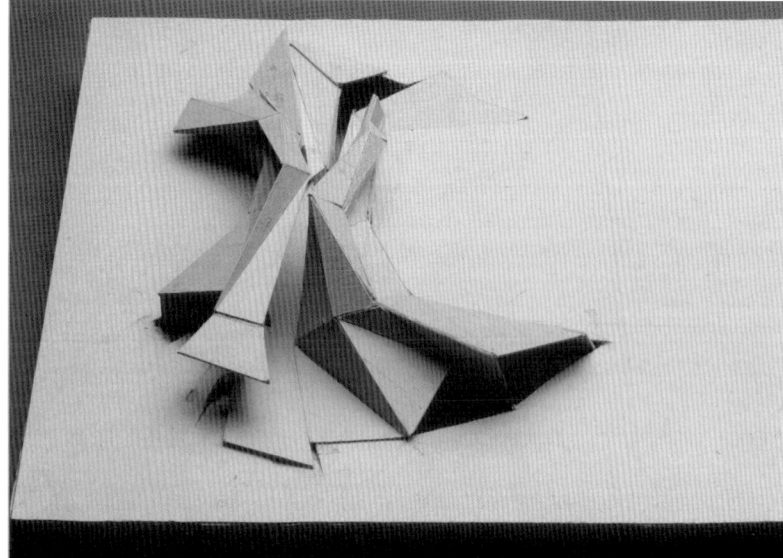

8.18 Study model.

8.19 Study model.

in the machinic process that it contains a condition of an already given difference which might lead to an *other* condition of architecture, that in its process lie new possibilities for the tropic. But the figural in itself does not necessarily embody the tropes of architecture. Thus far there is no a priori guarantee that a superposition, and a consequent blurring of the two diagrams mentioned above, would provide a modification of the traditional tropes of architecture, nor is there any mechanism which can move the process from forming to spacing.

What neither Deleuze and Guattari nor Zaera-Polo take into consideration in their proposition of the machinic is the necessity of producing what can be called a trope in architectural space. While a machinic process promises the possibility of such tropic conditions,

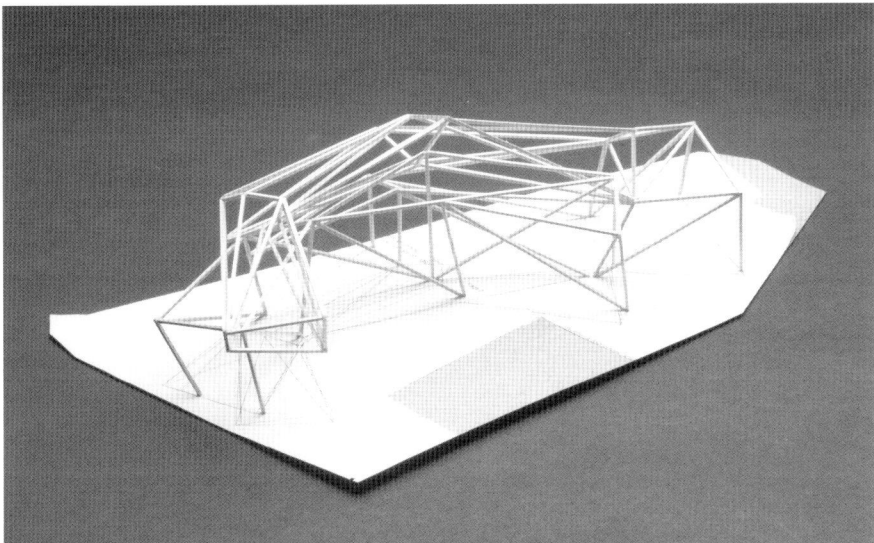

8.20 – 8.21 Stuctural study models.

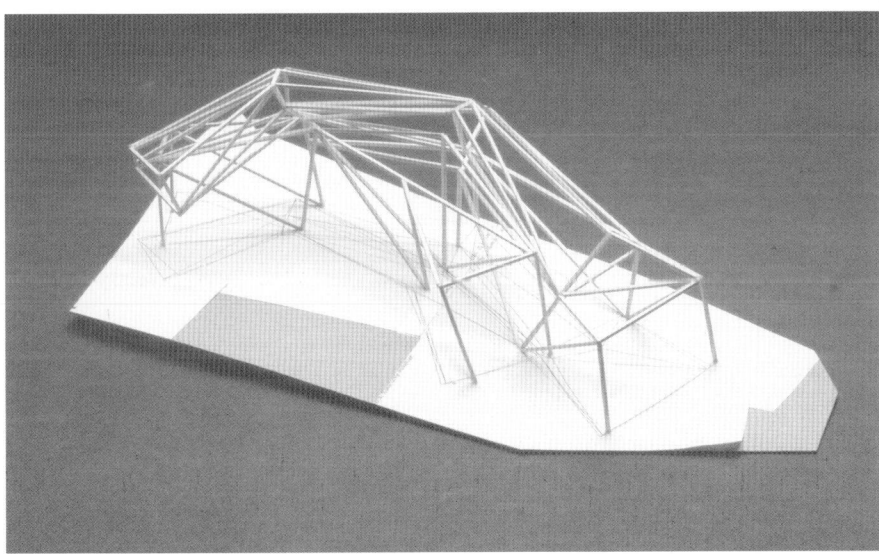

because such tropes already supposedly exist in the machinic process, these tropes are not necessarily the result of its processes.

Neither the process of the machinic nor any computer program can a priori produce such a trope. This is what young architects, weaned on computers, fail to realize. Computers may produce blobs and other self-generated formless aggregations, but these are in and of themselves no more architectural than they are graphic or illustrational. An architecture without its tropes would be similar to a painting without any pictorial conditions. While such pictorial tropes can be produced by a computer (one does not need to literally paint to produce edge stress) in two dimensions, similar spatial tropes may not necessarily produce

8.22 Western model view.

an edge stress in three dimensions. Thus, a third step in the process takes a turn away from an aspect of the machinic, its possibility of extraction, toward its more arbitrary and aleatory nature, by taking the blurred two-dimensional diagram of superpositions and projecting it into the third dimension. Since, a priori, such a process similar to the machinic cannot be expected to reveal in the third dimension the supposedly inherent figural possibilities of its process, another step is necessary. Here there is a necessary back and forth which comes between a physical, three-dimensional model and the composite diagram. Ultimately the intention is to make corrections in the diagram to incorporate the figural tropes so that the diagram can then run by itself, as it were, in a machinic way. This running by itself would give further smaller-scale articulations—windows, rooms, and corridors—which, because of the diagram, are no longer legitimized by function, aesthetics, or meaning. It is understood that the operations which modify the diagram in three dimensions may be already latent in the diagram, that it is merely a process of finding them. Thus this part of the process is both the most machinic and the most authorial, since it is a constant back and forth between processes.

Thus the third part of the process concerns the possibility of the production of tropes in real architectural space. However, if it is understood that these tropes could be considered as figural rather than formal, thus as other than the tradition of such tropes in architecture, then it is possible to introduce an other possibility for such tropes.

While the idea of a trope is clearly defined in literary terms—metaphor, metonymy, synecdoche—these terms do not define tropic conditions in architecture. This is because representation operates differently in architecture as opposed to literature or even painting.

Any system of representation is an image production, icons whose elementary units are signs, arrested images, as meaning effects, grasped as wholes composed of working parts between which analogical relations are established by a rhetorical transference. This is what is meant by a *trope*. Rhetorical transference and analogical relations are basically the tropes described above for literature. Conceivably any formal or figurative meaning mechanism could be considered a trope in architecture. These are relationships which in the past have created conceptual formal conditions such as shear, rotation, compression, and tension. While they may not be seen—there is no literal compression in the space—nevertheless they are affective in the space in that they can be sensed by the body. Thus what were formerly understood as architectural tropes can be seen as analogous to the pictorial in painting. Such things as flatness, edge stress, and picture plane are known as the pictorial, or the formal attributes of a canvas. In traditional architectural circumstances such tropic conditions were clearly operative. The difference, for example, between a space of Le Corbusier and a space of Adolf Loos would be in the different tropes used by each architect. However, when it comes to a machinic process, the making of a trope and thus the nature of its space are necessarily different.

Guattari says that spatial characteristics, such as what could be called tropes, already exist in the machinic environment. He says, "It possesses a core of consistency, insistence and ontological affirmation, which is prior to the unfolding into energetico-spatio-temporal coordinates."[10] Thus, what is being called here the figural could be considered differently from the traditional tropes in architecture, which are formal, in that the figural is in this sense marked by its processes of becoming, which already preexist in the machinic environment.[11] The figural is different from the formal in that it is the result of a pictorial act. The figural is a matrix of forces, a condition of becoming which uncovers potential attributes of space covered up by the formal. The figural uncovers these attributes in the formal through an act which is here called *spacing*. Spacing is a process which lies within forming. With the extraction of the figural it can no longer be seen as secondary to forming.

Machinic systems, Guattari says, are interfaces which are articulated to one another in what are called hypertexts. He writes, "The machine has something more than structure. It is 'more' than structure in that it does not limit itself to a game of interactions which develop in space and time between its component parts."[12] What this would mean for an architectural machine is that architecture's being already has an internal consistency which could be considered machinic, that is, there could be tropes, already given, which are not the same as a formal architectural trope, which is always added to a functional container. Rather, a figural trope would be one that already exists prior to its unfolding in spatio-temporal coordinates. That is to say, whether one considers figural tropes important to articulate or not is not the issue. Since their possibility already exists in a machinic process, they can be repressed only by choosing not to articulate them. If they are articulated, they will appear differently in space than they previously did as formal tropes. This difference can be seen, for example, in the trope of the *interstitial*.

Formerly, the interstitial as a formal trope was seen as a solid figuration usually known as *poché*. This was usually an articulated solid between two void conditions, either between

8.23 Eisenman Architects, BFL Software Headquarters, Bangalore, India, 1996. Interior perspective.

an interior and an exterior space or else between two interior spaces. The important condition of the interstitial was twofold. One, it was not merely a containing presence such as a wall, but also a figured or articulated presence. Two, this articulation was figurative and not figural, since it already embodied its content as a container which enclosed, sheltered, and had an aesthetic.

In order for the interstitial to be seen as something different from its condition as an articulated presence between two spaces, its status as an embodied figure would have to be changed. Such a change in status could be initially proposed as a presence within absence —a double absence. Such a condition of space might require a process which could begin from a process defined as *spacing* rather than a forming. Forming is a condition that is particular to architectural figuration, since a priori there must be a container which encloses and shelters. Thus forming as a process is presumed to be already preexistent in the idea of traditional architecture. It is this priority of forming that will be required to be displaced in what is described below.

In architecture, the container is always thought of first as an outline of a figure which contains a function and thus a meaning, as well as an aesthetic. The idea here is that since there will always be a container that exists a priori with a function and a meaning, somehow to cut this from its embodiment, while necessarily retaining function and some meaning, would mean to have both forming and a difference from forming. *The idea is to produce this already given difference of the machinic,* one which could extract something which lies within forming. Initially this process which is extracted can be called *spacing*.

Spacing is a term first suggested by Jacques Derrida with reference to writing. He attempts to differentiate between the notion of *écriture,* that is, writing in itself, and architectural writing. Derrida says that for him architectural writing implies a condition of inventive reading, that is, the possibility of a reading which had not previously existed. This is a reading by a subject who is no longer simply content to walk about and within architecture, but who would transform these elementary emotions into a condition of what Derrida calls a spacing. From this condition of spacing would derive the possibility of the invention of a system of writing from the gestures of the body, or of what Derrida calls "the spacing of another kind of writing." The term *espacement* for Derrida is distinguished from Martin Heidegger's use of the term as a gathering; Derrida's idea is more of a distancing. Here, spacing will be used in an entirely different way. In the context of architecture, spacing as opposed to forming begins to suggest a possible figure/figure relationship, which in turn suggests a new possibility for the interstitial. Spacing produces an other condition of the interstitial. The interstitial proposes a dissonant space of meaning. Where figure/ground was an abstraction, figure/figure is a figural condition that is no longer necessarily abstract. It is space as a matrix of forces and sense. It is affective in that it requires the body as well as the mind and the eye for its understanding. The interstitial, then, is the result of a process of extraction which produces a figural as opposed to a formal trope, and it exists as a condition of *spacing* as opposed to forming, as a presence in an absence, that is, between two conditions of figure as opposed to figure and ground. These conditions of the figure again can be directly related to Deleuze's idea of the relationship of the figurative to the figural explained above.

Such a removal of the interstitial from a process of forming, that is, from an embodied figuration, does not seem to be possible through an act of authorial expression or individual desire because all individual design processes, whether using the hand or the computer, end up as embodied systems; they are already conditioned by significance. In this sense, the interstitial has to be withdrawn from its figurative condition, that is, as a solid *poché*, where a meaning is already in place, to a condition of a spacing where it could be a void within a void, an overlapping within space of space, creating a density in space not given by the forming of a container with a profile.

The condition of this new idea of the interstitial is thus one of movement as opposed to its former condition of stasis. The interstitial as a static interval was held together through a rhetoric of reading. Here the interval assumes a new condition. As Deleuze says, it is no longer the material structure that curls around the contour in order to develop the figure. It is rather the figure (here it is assumed that we are talking about an interstitial figure) that wants to pass through the contour in order to dissipate into the material structure. Thus the contour assumes a new function, since it no longer lies flat between the exterior and the interior.

It is here that the process for the production of the interstitial becomes crucial. The interstitial can be understood in the same domain as inertia and entropy. While the interstitial cannot be produced within a system which relies on aesthetic value judgments, functional and representational criteria, it cannot be produced by mathematic or machinic processes either. While the machinic attempts to describe such an alternative idea of process, in order to produce this other interstitial, even the machinic process must be displaced as operational, because such other tropic conditions in architecture cannot be produced in the same way as they are in writing or in painting. In this sense, the production of the interstitial can be seen as a critique of the operational idea of the machinic proposed by Zaera-Polo.

What Deleuze and Guattari are saying is that the machinic process is neither mechanical nor organic, neither rational nor linear. The process does not operate between organism and mechanism, but between mechanism and organism on the one hand, and chaos on the other. Chaos is not what is seen as the final collapse of a system. Rather, chaos is something already given in the system that is building toward collapse.

It is not that one extra grain of sand at the moment of collapse in a landslide between a steady state and an unstable state. Most systems of description see the pile of sand as stable —its quantity and density can be measured through these traditional measurements. It cannot be known at what moment the next grain of sand is going to cause collapse. Through hypercomplex mathematics such measurements of inertia and entropy are possible.

Normal complexity is one that can be understood through a logical consistency. A cube is a simple form, but a hyperbolic paraboloid is a more complex form. It requires a more complex explanation. Hypercomplexity is something that is not explainable through the normal complex of logical mathematical equations. Spacing can be explained, but it requires a level of complexity not in conventional geometries. It is already another realm of description.

The machinic in this context can be seen as a condition of self-similar repetition as opposed to selfsame repetition, and thus it is neither mechanical nor organic. Equally, its objects must be seen as different from authorial or individual expression. In authorial expression the desire is for every result to be unique. In the machinic, the results are singular rather than unique. This is because the machinic contains an *already given difference* in architecture's interiority. Such a difference cannot be produced by a traditional authorial process of design, because the author only produces what is previously known.

The relationship of any subject to any object traditionally deals with a system of signification, or what Guattari calls a communicational reference. He says that we do not start off from signs and signifieds and then have a transfer. Rather, the regimen of the signified objects first suggests that something else is needed. That is, the signified suggest the signifiers. Guattari says that this condition could be reversed, that the implied mode of transfer or communication could come first, because the possibility of signification from the signifier to the signified is already given. If this is the case, then the machinic process can progressively develop possible different means of expression, ones that are different from the traditional means of architectural representation. In this context, it is possible to classify architectural signs in a different way. In fact, classification may not be the issue if architecture is thought in terms other than the traditional types of representation. Rather, it is possible that there are other conditions of signification repressed by these traditional classifications. Equally, if other modes of transfer can be proposed between the sign and the signified, then other means of expression, different conditions of signing, can be developed. While it is thought that one cannot change the object of architecture, only its means of signification, that is, the language with which one communicates, the above suggests this may be particularly true because of the embedded nature of the architectural sign in its being. If the means of communication in traditional language systems were limited by the regimens that were assumed to be in place, then it would seem that changing architecture from forming to spacing could change these systems of expression. While in architecture these conditions have always been more complex because of the icon/instrument relationship, the investigator of this complexity has been repressed in order to maintain the utility and clarity of architectural communication.

Ultimately, systems of clarification and utility create an excess in the space of power. The political system of transnational capital already suggests an organization of space and time, city, building, etc., which demands clarity and utility in order to create this excess. Standardization and technological processes are used to create the possibility of an excess which resides at present in capital. To suggest the possibility of an excess in the object, one that requires a radical change in the existing modes of production and consumption, becomes a political act. To produce a condition of spacing, of interstitiality, of something which cannot be consumed because it is no longer legitimated by utility and significance, is not merely an aesthetic argument, it is a political argument; it is speaking of a different kind of excess. Thus processes which produce difference can be seen to be resistant to the existing spaces of power. In architecture this would suggest that neither the author nor the machine can produce without some mutual interaction any condition of the figural.

Notes

1. Gilles Deleuze and Félix Guattari, *A Thousand Plateaus* (Minneapolis: University of Minnesota Press, 1987), trans. Brian Massumi, 7, 88–90, also chapter 3. Deleuze and Guattari primarily use the term to describe an *assemblage*, as in *machinic assemblage*.
2. Brian Massumi, *A User's Guide to Capitalism and Schizophrenia* (Cambridge: MIT Press, 1993), 192 n 45.
3. Ibid.
4. Felix Guattari, "On Machines," in *The Journal of Philosophy and Visual Arts*, no. 6 ("Complexity"), edited by Andrew Benjamin, 8. Trans. Vivian Constantinopoulos. Originally published in French in *Chimères*, no. 19 (Spring 1993).
5. Ibid., 9.
6. Ibid.
7. Ibid.
8. A singularity is a condition of self-similar repetition as opposed to selfsame repetition, and thus it is neither mechanical nor organic. In this sense it could be considered the result of a machinic process and not individual expression. This is because a singularity contains an *already given condition of difference* in its interiority.
9. Gilles Deleuze and Félix Guattari, *A Thousand Plateaus*.
10. Ibid.
11. Figural in this sense.
12. Ibid.

CHAPTER 9

SEPARATE TRICKS

Author's note. This essay was originally written in 1989. It remains largely intact from that date. The book for which this essay was intended, which supposedly is the actual record of a collaboration involving several different authors, can be seen instead as the trace of a future collaboration, one which does not require the participants to be actually present, working together. In one way or another, my work has always been a search for the trace, or what might be called the already given or the already present in architecture. While at different times I have called this search for the trace many different things, at one time formal absolutes or deep structure, at another time conceptual architecture or decomposition, it is here referred to as text. The idea of text concerned the two central conditions of my work: the relationship of the subject and the object. My work has always been about the denial of the traditional author architect, the originator architect, the expressionistic architect, at the same time that it concerned the effacement of the individual "I," the particular Peter Eisenman, whether in the form of the CASE group, the Five Architects, the Institute for Architecture and Urban Studies, *Oppositions*, Eisenman/Robertson, or now Eisenman Architects. Always there has been an attempt to define the work in terms of another author. Only recently has the idea of the trace as signature entered the work, and just recently there has been the effacement of that same signature.

Equally, the idea of the trace in the object can be seen throughout my projects; one has only to look at the outline of the missing column in the floor of House I; the redundant support structure of House II; the elaborate façade markings of House IV; the absent vertebrate center of House X; the inaccessible void of House 11a; the holes in the ground and the cutline peeling away of the ground of the Cannaregio project; the artificial excavation of Berlin or the Tokyo Opera House; and the scalings of the Romeo and Juliet project to understand the sustained development of a search for the signs of absence within the necessary presence of architecture.

Before our actual collaboration, my work with Jacques Derrida consisted in most cases of an attempt on my part to certify what I was already doing intuitively. Through a process of wishful and creative misreading, through the citation of quotations which may never have been read or could never be found, I had already established a collaboration of separate tricks, between fantasy and fact, between presence and absence. Thus, at the supposed beginning of our work together, when Derrida proposed that an essay he had been working on dealing with the Platonic idea of *chora* found in the *Timaeus* be the object of our collaboration, our program as it were in architectural terms, I willingly acceded. This was because, whether through another misreading or through a desire to protect the "I," or alternatively to search for its love, I thought that I was already working on such a concept, and had been for years. Thus the project for La Villette was initiated.

I could do what I always did, and by some misappropriation create the illusion of a collaboration, complete with a book. We could even record our being together and edit these voluminous ramblings to fit the traces of what we almost knew when we began. And this almost worked out but for the fact that several years elapsed between that time and the publication of *Chora L Works*. In the intervening time, slowly and unconsciously, I began to understand the manifold and subtle possibilities for the chora of Derrida's suggestion. Chora began to move my work toward our collaboration. This essay is an attempt to trace that movement between what we did together and what we did together/a Separatrix.

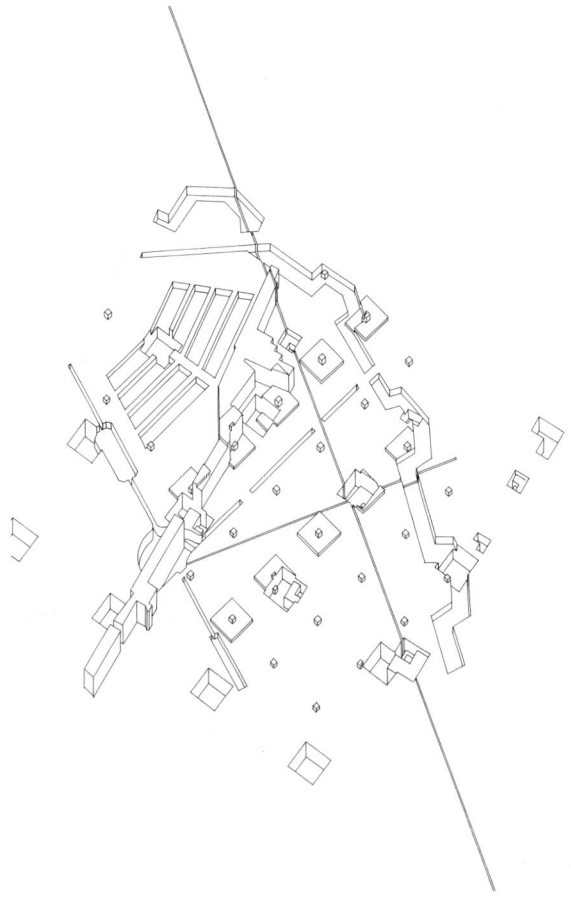

9.1 La Villette, Paris, 1987. Axonometric drawing.

In Edgar Allan Poe's story "The Black Cat," the convergence of the emotional and aesthetic energy of the story appears in the form of a bas relief on a newly plastered wall, the only standing remnant of a house gutted by fire. The image in this outline in the plaster is of a cat hung by a noose. This grim apparition appears as a haunting signal of the presence of a former actual cat that had been walled up by its master in this impromptu burial place. The reader's response to this image of an absent being is not so much to recall actual events —the murder of the cat or the torching of the house; a sentence or a real image could remind of those—it is a feeling of uncertain horror caused not by an actual image but rather by what can be called the trace of an image in the plaster. Was this trace real or imagined, how did it get there? Reason begins to ask, did the heat of the incinerated cat unwittingly leave this outline in the drying plaster? The irrational asks, was it the stain from the blood of the dying cat? In either case it is the inability to know for certain that creates the intense condition of response. Uncertainty is found because the image is produced in a condition that can be called a trace. Trace is a complex phenomenon—it is a suggestion of something before, or maybe the premonition of something after—the not yet present or the imagined past. The reader's reactions to a trace are not pure; they are charged with both uncertainty and fascination, complex reactions which elude the reactions to conditions of simple presence or reality.

In architecture, which is suffused with reality, can there be such traces? Certainly the outline of a door or a window is not a trace but a real marking of a functional element. More likely a string course or an entablature could be viewed as a trace, because they have no apparent function. However, as the idea of a trace will be thought of here, such architectural embellishments have little to do with the idea of text, being more the carrier of the aesthetic embellishment from one style or another. A trace in architecture can have a very precise function. It marks the presence of a text different from that of the traditional texts of architecture, which are usually grounded in symbolism, use, or some aesthetic function. While a trace must be some kind of form or mark, some physical presence, it is not a form in the traditional sense of an aesthetic presence in classical composition. Text in architecture could be considered more like what could be called an indexical as opposed to an iconic condition. The difference between the two is crucial for architecture. For while iconic relationships always refer outward from any form, architectural form poses a unique problem for such an outward looking in that any iconic condition in architecture lies within and thus contains its own instrumentality. A column is both a structural element and an iconic sign of its function. What the idea of trace proposes is to insert a third condition into the presence of the column, or the wall, a presence which marks an index about the possibility of the wall or column, an index of its own being and the processes by which it came to be.

Traditionally, the content of architecture, its meaning and symbolism, has been based on metaphors of the body and the natural. Nature was used to explain the world metaphorically as both a process and an object to be emulated. Like architecture, the foundations of modern science, biology, physics, genetics, etc., were based on the need for man to overcome the natural. It followed because architecture symbolizes and mirrors the attitudes of society, that architecture, perhaps not explicitly, has represented and symbolized the struggle of humanity to overcome nature. That is, since the Renaissance, when humans became self-conscious, architecture became a representational act. Architecture became consciously more than commodity, firmness, and delight.

Today, and for the past forty years, science has borne witness to a cultural shift. This can be seen, for example, in Newtonian physics, which was once considered the basis for a universal system of thought. While there is still Newtonian physics, it is no longer seen as a universal. Such displacement of universals has had a far-reaching effect in many discourses. But more problematic for architecture is that science is no longer focused on the problem of man and nature. Rather, science is concerned with the problem of the struggle of man to overcome knowledge. Such an important epistemological shift from man/nature to man/knowledge has created a unique problem for architecture as for no other discipline, because architecture must continue to stand against gravity, to shelter against the forces of nature. However, the displacement has caused the significance of the symbolism of overcoming the natural to be trivialized. When the body, anthropomorphism, and the natural are taken away from architecture, it is left with no object.

This condition is further problematized by the role of place in an age of information. An idea of place, or *topos*, has always been seen as a universal in man's relationship to the environment. Since the time of the Romans, when the crossing of the *cardo* and the *decumanus* marked the topos of the Roman encampment, humanity has been defining place as the mark—whether a cross or a square, a clearing in the forest or a bridge over a river—of the struggle to overcome nature. Today, two things have happened to bring traditional forms of place-making into question. First, technology has overwhelmed nature—the automobile and the airplane, with their potential for unlimited accessibility, have made grids and radial patterns of the nineteenth century obsolete; second, modern thought has found "unreasonableness" within traditional reason, and logic has been seen to contain the illogical.

These challenges to the traditional or universal order of architecture have been repressed by traditional reason. But with the displacement of universals these ideas can no longer be repressed. In architecture this can be seen in the question of whether man's marking of his conquest of nature is still significant, and in the acknowledgment that place (topos) has always contained "no place" (*atopia*). With this breakdown of the traditional forms of place has come a concurrent breakdown of the traditional categories of figure/ground and frame/object.

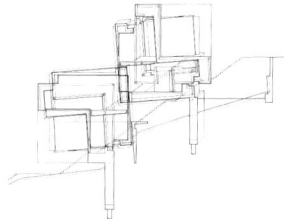

9.2 Guardiola House, Cadiz, Spain, 1988. Section drawing.

Since classical times there has been an *other* definition of place, which suggested such a simultaneity of two traditionally contradictory states. This is found in Plato's *Timaeus* in the definition of the receptacle (chora) as something between place and object, between container and contained. For Derrida, chora is spacing, not a between, but a neither nor, neither a space, nor a place. For an architect who needs to "ground" a concept, chora is like the sand on the beach: it is not an object or a place, but merely the record of the movement of water, which leaves traces of high-tide lines and imprints—erosions—with each successive wave receding into the water. Much as the foot leaves its trace imprint in the sand, and as the sand remains as a trace on the foot, each of these residues and actions is outside of any rational, predictable, or natural order; they are neither and nor at the same time.

Chora introduces another possible conception of space as the distinction between trace and imprint. In my earlier projects, because there was no idea of receptacle, all of the marks were essentially traces, that is, the residue of something that was formerly present. In the sense that the term is used here, what was formerly seen as a trace can now be called an imprint. Since the receptacle, according to Derrida, does not influence by its own substance the trace, the material of the receptacle can be thought of as some malleable, putty-like substance. The receptacle, conceptually, is then a construction that has the potential to constantly change its shape as well as to change the shape of another object, without being material itself. Thus when something is pressed into the chora or receptacle, an imprint (and not a trace) is left, while simultaneously a trace of the receptacle is left in the imprinting object. This idea of trace and imprint was first attempted in the project for the Guardiola House. This project was conceived of as two figural L-shaped volumes lying within one another. At some moment in their history there is an oscillation or a reverberation between them that causes them to react to one another. In doing so, the one leaves an imprint on the other, but at the same time loses some of its original figural presence. The outline of this lost presence is then recorded in a series of traces, frame structures, which bear witness to the former volume. These notations resonate in the material of the house. In the floors, walls, ceilings, even in the space itself. The initial oscillation is arbitrary, as are the L-shaped volumes. Equally, each succeeding trace becomes a new, initial yet arbitrary but somehow necessary condition, responding to and preempting a continuing sequence of new initial arbitrary conditions. Now, unlike a traditional idea of place, which originates somewhere and is a linear, rational, narrative record of the transformation of that initial condition, this sequence of arbitrary initial conditions produces a dense series of markings in space. They do not embody place as their object. Here, walls, floors, and ceilings do not only contain and shelter; they also become a condition of excess, neither containing nor contained, neither inside nor out, frame nor object, figure nor ground. The house no longer can be read iconically, because the traces and imprints which saturate the house have no iconic value, do not refer outward. Nor can they be read as merely the result of functional necessity. Rather, they become intelligible only by understanding their own internal, indexical logic. The resultant space is clearly different from the space of a house, even though it may function as a house. It only does so in the same way that a table, which is a concept, can also be used as a place to eat.

The idea of trace and imprint was therefore an important operating mechanism in the conception of the La Villette project, because it was the first time that it was being used at an urban as opposed to building scale. While the idea of a palimpsest and layers of superpositions had been employed in previous projects, La Villette was the first project to distinguish between mere superpositions and traces and imprints.

The idea of chora also introduces a new condition into the relationship between figuration and abstraction. This is particularly true in the third dimension of the La Villette project. Like other projects prior to it which dealt with conditions of trace, they did so primarily in plan. Any notations in the third dimension were merely extrusions of what could easily be seen in two dimensions. Trace did not seem to provide any way for mapping in the third dimension. With the introduction of the idea of chora, and thus of imprints, the third dimension became a possibility in the notational system. This was particularly true when it came to the use of the grid. The grid, whether in its two- or three-dimensional manifestations, is usually considered as an abstraction, as a ground by which figuration can be seen. In the use of imprints the role of the grid becomes potentially ambivalent. For example, in the Guardiola House, the grid becomes a series of frames which are warped and distorted; instead of being structural integers they are now traces and imprints, traces which reveal the condition of the imprint as the intersection of the two figural elements.

In the La Villette project the idea of imprint was used to distinguish the literal imprinting of the ground in the voids of the Cannaregio project, which was used as both an iconic and indexical referent for the work at La Villette. Here the superposition of imprints, like Freud's dreamwork, is one of condensation and displacement. From these, new icons and indices reverberate at displaced and condensed scales, as if there were infinite reflections in an imperfect mirror. It is a cut between icon and index, between metaphor and metonymy. It is the "difference between" that was being sought.

Other conceptions of place similar to the idea of chora enter into the La Villette project. The idea of atopia is one. Atopia is literally "no place" or "without place." The relationship between chora and atopia is that they both propose a displacement of the traditional concept of place. In order to understand the nature of this displacement, the nature of traditional place must be defined. The concept of urban place has been associated with a bounded or framed unitary condition of presence. Unlike the Japanese conception of *ma* as "space between" and *mu* as "no place," both of which imply a very real condition of a presence in a condition of absence, Western conceptions of place are always presence bounded as well as grounded to a specific location. Even in the supposed binary terms of figure/ground and solid/void, both ground and void are always defined as conditions of presence. The dominance in the architectural language of figure/ground gestalts, where place is usually seen as a figural void, has caused an undermining of the possibility of conceptualizing absence as well as any other interpretation of absence. In this sense, what is in reality a classical convention of reading place has come, because of this idea of gestalt, to be seen as natural. In order to displace place, to introduce the possibility of some other conception of what is an alternative condition of architectural space, the following seems to be a possible agenda.

9.3 Cannaregio, Venice, Italy, 1978. Presentation model.

First, one must be able to displace the idea of gestalt as a basis for conceptualizing place. Second, one must attempt to displace the dominance and monovalency of presence. Third, one must be able to displace metaphoric meaning and classical aesthetics as the basis for reading architecture. These were the issues that defined the architectural programs of the La Villette project as it began.

The third of these concerns appears as an attempt to dislocate the ideas of metaphor and metonymy so that actual time, place, and scale are replaced by analogies of these conditions. For example, while the site was considered as an actual place, it was also given a series of other times, places, and scales through a series of superpositions termed scaling. Scaling is a process that uses analogous material at differing scales to reveal previously hidden relationships between the site of La Villette and the project for Cannaregio. For example, the grid of my Cannaregio project was derived from, and seen as an extension of, Le Corbusier's hospital project for the same site in Venice. The Le Corbusier project was to have replaced the slaughterhouses which were then on the site. Similarly, Bernard Tschumi's project replaced the slaughterhouses of La Villette. Coincidentally, Tschumi's grid was also similar to Le Corbusier's grid at Cannaregio. Thus the superpositions of our Cannaregio grid onto Tschumi's grid at La Villette denied the primacy or originary value of either, causing their spacing to fluctuate between many different times, places, and scales. This fluctuation displaced the grounding dialectic present in the binary convention of figure and ground. It showed it to be what it is, a convention, one of many possible, rather than a natural condition of architecture. This new topos no longer contains specific place, scale, and time but can be seen as a continuous blurring of the two.

The dominant strategy of postmodernist urbanism has been the idea of contextualism as put forward by Colin Rowe and others. Contextualism purported to find latent figures in any existing context, giving those figures value by virtue of their prior presence on the site. What exists was given a value over the modernist doctrine of every site as a possible tabula rasa. This idea of an already present can be seen to be similar to the idea of chora, which also finds an already present in its receptacle or context. The difference between the two is significant. The Rowe doctrine, largely based on gestalt phenomenology, reifies the object, gives it presence, while chora attempts to destabilize and subvert presence. Chora finds the already given in order to destabilize its being. It is not at issue that both strategies have conditions of origin. It is not so much the material of the originary that is at issue, but rather how it is operated on. Chora exposes the contingency and conventionality in the value of place but does not neutralize it. Rather, it allows it to be active within a multivalency that is no longer dialectical, that is no longer concerned with resolution.

Trick: An illusion or stratagem. A trick is a sexual act turned by a prostitute. A trick is a device for counting in the game of bridge. A trickster, according to C. G. Jung, is a complex, archetypal character. It has both positive and negative connotations. In the negative sense it is a person who is always playing games, who cannot face reality. For Jung it has qualities of the eternal boy. On the psychologically positive side, a trickster is one who when confronted with power is able to undermine through guile the force of the power, to divert or subvert it without direct confrontation.

As Jean-Louis Cohen has written, "But a common penchant for playing with words and meanings (and most likely inherited from Jewish traditions, albeit quite *separate* ones) was as much in evidence as a predilection for conspiracy and the subversion of institutions." Derrida, when asked if we had had a collaboration, replied that it was not a collaboration or an exchange, but rather a double, parasitic laziness; separate tricks.

CHAPTER 10

WRITTEN INTO THE VOID

In his foreword to *Spoken Into the Void* (*Ins Leere Gesprochen*), Adolf Loos says of the German language that the "rigid clinging to the practice of capitalizing nouns has as its consequence the return of language to a barbaric state." This "derives from the abyss that opens up in the German mind [the void] between the written and spoken word." For Loos, the choice of the words *spoken* (*gesprochen*) and *void* (*Leere*) is charged with a very specific meaning. The architectural historian Manfredo Tafuri has said that Loos had a problem with Josef Hoffmann's belief in the fullness of the written word (or writing). This was opposed to Loos's idea of speech, which he felt had the immediacy of the now, the capacity to erode the sedimented and encrusted history of the culture that he saw in the written. Thus for Loos, *spoken* is analogous to what is free and unencumbered. It seems clear that Loos's anxiety with writing began with the German *faktur*, the process of writing every noun with a capital letter. This procedure, he said, quoting Jacob Grimm, derives from a time when all writing was originally done in capital letters, after the manner in which they were inscribed in stone. Loos, however, says it is impossible to utter a capital letter. "Every one of us speaks without ever thinking of capital letters."

Tafuri says that despite the environment of new "languages" created in the Vienna of Ludwig Wittgenstein, Karl Kraus, Sigmund Freud, and others, Loos can be spoken about in many ways, but not in terms of a new language. If Hoffmann's work can be seen as the practice of writing, Tafuri writes, one could say that writing disappeared in Loos. He adds, "If we eliminate the late nostalgia for the fullness of the word pronounced by Hoffmann, we could find Loos." Loos's prioritizing of the spoken over the written recalls similar traditional ideas held in formal or structural linguistics. Today the opposition between the written and spoken has been shown to be problematic by poststructuralist thought.

Writing and speaking once defined the poles of a hierarchical dialectic, with speaking as primary and writing, secondary. This dialectic, as Jacques Derrida has shown, no longer defines a hierarchy in the space of language because in poststructuralist thought, writing is no longer considered secondary to speaking. This puts into question the former primacy of the idea of speaking, which in architectural terms was translated as *architecture parlante*. In architecture, both speaking and writing are useful terms because they also open up ways to question the prevailing ideas concerning the discipline of architecture without necessarily returning to a linguistic or semiotic model.

In his book *The Postmodern Condition*, Jean-François Lyotard writes, "We can distinguish an oral culture from a written culture through the idea of memory." In an oral culture, he says, the idea of memory lies outside the individual like a collective body waiting to be activated by communication from some external subject. In a written culture, the subject is constituted by contact with and through a preexisting body of memory. This preexisting memory is activated through a writing which must be read. In other words, according to Lyotard, the consciousness of a subject external to this memory is created through reading and writing. The constitution of the subject and a preexistent body of memory will become important below, when these ideas are examined in terms of architecture.

In Lyotard's terms, architecture would be traditionally thought of as an oral culture; that is, a culture activated by a set of external rules and regulations for communication with some external subject. Architecture has rarely been thought of in terms of a written culture, that is, in terms of creating a consciousness of its object or, for that matter, of the subject through the possibility of reading and writing. While architecture has always had the possibility of being read, this reading is very different from the possibility of writing. Even with the idea of an *architecture parlante*, or spoken architecture, in which architecture attempts to acquire a status similar to that of words on a page, it is necessary to distinguish the possibility of reading for narrative and iconographic content or aesthetic appreciation—the traditional readings of architecture—from a kind of writing that is possibly a displacement from these assumed-to-be normative conditions of function, meaning, and aesthetics.

Gilles Deleuze also deals with the question of writing as a form of memory in his discussion of Marcel Proust's *In Search of Lost Time*. For Deleuze, Proust's idea of the past does not represent something which has been, but something which is and which coexists with itself as a past in the present. In other words, Proust's past is not a past of memory as a past perfect but a past which coexists with the present as a reality. Proust speaks of this past-present writing as a sign of memory. He says it is the real without being present and the ideal without being abstract.

Deleuze supports this distinction using an argument from Henri Bergson's *Matter and Memory*. Bergson says that the past does not have to perceive itself in anything but itself, because it survives and preserves itself in itself. This being of the past in itself is what Bergson calls "the virtual." The notion of the virtual as an active memory of the past in the present is from today's use of the virtual, as in virtual reality.

The virtual as a reality in the space of architecture is not the same virtual as virtual reality. A reality of the virtual, that is, a condition of the virtual in real space, would be produced by what is called here a *writing*, which conveys memory as an aspect of the interiority of architecture, not as the preservation of the past in the sedimented history of architecture, or the past as it actually was, but rather as it could exist in the present. The virtual is that part of the present that contains a past memory. The virtual, or writing, of architecture thus deals with the memory that exists in the interiority of architecture projected into the present. For example, G. B. Piranesi's *Campo Marzio* is a writing of the virtual in the sense that Proust, Bergson, and Deleuze discuss, that is, it presents several conditions of time. There is real time past in the actual monuments that existed in ancient Rome; there are buildings that existed in Piranesi's present Rome of 1762, which remain in place from the past; there are buildings from the past that no longer exist but are present as traces or ruins. In addition, some of the buildings from the past that no longer exist are moved from their past real location to a new place in the plan. Finally, Piranesi invents buildings that never existed in any time, past or present. These invented buildings look like real buildings, even when they are examined closely. But when one attempts to give function to them, they do not work. In this sense, they are the simulacra of buildings. They may seem to be buildings from the past, but they are produced from an interiority of memory. This memory does not consider buildings as a form of nostalgia because they never existed; they are phantasms, diagrams, simulacra—all conditions of virtuality.

This idea of architectural writing as a simulacrum differentiates the architectural object from its thought-to-be functional, aesthetic, and meaningful nature. Such a simulacrum would be articulated in a writing that contains the traces of a memory not only from architecture's interiority but also of the way an object comes into being, that is, its process of making. An example of such a process could begin with a piece of clay that, when molded into a shape, has a form. If a stone is thrown at that piece of clay, it deforms the piece of clay. When the stone is removed, it leaves in the clay a trace of the collision between the stone and the clay, and conversely, the stone retains a residue of clay. Until now, this dimension of memory as a trace has not been fully recognized in architecture. In its sedimented memory, most architecture marks those kinds of processes through axes, places, etc. The difference between an axis and the thrown stone is the difference between a straight line and a vector. A vector has speed and density. The particular density of the rock that is thrown at the clay and the speed at which it is thrown will mark the clay differently each time.

Architecture has the capacity to produce writings that deal with time and space, intensity and extensity, in terms of weight, material, and speed. The way in which X impacts Y — the extensity of the impact and the intensity of the speed — is rarely measured in architecture. The idea of the vector, as opposed to the axis, is a possible condition of writing. However, to have both the writing of a vector and the writing of an axis creates a problem in the interiority of architecture. An axis already exists as a presence in the memory of an architectural interiority, and a vector does not. This means that a vector might exist (though repressed) in the memory of an interiority (it cannot be repressed if it does not exist, even as a mere possibility). In order to write a vector, one first has to sublimate the embodied and motivated relationship of the axis and then begin to define an interiority in which the vector is not a repressed condition of the axis. This begins to suggest another opening in the interiority of architecture, one that relates the virtual to the problem of presence.

Thus one aspect of a writing is the possibility of inventing the conventions of the past in the present, not merely retrieving them. The architect can write something that does not exist. Rudolph Gasché, in his essay on Herman Melville's *Moby-Dick*, says that an architect feels about blindly for the "already drafted" but hidden foundations of his discipline. The architect, blinded from the beginning, is meant to outline in his draft nothing less than the chaotic structure of this already given. In other words, the architect, like any other subject, is blinded today by the notion of nineteenth-century causality in the system of Western metaphysics. This produces the received and commonly accepted idea that architecture is the locus of the metaphysics of presence. This idea blinds the architect to what Derrida and Gasché speak of as an already given (or what I call the interiority of architecture). Because of this blinding, the architect can only write from an interiority that is known as presence. Gasché says that all the architect can do is outline in his writing the possible conditions of this "already given" architecture, which, as an interiority, does not conform to the ideas of presence or absence fundamental to Western metaphysics, but exists on the edge of chaos, as a between condition, in the void. This outline of the void as a writing can also be considered as a diagram.

Derrida's idea of a writing becomes crucial to what follows. A diagram is a writing which acts as a template of possibilities, a tissue of traces. The diagram is not a manifestation of form or function or even presence, but rather a possibility of each of these. As such, because it is manifest in physical presence, the diagram stands as a critique of the assumed idea that it is a locus of presence. Architecture, in this sense, has always been a primary locus of a nostalgia for presence. Derrida's idea of writing counters Heidegger's idea of being as a primary presence, as a transcendental signified, as containing a nostalgia for presence. Derrida's concept of a sign is a heterogeneity, not a unity (or a nostalgia for unity) but a structure of difference. Word and thing are never one but are enfolded within one another, in an original difference. As such, this original condition is no longer a primary presence but rather something different from presence. In architecture, a presence such as a platonic solid or type form has always been held as an anterior condition. In the view of a writing as proposed here, an architectural interiority could be conceptualized as an original absence. If architecture's interiority can be conceptualized as not only an original difference but also as an original and perhaps unstable absence, then writing could be understood as articulating something different from a sign of presence. It could signal that the interiority of architecture could be understood as an absence enfolded within presence and not as something beginning from geometry. Here the singular interiority of architecture, one which already contains an idea of a necessarily occupiable space, becomes important. First, there is always already an absence-space, yet this space is always seen as being defined by a presence or a unity, such as a profile, contour, or exterior container. Second, if the idea of the interiority of architecture could also be considered as a difference from space, then this difference could be considered as a void—the absence of the presence of space. This void could be seen as enfolded in presence, or as other than presence. Such an anterior condition might require an alternative process of translation from this interiority to real space, that is, an alternative to designing. This suggests that writing must be seen differently from designing: first, as already given in and defining such an interiority; and second, that how something is written is different from how something is designed. The difference between writing and designing in this context is important.

Designing attempts to resolve, ameliorate, organize, etc., problems of site, shelter, function, and meaning, and to do so in a way that is aesthetically pleasing to both the client and the architect. While writing must in some fashion do all of the above, it does not make these conditions thematic. As in literature, where writing is more than narrative storytelling, writing in architecture is more than problem solving; it is an excess. While designing aestheticizes problem solving, writing theorizes problem solving and makes it operative in a project. Writing is therefore also a critical and autonomous function in architecture, in that of necessity it acts differently from the writing of literature. It must countermand designing while at the same time performing similar functions.

Writing as architecture proposes three conditions of difference. The first is a difference from the design process of solving the problems of site, shelter, aesthetics, functions, and meaning, that is, the difference from the reality of presence and the truth of what is seen as present. Second, writing implies a difference from full presence in the idea of a simulacrum, which includes the past as an act in a process of making, internalized in the reality of a present. Writing in architecture, therefore, begins with an idea of the void as a potential fullness, a heuristic or virtual condition that can reveal a figural space cut off from its previous modes of legitimation. The third difference in writing architecture concerns the idea of the invention of the self, particularly in relation to the idea of authorial expression and the signature, signing, and designing. While writing often implies signing, the signature is an expression of an author as opposed to some manifestation of architectural interiority. Signature signals a personal expression, while writing constitutes the writer/subject. In a sense, signing is an oral condition, because in signing, the subject/author is already constituted by the mere fact that the subject is aware of being able to sign. That is, the subject is already constituted in relationship to a body of knowledge. Lyotard describes this relationship as oral. In this sense the signature is always involved in orality.

Piranesi's signature is in his *vedute* of Roman antiquity. They are a literal presentation of what he saw in Rome or in books. His *Campo Marzio* drawing, on the other hand, is different; it is a drawing as a diagram, a writing as a condition of Piranesi constituting himself as a subject. The *Campo Marzio* uses the past as a vehicle for inventing Piranesi in the present. Neither Piranesi nor Rome existed as other than unconscious fragments before they were invented through the possibility of Piranesi's writing. That is, Piranesi wrote himself at the same time as he wrote Rome. His was an expression of a preexistent, or unconscious, universe as opposed to an expression of a personal aesthetic.

Writing or signing oneself requires an external condition from which the subject can be seen to be a deformation, deflection, displacement, etc., an already constituted knowledge of self to be able to sign—an oral relationship. Writing oneself means constituting oneself through a body of memory that through writing constitutes the subject. Therefore, a writing in architecture is also the constitution of the author/subject as well as that of its object.

When the self is constituted in the signature, it is not writing, it is a form of personal expression. Writing in this sense is a very specific condition of involuntary memory. It is used to constitute something that does not consciously exist in the present. In this sense writing is not only formal, geometric, aesthetic, functional, or structural but displaces these through the institution in presence of the virtual.

For example, the writing of self is different from the idea of signature. Whereas Proust constitutes himself by writing *In Search of Lost Time*, Gasché says that Melville constitutes himself as a subject through the writing of *Moby-Dick*. Gasché says that *Moby-Dick* could be read as merely a linear narrative, and that it exists as a signature of Melville except for the chapter on cetology, which demonstrates that Melville was trying to create a writing rather than a signature. This chapter, which deals with the classification of whales, is outside of the narrative story. Gasché says that Melville writes about the classification of whales precisely because whales are impossible to classify. That is, classification is such that every whale has its own distinct character; there is no generic whale. Any attempt to classify a whale produces a simulacrum of whales because classification does not represent any one whale but rather an invention of some composite whale. In order to make a typology of whales, one, in a sense, restructures the whale. In other words, one is writing the whale, thus in doing so, Melville also writes himself. For Gasché, Melville the subject/author is defined through writing a memory in the present of a preexistent idea of a virtual whale.

The difference between a writing and signature is the difference between unconscious invention of an already given difference, of a simulacrum of memory, and conscious invention, which involves an actual personal memory. Unconscious invention concerns the constitution of consciousness through the process of this invention. When an author/subject is consciously attempting to make something new, it is a signature; when he is involved in a writing, it is not a totally conscious activity.

This unconscious activity, this "blindness," as Gasché terms it, poses two questions. First, it only allows the making of an outline—what I have called a diagram—of this already given, or what can be called the immanent structure of architecture. Second, this outline or diagram is no longer within the realm of metaphysics; it borders on the edge of chaos. This is a different problem in architecture, the theme of writing and of interiority. Gasché makes an important distinction for architecture between interiority and insidedness. Interiority is something known to exist and which defines any discourse. Insidedness is that which is unknown, repressed by what is known of the interiority. Insidedness, therefore, is a prior condition, an already given difference within the interiority of architecture.

What is being argued here is that architectural writing is an aspect of that already given, a priori condition, that is, it is already a condition of difference, an insidedness, in the interiority of architecture. For such a writing to be deployed as both a simulacrum and a memory, it must already have the possibility to be written; otherwise it could not be thought. Since it has a possibility to be written, it exists prior to its interiority, that is, prior to its possibility to manifest itself as a simulacrum. It is this state that can be called architecture's insidedness.

Writing in architecture, therefore, could be considered as both an exteriority with no origin at the same time that it participates within, that is, as the only possibility to access the preexistent insidedness of the interiority of architecture. Thus writing in the space of architecture is as an already written. It is this idea of the already written which has the possibility of being unique in its architectural manifestation.

Here the idea of a preexistent inscription of the possibility of an insidedness of a writing, an inside of an interior, is not the notion of a dialectical opposition of a literal outside to a literal inside, but rather something which is always enfolded in an exteriority; that is, an idea of enfolding in writing the past within the reality of the present as a condition of this memory. This is a condition of a singular immanence in architecture, of architecture as the manifestation of a void interiority.

It is necessary to differentiate between Derrida's notion of *écriture*—for example, writing in itself in literature—and architectural writing. For Derrida, architectural writing implies a condition of inventive reading, that is, the possibility for reading a writing which had not previously existed, a writing which is unique to architecture, a writing which is not a representation of architecture but is architecture itself. In reading literature, for example, there is a direct relationship between what is seen on the page and what is received by the mind. While syntax and grammar provide a certain opacity, the sign system of language is relatively transparent. There is a one-to-one correspondence between what is read, or seen, and what the mind understands. Such a one-to-one correspondence does not exist in architecture, not only because there is no agreed-upon sign system in architecture but also because the body enters in and "sees" in a different way than the eyes. The somatic, apperceptive experience of the body is different from the recognition of the visible by the eye. Literature loses the affective dimension of speech, that is, the way speech is articulated through gesture or bodily sensations. These gestures only occur in an oral presentation. It is possible to argue that writing architecture already contains the necessary condition of this oral culture in the bodily experience. Writing architecture cannot be thought without the already given physical experience of the body. Thus the notion of architectural writing is incomplete without its orality, without its being experienced by an affecting body. Therefore, the concept of writing in architecture distinguishes itself from writing in language precisely because it must incorporate its oral dimension. The writing of architecture will always be spoken as if it is read. Any architectural writing must take into account this possibility of its condition of being spoken.

The insistence here on a notion of writing in architecture is not a passing contemporary fashion or new style. If anything, it is an idea that is suppressed by fashion and style, suppressed as well by memory of what architecture is thought to be, a transcendental memory of cause and effect. To insist on the idea of writing architecture as proposed here becomes important precisely because it has been repressed by this memory. The idea of a writing of architecture as a virtual condition introduces a critical dimension to the relationship between the body of the subject and the body of the object. This critical dimension ultimately must be seen as political.

The writing of Proust and Melville, of any poetic discourse that contains an affective dimension of a sensuous sign and an involuntary memory, is always in excess of writing that is merely narrative and scientific. The primacy of critical content in architecture, as opposed to an architecture that is only aesthetic, causes an affective and spatial dimension to come into being, which is ultimately political. This is because a writing fundamentally disturbs a received notion of what constitutes the architectural project. It is this disturbance, or displacement, that becomes a political act.

CHAPTER 11

DIAGRAM An Original Scene of Writing

DIAGRAM

As in all periods of supposed change, new icons are thrust forward as beacons of illumination. So it is with the idea of the diagram. While it can be argued that the diagram is as old as architecture itself, many see its initial emergence in Rudolf Wittkower's use of the nine-square grid in the late 1940s to describe Palladian villas. This pedigree continued to develop in the form of the nine-square problem as practiced in the American architectural academy of the late 1950s and early 1960s, a practice seen then as an antidote to the bubble diagraming of Bauhaus functionalism rampant at Harvard in the late 1940s and to the *parti* of the French academy that was still in vogue at several East Coast schools well into the late 1960s. As a classical architectural diagram, the *parti* was embodied with a set of preexistent values such as symmetry, the *marche*, and *poché*, which constituted the bases of its organizing strategy. The bubble diagram attempted to erase all vestiges of an embodied academicism in the *parti*. In so doing, it also erased the abstract geometric content of the nine-square.

Generically, a diagram is a graphic shorthand. Though it is an ideogram, it is not necessarily an abstraction. It is a representation of something in that it is not the thing itself. In this sense, it cannot help but be embodied. It can never be free of value or meaning, even when it attempts to express relationships of formation and their processes. At the same time, a diagram is neither a structure nor an abstraction of structure. While it explains relationships in an architectural object, it is not isomorphic with it.

In architecture the diagram is historically understood in two ways: as an explanatory or analytical device and as a generative device. Although it is often argued that the diagram is a postrepresentational form, in instances of explanation and analysis the diagram is a form of representation. In an analytical role, the diagram represents in a different way than a sketch or a plan of a building. For example, a diagram attempts to uncover latent structures of organization, like the nine-square, even though it is not a conventional structure itself. As a generative device in a process of design, the diagram is also a form of representation. But unlike traditional forms of representation, the diagram as a generator is a meditation between a palpable object, a real building, and what can be called architecture's interiority. Clearly this generative role is different from the diagram in other discourses, such as the parsing of a sentence or a mathematical or scientific equation, where the diagram may reveal latent structures but does not explain how those structures generate other sentences or equations. Similarly, in an architectural context, we must ask what the difference is between a diagram and a geometric scheme. In other words, when do nine squares become a diagram and thus more than mere geometry?

Wittkower's nine-square drawings of Palladio's projects are diagrams in that they help to explain Palladio's work, but they do not show *how* Palladio worked. Palladio and Serlio had geometric schemas in mind, sometimes explicit and sometimes implicit, which they drew into their projects. The notations of dimensions on the Palladian plans do not correspond to the actual project but to the diagram that is never drawn. A diagram implicit in the work is often never made explicit. For example, as Kurt Forster has noted, in the earliest parchment drawings in architecture, a diagrammatic schema is often drawn or etched into the surface with a stylus without being inked. The later inking of the actual project over this then becomes a superposition of a diagrammatic trace. In many of these drawings—from late Gothic architecture to the Renaissance—the overlay does not actually take all of the diagrammatic imprint, only partial traces of it. The quality of the ink on the page changes where it runs over the diagram as opposed to the places where the diagram is actually part of the plan of the building. Thus, there is a history of an architecture of traces, of invisible lines and diagrams that become visible only through various means. These lines are the trace of an intermediary condition (that is, the diagram) that exists between what can be called the anteriority and the interiority of architecture; the summation of its history as well as the projects that could exist are indexed in the traces and the actual building.

The diagram not only is an explanation, as something that comes after, but also acts as an intermediary in the process of generation of real space and time. As a generator there is not necessarily a one-to-one correspondence between the diagram and the resultant form. There are many instances, for example, in Le Corbusier's Modulor, where the diagram is invisible in the object yet appears as a generative element that occurs at many different scales, such as in the facades as well as in segments of urban plans, yet it is rarely an explicit form. Any preconception that the plan is the generator will be seen to be different from the diagrammatic other. There are many examples of diagrams in which a variety of processes are generated through a geometry that is exfoliated into different shapes. For example, Leonard Goldburt used geometric matrices to evolve natural and animal forms. Perhaps the most interesting is the manifestation of a camel drawn from interlocking squares and triangles. Also in the chateau architecture of the Loire Valley in the sixteenth century there are highly complex forms that could only have been produced though the manipulation and transformation of a diagrammatic geometry into a three-dimensional process. There are literally stone vault templates generated by these kinds of diagrams. In late Gothic cathedral architecture, for example, there is a diagrammatic process that leads to the attempt to allow, for example, column capitals to change from a stylized or canonical, natural sculpted quality, that tries to a more naturalistic, free-form nature. Such a process is not from straightforward manipulation of geometry that was the tradition in Gothic cathedrals. Rather, the plastic evolution of these other capitals comes not from geometry but from a diagram. In this sense, the diagram becomes an intermediary condition between a regular base geometry and the capital itself. Here the diagram acts neither as geometry nor as the existent capital. It is a trace or phantom, which acts between something which can be called the interiority of architecture and the specific capital; between some explicit geometric formation which is then transformed by the diagram or intermediary process onto a result.

Reacting against an understanding of the diagram as what was thought to be an apparently essentialist tool, a new generation, fueled by new computer techniques and a desire to escape its perceived Oedipal anxieties—the generation of their mentors—is today proposing a new theory of the diagram based partly on Gilles Deleuze's interpretation of Foucault's recasting of the diagram as "a series of machinic forces" and partly on their own cybernetic hallucinations. In their polemic, the diagram has become a key word in the interpretation of the new. They challenge both the traditional geometric bases of the diagram and the sedimented history of architecture, and in so doing they question any relation of the diagram to architecture's anteriority or interiority.

The second point Deleuze makes is that the diagram is different from structure. The classical architectural idea of a diagram exhibits a belief in structure as something that is hierarchical, static, and has a point of origin. Deleuze says that a diagram is a supple set of relationships between forces. It forms unstable physical systems that are in a perpetual disequilibrium. Deleuze says that diagrams that deal with distribution, serialization, and formalization are all structural mechanisms in that they lead to structure and a belief in structuring as an underlying principle of organization. If a structure is seen as a vertical or hierarchical ordering of its constituent parts, the diagram must be conceived both horizontally and vertically, both as a structure and as something which resists structuring: "From one diagram to the next, new maps are drawn; thus there is no diagram that does not also include besides the points which it connects up (that is, besides its structural component) certain relatively free or unbound points, points of creativity, change, and resistance to that existing building." In this sense, diagrams are those forces which appear in every relation from one point to another, as superimposed maps. The distinction between Deleuze's idea of superimposition and my use of the term *superposition* is critical in this context. Superimposition refers to a vertical layering differentiating between ground and figure. Superposition refers to a coextensive, horizontal layering in which there is no stable ground or origin, where ground and figure fluctuate between one another.

Thus diagrams for Deleuze must have a nonstructuring or informal dimension. It is "a functioning abstracted from any obstacle or friction, detached from specific use." This is an important movement away from the classical idea of an architectural diagram. Deleuze says that "a diagram is no longer an auditory or visual archive, but a map, a cartography that is coextensive with the whole social field. It is an abstract machine." This abstract machine is defined by its functioning in unformed matter, as a series of processes that are neither mechanical nor organic. The diagram, then, is both form and matter, the visible and the articulable. Diagrams for Deleuze do not attempt to bridge the gap between these pairs but rather attempt to widen it, to open the gap to other unformed matters and functions which will become formed. Diagrams, then, form visible matter and formalize articulable functions.

R. E. Somol follows Deleuze in situating these ideas of the diagram in architecture. For Somol, diagrams are any kind of explanatory abstraction: "cartoons, formulas, diagrams, machines, both abstract and concrete. Sometimes they are simply found and other times they are manipulated." A partial list of what Somol labels as "previous" diagrams includes the nine-square, the Panopticon, the Dom-ino, the skyscraper, the duck and the decorated shed, the fold, and bachelor machines. Somol says that he is searching for an alternative way of dealing with architecture's history, "one not founded on resemblance and return to origins but on modes of becoming an emergence of difference." The problem with this idea of the diagram as matter, as flows and forces, is that it is indifferent to the relationship between the diagram and architecture's interiority, and in particular to three conditions unique to architecture: (1) architecture's compliance with the metaphysics of presence; (2)

the already motivated condition of the sign; and (3) the necessary relationship of architecture to a desiring subject.

Somol's argument for a diagrammatic project takes as axiomatic that every design project, whether in practice or in the university, needs to take up anew the issue of what constitutes the discipline or, in other words, that architecture both as a discipline and a social project needs to suspend and rearrange ruling oppositions and hierarchies currently in operation. This would suggest that design projects and processes cannot simply be derived from their contexts, but rather must *transform* their very social and intellectual contexts. In this sense, Somol's diagrammatic process, as a machinic environment, is already given as a social project. That is, it is not abstract or autonomous, but rather presumes that architecture already contains in its being (that is, its interiority) the condition of the social.

If in the interiority of architecture there is a potential autonomous condition that is not already socialized or that is not already historicized, one which can be distilled from a historicized and socialized interiority, then all diagrams do not necessarily take up new disciplinary and social issues. Rather, diagrams can be used to open up such an autonomy to understand its nature. If this autonomy can be defined as singular because of the relationship in architecture between sign and signified, and if singularity is also a repetition of difference, then there must be some existing condition of architecture in order for it to be repeated differently. This existing condition can be called architecture's interiority. When there is no interiority, that is, if there is no relationship between interiority and the diagram, there is no singularity which defines architecture.

If architecture's interiority can be said to exist as a singular rather than dialectical manifestation of a sign that contains its own signified, the motivation of its sign is already internalized and thus autonomous. Yet if the diagram is already social, as Somol suggests, this definition immediately historicizes autonomy. The notion of the diagram being proposed here attempts to overcome the historicization of the autonomy of architecture, that is, the already motivated nature of architecture's sign.

In this context, the relation between the diagram and architecture's interiority is crucial. Foucault's understanding of an archive as the historical record of a culture, and of an archaeology as the scientific study of archival material, can be translated as architecture's anteriority and interiority. These cannot by their very nature be constituted merely by unformed matter, as Somol suggests, but in fact already contain presence, motivated signs, and a psychical desire for delineation by the subject of both ground and figure. A diagram of instability, of matter and flows, must find a way to accommodate these concerns specific to architecture. In this context, another idea of the diagram can be proposed, one which begins from Jacques Derrida's idea of writing as an opening of pure presence.

For Derrida, writing is initially a condition of repressed memory. The repression of writing is also the repression of that which threatens presence, and since architecture is the sine qua non of the metaphysics of presence, anything that threatens presence would be presumed to be repressed in architecture's interiority. In this sense, architecture's anteriority and interiority can be seen as a sum of repressions. While all discourses, Derrida would argue, contain repressions that in turn contain an alternative interior representation, architecture must be seen as a special case because of its privileging of presence. If Derrida is correct, there is already given in the interiority of architecture a form of representation, perhaps as the becoming unmotivated of the architectural sign. This repressed form of representation is not only interior to architecture, but anterior to it. It is this representation in architecture that could also be called a writing. How this writing enters into the diagram becomes a critical issue for architecture.

One way that memory overcomes forgetting is through mnemonic devices. Written lists are a form of mnemonic device, but one that is graphic and literal; they do not represent or contain a trace. In architecture, literal notations can produce a plan, but they have nothing to do with the diagram, because a plan is a literal mnemonic device. A plan is a finite condition of writing, but the traces of writing suggest many different plans. It is the idea of the trace that is important for any concept of the diagram, because unlike a plan, traces are neither fully structural presences nor motivated signs. Rather, traces suggest potential relationships, which may both generate and emerge from previously repressed or unarticulated figures. But traces in themselves are not generative, transformative, or even critical. A diagrammatic mechanism is needed that will allow for both preservation and erasure and that can simultaneously open up repression to the possibility of generating alternative architectural figures which contain these traces.

Derrida says, "We need a single apparatus that contains a double system, a perpetually available innocence and an infinite reserve of traces." A diagram in architecture can also be seen as a double system that operates as a writing both from the anteriority and the interiority of architecture as well as from the requirements of a specific project. The diagram acts like a surface that receives inscriptions from the memory of that which does not yet exist —that is, of the potential architectural object. This provides traces of function, enclosure, meaning, and site from the specific conditions. These traces interact with the traces from the interiority and the anteriority to form a superposition of traces. This superposition provides a means for looking at a specific project that is neither condemned to the literal history of the anteriority of architecture, nor limited by facts, the reality of the particular site, program, context, or meaning of the project itself. Both the specific project and its interiority can be written onto the surface of the diagram that has the infinite possibility of inscribing impermanent marks and permanent traces. Without these permanent traces there is no possibility of writing in the architectural object itself.

If architecture's interiority is seen as already-written, then Derrida's use of Freud's double-sided Mystic Writing Pad could be one model for describing a conception of a diagram different from both the traditional one in classical architecture and the one proposed by Somol. Neither of these considers in any detail architecture's problem with the metaphysics of presence, the unmotivating of the sign, or the psychical problem of repression in both the interiority of architecture and in the subject. The analogy of the Mystic Writing Pad is useful because the specific conditions of site and the anteriority of architecture both constitute a form of psychical repression.

The Mystic Writing Pad, as proposed in Freud's analogy, consists of three layers: the outer layer or surface where the original writing takes place, a middle layer on which the writing is transcribed, and underneath, a tablet of impressionable material. Using a stylus, one writes on the top surface. Because of the surface underneath, the top surface reveals a series of black lines. When the top surface is lifted from the other two, the black lines disappear. What remains is the inscription on the bottom surface, the trace of the lines that have been drawn. The indentations made by the stylus remain, always present. Thus there are infinite possibilities for writing and rewriting on the top surface and a means of recording the traces of this writing as a series of superpositions on the tablet underneath. This recalls the traces of the earliest incisions on parchment that already exist in the anteriority of architecture as described above.

The architectural diagram, like the Mystic Writing Pad, can be conceived of as a series of surfaces or layers which are both constantly regenerated and at the same time capable of retaining multiple series of traces. Thus, what would be seen in an architectural object is both the first perceptual stimulus, the object itself, along with its aesthetic and iconic qualities, and another layer, the trace, a written index that would supplement this perception. Such a trace would be understood to exist before perception, in other words, before a perception is conscious of itself.

Derrida says, "Memory or writing is the opening of that process of appearance itself. The 'perceived' may only be read in the past, beneath perception and after it." The diagram understood as a stratum of superposed traces offers the possibility of opening up the visible to the articulable, to what is within the visible. In this context, architecture becomes more than that which is seen or which is present; it is no longer entirely a representation or an illustration of presence. Rather, architecture can be a re-presentation of this intervening apparatus called the diagram. In this sense, the diagram could be understood to exist before the anteriority and the interiority of architecture. It exists as the potential space of writing, a writing which supplements the idea of an interiority before perception. This idea of an interiority as containing a palimpsest of an already-written undercuts the premise of architecture's origin in presence.

But there is also a temporality involved in the processes of the diagram. Derrida says that the Mystic Pad includes in its structure what Kant describes as the three modes of time: permanence, succession, and simultaneity. The diagram, like the writing pad, contains the simultaneity of the appearance on its surface, what would be akin to the black lines on the top layer of the pad, as well as the indentations in the wax below; the second aspect of the time of the diagram is succession, which is akin to the lifting up of the pad and is involved in erasure and the posting of a new image. This is the permanence in the wax itself. The diagram presents in such a context a discontinuous conception of time as the periodicity and the spacing of writing. These three conditions of time are not linear or connected in a narrative way. Thus, the diagram is an intermediate or interstitial condition which lies between in space and time—between the architectural object and the interiority of architecture.

Writing implies that in an architectural object, the object's presence would already contain a repetition. In this sense an architectural object would no longer be merely a condition of being, but a condition which has within itself both a repetition of its being and a representation of that repetition. If the interiority of architecture is singular as opposed to dialectical, and if that singularity can be defined as a repetition of difference, then architecture's interiority may be already written.

There is a second concern that the diagram must address, and that is the potential for the becoming unmotivated of the sign. The already-written introduces the idea of the index into the architectural object. The index is the first movement away from a motivated sign. Here, another layer must be added to the strata of the diagram, one which, through a process of blurring, finds new possibilities for the figural within architecture's interiority that could not have come from that interiority. An external condition is required in the process, something that will introduce a generative or transformative agent as a final layer in the diagrammatic strata. This external agent is not the expression of a desiring subject, but rather must come from outside of architecture as some previously unfigured, yet immanent agent in either the specific site, the program, or the history. It could take the form of a transparent pattern or screen, which causes the already imprinted to appear as other figurations, both blurring and revealing what already exists. This is similar to the action of a moiré pattern or filter, which permits these external traces to be seen free of their former architectural contexts.

The diagram acts as an agency which focuses the relationship between an authorial subject, an architecture object, and a receiving subject; it is the strata that exist between them. Derrida says that "Freud, evoking his representation of the psychical apparatus, had the impression of being faced with a machine which would soon run by itself. But what was to run by itself was not a mechanical re-presentation or its imitation but the psyche itself." The diagrammatic process will never run without some psychical input from a subject. The diagram cannot "reproduce" from within these psychical conditions. The diagram does not generate in and of itself. It opens up the repression that limits a generative and transformative capacity, a repression that is constituted in both the anteriority of architecture and in the subject. The diagram does not in itself contain a process of overcoming repression. Rather, the diagram enables an author to overcome and access the history of the discourse while simultaneously overcoming his or her own psychical resistance to such an act. Here, the diagram takes on the distancing of the subject-author. It becomes both rational and mystical, a strange superposition of the two. Yet according to Freud, only the subject is able to reconstitute the past; the diagram does not do this. He says, "There must come a time when the analogy between this apparatus and the prototype will cease to apply. This is true that once writing has been erased the Mystic Pad cannot 'reproduce' it from within; it could be a Mystic Pad indeed if, like our memory, it could accomplish that."

CHAPTER 12

AUTONOMY AND THE WILL TO THE CRITICAL

Within current debates on architecture, one topic seems to be in question more than ever and that is a concern for the critical. Our understanding of the critical previously rested upon Immanuel Kant's conviction that the critical represented the possibility of knowledge within knowledge. In other words, the critical traditionally meant a possibility lying within any discourse. In architecture, for example, this might mean the possibility of being within being. Because the nature of possibility implies options, it relies on some form of judgment that could be seen to modify, question, or change the dominant space/time condition at any moment in history. Consequently, the critical was often understood to be the new and the original. This correspondence can easily be confirmed by looking at the various avant-garde movements of the twentieth century. Today, poststructuralism's critique of history both as progressive—that is, as an agent that historicizes time in the form of the zeitgeist—and, simultaneously, as a construct that depends on an origin of value has problematized the idea of the new and the original. In architecture the repercussions of poststructuralism's upending of the given Kantian definition of the critical have generated two important responses, one articulated by R. E. Somol and the other by Jeffrey Kipnis.

Somol defines his position as the "postcritical." For him, the critical is something reactive, dialectical, or oppositional and thereby requires something in place to which it can then respond. Somol's opposition to the critical is grounded in the literal, the matter-of-fact, the "just life." The critical, he says, turns up attention, causing an awareness, a self-reflexive search for meaning, as in a formalism or in a writing. Somol's postcritical instead attempts to privilege the literal or the sensible over the abstract; it produces multiple kinds of subjects who are at once intoxicated, numb, fascinated, and seduced. For him, the postcritical is not about the representation of a *meaning*, but rather, concerns the performance of what something *does*. For example, he advocates increasing background noise so as to blur focus and attention. This last point constitutes my initial difference with Somol. I, too, am not interested in the message, or for that matter in the visual. The critical, in my terms, begins with the *becoming unmotivated* of the sign, the potential reduction of the culturally sedimented meaning of signs, so that the message itself becomes the interference. It is interference as *foreground* and not background that begins to define a fundamental characteristic of the processes of what is, for me, a necessarily existent critical project in architecture.

Unlike Somol, Jeffrey Kipnis argues that the critical is not merely reactive but that it always constitutes some form of resistance to the status quo. As such, it questions, explores, and proposes strategies that make manifest these resistances. These manifestations, while not dependent on, clearly relate to judgments that question the space/time regimes that are in place at any given time. In modernist thought, for example, abstraction was seen as a resistance to figuration. But eventually abstraction became absorbed into and identified as a trope of modernism. Clearly, when modernism became the dominant space/time regime, abstraction was no longer a resistant trope. The same can be said of collage as a process of abstracting one form of meaning and narrative into a non-narrative but still meaningful context. Today, collage, like montage, has been absorbed into every form of media as the dominant means of deploying visual information. If abstraction and collage no longer provide forms and processes of resistance, then the question that Kipnis would ask is, what are the forms of resistance today?

Kipnis rightly argues that there always will be two forms of resistance: one that resists change, that attempts to maintain the status quo—in this case, the sedimented interiority of architecture at any given time—and the other that resists and thus displaces the status quo. He then again rightly asks what is the nature of the judgment that decides what remains and what is displaced. For him, it is this judgment that constitutes the possibility of criticality today. For example, Jacques Derrida's claim that "architecture will always mean" and Rosalind Krauss's statement that "architecture will always have four walls" are the kinds of judgments that Kipnis's idea of criticality would challenge. He replaces the former conceptual and mental domains of the critical with the sensible and the affective. My differences with Kipnis lie with his idea that such external judgments—judgments of a subjective sensibility as opposed to judgments of architecture's interiority—are primary critical tools. For me, Kipnis's critical ignores the possible inherent criticality that is unique to architecture.

To understand this idea of a unique criticality within architecture, it is necessary to turn to the question of signs and their meaning. While signs play a role in all of the arts—music, literature, painting, and sculpture—they do not contain an immanence in these various disciplines as they do within architecture. A figurative or abstract piece of sculpture is not the *sign* of sculpture; it is the thing itself, because it is self-evidently so. A column in architecture, on the other hand, is *both* a structural element and the sign of that structure; that is, the sign is immanent to its own being. Their distinction is not self-evident. This is a unique condition, because unlike the other arts, such conditions as abstraction and figuration in architecture are both the sign and the form of the sign. Such a condition constitutes a singularity of architecture, in that, while it is a unique instance, it is not an original one.

Singularity is a useful term for understanding criticality; it distinguishes a unique instance, like a black hole, from an original instance, such as the beginning of something. A black hole is unique but not original. Krauss has said that to preserve the singularity of objects we must cut them off from their previous modes of legitimation. This idea will be seen to be important to any project of autonomy. Originality and newness have traditionally comprised the two dominant modes of legitimation in architecture. Radical or resistant behavior was always linked with the avant-garde, with the pursuit of the ever new and thus the original. With the loss of the continuity of history as a value of the origin, and the weakening of the dialectic economy of the model and its copy, the question of singularity becomes relevant, in particular in architecture's condition of the sign. Singularity does not displace the thing itself—a column, for example—nor deny its usefulness, but rather, denies that which formerly legitimated the thing's being—the sign of the column's structuring function. It is this possible singularity that evolves from the cutting off of the sign function—in other words, architecture's sedimented history as meaning—that begins to suggest architecture's autonomy. While traditionally any project of autonomy was primarily formal, autonomy is being proposed here as a means of unmotivating the architectural sign; that is, as a means of cutting the sign off from its previous value in function and meaning. This autonomy is neither formal nor semiotic per se; rather, it opens the internal processes of architecture to their own internal possibilities. It is the manifestation of these processes that will constitute the critical.

There have been two previous projects that posited a nonformal autonomy. Both occurred almost simultaneously in the late 1960s. The first was the Italian project of Aldo Rossi and Manfredo Tafuri. While their objectives were quite different, they nevertheless both relied on the reintroduction of history. Rossi's project concerned the development of archetypal elements that iterate in the course of history—domes, pediments, cylinders, and the like—while Tafuri proposed history as an autonomous condition outside of the architectural project. The second project of autonomy, which was entirely different from the Italian ones, was the architectural analogy to linguistic and semiotic "deep structures." What these two projects had in common was their denial of the historicist propelling energies of the zeitgeist in favor of something more permanent, essential, and universal: for Rossi and Tafuri, that essential was the autonomy of history; for the structuralists, it was language per se. The latter translated into architecture as the supposedly given structural relationship between the sign and the object. In other words, while both projects went beyond modernist formalism, they nevertheless had a more conventional conception of autonomy than can be conceived today. This is because with the weakening of dialectics and the advent of computational technology, architecture's interiority has been expanded to include previously repressed possibilities. Whereas prior autonomies were created between architecture and other disciplines as difference for its own sake, today, autonomy—and thus architecture's criticality—is the possible articulation of dynamic processes of difference between being and sign within architecture itself. Computation has opened up these possibilities to a performance, which allows autonomy to be the *continuous unfolding of possible being*, wrested from any preference for the functioning of the sign. In other words, criticality can be understood as the striving or the will to *perform* or manifest architecture's autonomy.

Today, it is possible to see autonomy in a new light, not as categorical permanencies and universals, but as dynamic processes of difference. In this sense, criticality can be further understood as the striving to perform this difference in architecture's autonomy. For Walter Benjamin, this striving in architecture was a will to the consciousness of the image in order to compensate for its lack, or its repression, in the zeitgeist (which defines itself by manifesting its normality as a form of repression). It is helpful here to read Benjamin's use of the term *image* in the larger sense as architecture's necessarily *figural* condition.

These processes of architecture's autonomous will lie primarily in the becoming unmotivated of the sign; that is, the sign no longer manifests only use, meaning, and structure, but also this will to difference. This will to difference, which remains as the sign's internal motivation, will be seen to be the processes of its becoming, of its becoming figural, the ebb and flow between abstraction and figuration. To become unmotivated, then, is to become both autonomous and singular: to cut from previous modes of legitimation and, simultaneously, to unmotivate. Autonomy thus becomes a critical project when it performs this will to either figuration or abstraction; that is, as a condition of possible being. This is not an external judgment, but an inevitable internal process.

The critical is an inevitable condition of autonomy, but is not synonymous with it. The critical determines how disciplinary processes such as abstraction and figuration are deployed and displayed. The locus and nature of such displays clearly change in relationship to the existing space/time regime. The display of criticality is not merely the performance of an architectural trope, such as abstraction, but also the display of the struggle between that which is in place and that which is being abstracted from it. Architectural autonomy, on the other hand, is always the struggle between a dominant mode—abstraction, for example—and the latent figural.

In and of themselves, abstraction and figuration are neither resistant nor compliant; these determinations depend on external conditions. The becoming figural does not. It is a will always attempting to overcome the normal relationship to the architectural sign. Thus it is similar to Gilles Deleuze's idea that the figural lies as an immanent condition within the plane of the unpainted canvas. In this sense, there can be no sign within architecture without some form of figuration. The autonomous is what always strives to overcome the sign's resistance to this figuration. When the figural is performed not as a model—that is, as the maintenance of the existing values of the discourse—but rather, as a unique instance—that is, as a singular difference lying within architecture as an enfolded figural possibility—the *presentation* of this autonomy then becomes critical.

According to this logic, the critical does not rely on an external, subjective judgment of taste or value, but a necessary internal articulation of a figural condition, which is singular to architecture's autonomy. While a choice of one thing over another will always involve a judgment—how and why one chooses—architecture's autonomy presents no need for judgment. It is precisely autonomy's inexorable will to manifest its singularity as the becoming unmotivated of the sign, and the cutting off of the object from previous modes of legitimation, that becomes a constant repetition within architecture. This repetition becomes a critical vehicle that disrupts the economy of the idea of the original and its copy, which exists as a present mode of legitimation. Architecture's singularity is, in a sense, an autonomy from which there can be no copy. Instead, it generates a constant iteration of internal difference between its sign and the form of its being. It is this difference that articulates the becoming unmotivated of the sign.

Here, autonomy is seen in a new light, as engaged in the survival of the discipline. The discipline is critical within its own project when it detaches itself from other projects rather than from difference in itself. Here, the critical becomes generative as opposed to being reactive or resistant. It becomes part of a dynamic internal condition, continually opening architecture's discourse.

CHAPTER 13

MIES AND THE FIGURING OF ABSENCE

Author's note: The following text is a fragment. It represents two interrelated concerns: the first is my long-standing interest in the permeability of the concepts of figure and ground, and how Mies's work—in particular the evolution of his column section—can be taken as a symptom of his concern for this problem; second, this text was a background for an architectural project my office submitted to the Illinois Institute of Technology (IIT) Student Center competition. In a sense, this text became the point of departure for what was to be construed as the radical nature of our projects with respect to Mies's project for the IIT campus. Without this text our project would seem to make little sense. Conversely, without our project this text may seem to be totally ungrounded. This project and the text are only part of a continuing fascination I have as an architect with the Miesian project, in particular, how it intersects my own concerns with figuring the ground, with blurring the distinction between the two poles. It is in this context that the following fragment is presented.

MIES AND THE FIGURING OF ABSENCE

Mies van der Rohe's idealism is never sentimental, but is more like the Nietzschean idealization of the Greek state. Mies' idealism is a solitude. It is a solitude without nostalgia, but one that illuminates the profane.
—Massimo Cacciari

Richard Serra's gesture of smashing a seventy-ton cube of black steel into the plinth of Mies van der Rohe's New National Gallery in Berlin gave the lie to two of the received myths about Mies's work, thus opening up the possibility of looking at the Miesian project from another perspective (fig. 13.1). The gesture first questions the supposed ideality of the work as embodied in the symbolic presence of a classical plinth. It is obvious to anyone visiting the museum that much of the ideality of the plinth and its "black box" superstructure masks a displaced functionality, which must find its life in the underground recesses of the building. Serra's block of steel repudiates the ideality by making what was formerly an ideal podium seem thin and brittle. In this context, architect and sculptor, Mies and Serra, ground and figure frame and reframe each other: site and object become part of a constant dialogue. As the art historian Hal Foster has written, "This slows down the becoming image of the object [figuration] and restores the body [the figural] against the abstract objectivity of Mies." This slowing down reduces and questions the immediate visual recognition of plinth as ground, forcing us to reconsider its grounding value.

13.1 Richard Serra, Block for Charlie Chaplin on podium of the New National Gallery, Berlin, 1977. Photo: Laurenz Berges.

A second and potentially more important question made possible by the Serra gesture concerns the historiography of the first half of the century, which often invested Mies with a simplified ideality. This caused many of the subtle nuances of his work such as the shape and placement of columns to be processed in the context of a master narrative. These narratives were characteristic of the tradition of German art history from the nineteenth century through the period preceding the Second World War, and attempted to explain the work of an architect as a seamless, often uninterrupted flow of history, despite stylistic and social evidence to the contrary. It was not until Massimo Cacciari, Manfredo Tafuri, and others began to question what came to be called "operative criticism," the kind supposedly practiced by Bruno Zevi and others in the late 1960s, that the material of previous historiographies was challenged. Tafuri argued that such operative histories often attempted to make the facts fit a grand historical abstraction, whereas he believed that the actual facts should be allowed to remain as facts, without these interpretations. Emerging from Tafuri's critique was the idea of an autonomous historical practice, where architects would simply pay attention to the facts of their building craft and leave the critical constructs to the historians. Underlying this idea of an autonomous historical practice was the concept of the negative, as a matrix of critical thought taken from Theodor Adorno's *Negative Dialectics* and filtered through the writings of Walter Benjamin and Martin Heidegger. The negative project essentially undercut the myth of architecture's supposed utopian and idealist aspirations, and suggested that any project of architecture, in particular those of the radical avant-garde, was bound to be consumed by expansionist capital. It is the intersection of the negative project and the "absence" of figuration that is of particular interest here. This is not the Mies and Adolf Loos of Tafuri and Cacciari who are used as examples of the ideology of the negative; rather, here the negative project will be used to calibrate spatial dissonances found in Mies's project, with particular reference to his work at IIT.

This having been said, it is worth noting that today there has been a further critique of both Zevi's operative criticism and Tafuri's autonomous historical practice, a critique concerned with the problematics of a history conceived as outside of a disciplinary practice. Much of the work of poststructuralism has demonstrated how dialectical and metaphysical projects are no longer adequate as operative critical tools. Yet in this postideological moment, much of the critique of the grand historical narrative embodied in the negative project still warrants some attention, particularly as it helps to open up Mies's use of the figural to contemporary practice.

Therefore, this essay proposes to question some of the received notions of Mies's spatiality in relation to the negative project. It will focus only on his IIT campus proposals of the late 1930s and early 1940s. One obvious issue, when looking at the many variations of the project, is the implied intention to make a paradigmatic image using closed, geometric, block forms, despite the problems that these forms created for the placement of functions. It is the conventional wisdom implied by these static block forms that will be questioned. Any such crucial reassessment of the IIT campus needs to consider three scale relationships: (1) the relationship of the urban fabric to the campus; (2) the relationship of the campus to the individual buildings; and (3) the relationship of building to building. In the case of the latter, there is a particular focus on the space between one building and another, and the way in which this space becomes figures through the implication in the detailing of the corner of individual buildings.

At the first scale, Mies's "solitude," as Cacciari calls it, can be seen in the isolation of the central campus from the urban fabric. While such isolation has been a tradition in many urban campuses (notably at Harvard and Columbia, where literal walls surround the university precinct), Mies suspended the tradition of the walled enclosure at IIT. Instead the plan relies on the voids—the empty spaces between and around the buildings—to serve as the conceptual and visual edge of the campus precinct. While such a strategy was also present in many of Le Corbusier's insertions into the fabric of Paris, Mies's use of the void is quite different. Le Corbusier's intention was to open up the city to a new connective tissue of light, air, and green space. Mies's plan, on the other hand, proposed an autonomy of the image, oblivious to the sense of polis; the campus was to be seen as profane with respect to the city. If anything, his was the void as a manifestation of the negative, of a lack; it suggested the impossibility of a connection to the old. Cacciari has stated that no other work in the city possesses the force of Mies's work, precisely because it is radically detached from the city, not only as an image but as a spatial and conceptual construct. This radical detachment derives not only from the different relationships of figural buildings to their ground, but also in the buildings' implication of an anticlassical, anti-ideal, antiprogressive utopian project at odds with the main tenets of modernism's insurgency.

In this sense, the modern project was dominated by the attempted amelioration of the city and its social relations with the individual and the groups. This attempt acknowledged the necessary duality of inclusiveness and separation. On the one hand, it was necessary to allow the new psychological subject, the individual, to "enter" the city and participate in its evolution. This required a certain openness and a fluidity of access and motion. On the other hand, the city needed to find separate places within its structure for the different psychological collectives: the new ethnicities, the defining classes, etc. In this context, the issue was not the simple matter of inclusion versus exclusion, but rather the nature of the new boundaries themselves, able to accommodate the desires of these groups and define their own identifiable urban places. The conflict inherent in the modern urban project can be seen to occur between these two limits: the needs of the individual and the needs of the group with respect to the city. Within these limits was the difficulty of provision, in the modern city, for both conjoining and separating the individual and the collective. A possible resolution of that conflict is simultaneously proposed and denied in Mies's campus. The individual is clearly symbolized in the freestanding object blocks and in the flowing and dynamic relationships of spaces to their virtual connection to these blocks, free of axial hierarchies. The definition of place for the collective can be found in more subtle distinctions. It is achieved not with traditional physical boundaries, but rather by a texture of buildings and open spaces, which in its stark contrast to the traditional fabric of the Near South Side of Chicago marks the difference not only between *civitas* and *universitas*, but also between Mies and Le Corbusier.

In the urban isolation of the campus and its buildings there was a seeming unity of thought, supposedly generating urban space that could also modify city form. The differences between the open spaces of Mies and those of Le Corbusier's Plan Voisin are salutary in this context. While Le Corbusier's blocks are vertical extrusions, bearing little relationship to the void spaces between them, Mies's buildings establish a horizontal, continuous datum for both building and space. The conceptual plane is no longer the ideal ground zero as manifested in a single, dominant ground plane, but is rather a zone of many layers extending from below ground in section to the tops of the buildings, with no single layer becoming dominant. This idea requires the disparate buildings to be seen as part of a continuous fabric, which in the specific case of IIT is also a metaphoric extension of the prairie into the city. But this metaphor is a red herring, because it returns space (the horizontal) to a single, dominant dimension. And it is through this dominant datum that the concept of figure/ground persists as a master narrative. Mies's buildings, which seem to reinforce this idea of datum, have in reality disrupted it. At the time of their construction, perhaps such a disruption could be seen as a negative gesture toward the city. But the proliferation of such gestures over the last decades—in particular the high-rise public housing that dominates the landscape of many of our cities—has turned this negativity into a hollow triumph and nullified any critical act. However, even a surplus of high-rise urban housing projects, with their barren stretches of open space, cannot erode the delicate interaction Mies proposed between void and solid at IIT. Instead, these high-rise projects stand as mute testimony to their misunderstanding of the Miesian project.

It is at the scale of void and solid that IIT is most revealing. If the history of architecture is marked by two different kinds of energy—one negative, transgressive of the status quo, and the other attempting to normalize and typify all transgressions and restore some stability

—then Mies's project between the two wars was in essence a transgressive one. Nowhere is this more evident than in the juxtaposition of elements in plan and section at IIT. Eschewing traditional campus planning ideas, from the walled monastic enclosures of the Cambridge colleges to the axial great lawn of the University of Virginia, Mies projected a campus that, in its denial of its urban context in setting its own interior rhythms, forever radicalized and transgressed existing collegiate typologies, both urban and pastoral.

Mies begins his project by setting up an overall twenty-four-foot-square grid that would seem to unify and organize the site. While this grid gives dimension to the object-buildings, when these dimensions take physical reality, the spatial grid becomes virtual as the buildings slip and slide past one another. The figural elements of the grid seem to appear only within the building blocks, as a literal column grid, while not appearing in the spaces between them. However, the apparent symmetry of the central campus in the preliminary scheme of 1939 and in the revised scheme of 1940 is not carried out in the detailing of the columns in the buildings themselves. It is interesting to note, in this context, that in the symmetrical scheme of 1939 the figural elements, the auditoria, were placed outside the building envelopes. In the later schemes, when the dominant symmetry is disrupted the figural elements are subsumed within the building volumes. When the figural elements arise within the void spaces, they displace this space, causing it to be seen as residual. When these elements are inserted within the buildings, it allows for another interpretation of the void spaces.

Again, it is useful to compare Mies's idea of a horizontal datum with Le Corbusier's. For Le Corbusier, space was sometimes conceived as horizontal lateral extension, for example, in the Maison Dom-ino project of 1914 and in the villa at Garches of 1929, or it was a horizontal extrusion, as in the radical section of Project A for Algiers of 1931–32. Mies's idea of a multilayered horizontal datum, while similar to Le Corbusier's, rarely included extension. There was always an articulate distinction between roof and floor, oftentimes with the roof acting as an umbrella hovering over the floor plane. This has given rise to an oversimplified reading of the discrete blocks, but upon closer inspection (particularly at IIT) the discrete quality of these elements with respect to the void must be questioned.

As has been said, at first glance, Mies's grid at IIT would seem to define the object-buildings, but in fact, as in the Barcelona Pavilion, this initial impression does not reveal Mies's questioning of presence in the void space. The building blocks, both positive and negative (solid and void), demonstrate a direct relationship to the columnar articulation of the twenty-four-foot-square grid. This articulation, usually seen at the corners or ends of the building blocks, thus causes a horizontal striation to occur in the plan of the supposedly neutral grid. Mies's articulation of the corner, particularly at IIT, must first be distinguished from a similar concern that inhabits the major narrative of architecture's discourse from the Renaissance onward. This history is usually cited with reference to the courtyard of the Palazzo Ducale in Urbino (fig. 13.2) and the courtyard of Bramante's Santa Maria della Pace in Rome (fig. 13.3). Both of these examples reflect a thought-to-be generic architectural problem: the intersection of the two walls of an interior courtyard space and how they articulate (turn, interrupt) the corner as an aspect of the building's discourse. In these examples it is always assumed that the building is a frame and the interior space is residual.

While Colin Rowe understood this problem when he attempted in his figure/ground reversals to give a positive value to the void, he succeeded only in restoring a phenomenological basis for what was in reality an idealist figure/ground dialectic.

For Mies, the problem at IIT would initially seem to be merely a different formal one, that is, the meeting and turning of an external corner. However, this is only part of Mies's concern. To understand the discursive strategy of the corners at IIT one has to go back to the Barcelona Pavilion. There, the cruciform stainless-steel columns seem to form a free-plan field. But unlike Le Corbusier's circular sectioned pilotis, which allow space to flow freely between them, Mies's Barcelona Pavilion columns define a series of square bay volumes, the corners of which seem to have disappeared because of the mirrorlike quality of the inboard intersection of the cruciform. From the Barcelona Pavilion on, the material and shape of Mies's column section define a continuing evolution in his work. But at IIT they enter a new phase: they become implicated in the horizontal zone of layers, not only in the physical presence of the building blocks but also in the void spaces between the buildings.

In the Library and Administration Building, only the four corners and the intermediate columns at the two ends (the north and south elevations) are articulated. In the initial plan, this building was paired with the Student Union Building, forming the major centerpieces of the campus. Their columnar organization sets up a linear north-south striation of space between them because both buildings are aligned north-south and east-west along a virtual axis produced by their placement at the conceptual center of the plan.

At the Navy Building (Alumni Memorial Hall) and the Metallurgy and Chemical Engineering Building (Perlstein Hall) (fig. 13.4), a similar phenomenon can be seen. The void L of space that the columns articulate at the corners produces a directional as opposed to gridded reading of the space. That is, the actual buildings and, by extension, their adjacent voids, which are "clipped" to the corners through the articulated columns, deny in their material presence the ideal condition of the underlying grid. Nowhere is the ideology of the negative more obvious than in these exposed column details. Several explanations are usually offered for these, many treating these details as a manifestation of the continuing cultural struggle between idealist and materialist impulses. The contradiction between the idealist and the materialist impulses in modern society has taken the form of the division of labor between the artisanal and the technological. This division has never been more evident than in twentieth-century architecture, which turned away from the artisanal—the bricklayer, the stonecutter, the plasterer—in favor of industrialized production. At IIT, Mies sought to overcome this duality, to retain some ideal of machine perfection and inscribe it into the form of the tectonic, as well as the articulation of the connections of frame to infill panel (particularly at corners) so as to declare the corner as something other than such an icon.

When considering the tectonic today, however, one must consider the impossibility of redeeming or even representing the Hegelian synthesis. This is especially relevant for architecture precisely because, as Kenneth Frampton has noted, "The structural unit is the irreducible essence of architectural form." For Frampton, the tectonic is not the technocratic but the poetic manifestation of structure in the original Greek sense of *poesis*, as an act of making and revealing. Clearly, this idea of making and revealing was also at work in

13.2 Luciano Laurana, Courtyard of Palazzo Ducale, Urbino, 1465, c. 1992. Photo: Luciana Miotto.

13.3 Donato Bramante, Interior Courtyard of Santa Maria della Pace, Rome, 1501–04.

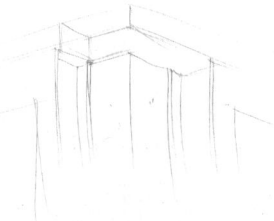

13.4 Mies van der Rohe, IIT Metallurgy and Chemical Engineering Building, 1994. Perspective sketch for symmetrical corner. Red pencil on Apex notepaper, 6 x 8½ in.
The MvdR Archive, The Museum of Modern Art, New York. Gift of the architect. © 2001 The Museum of Modern Art, New York.

Mies's corner: in the tectonic steel frame and the compressive mass of brick. But for Frampton, the moment of architecture is the generic joint between these two, a point of "ontological condensation." While Frampton dreams of a reassociation of architecture and engineering, this split, as Hal Foster has observed, cannot be redeemed but only exploited to make its conditions somehow more relevant to a postindustrial age. In fact, the exploitation of this split between the icons of the tectonic and its material presence has become a new internal necessity for architecture.

It is perhaps more useful to look at the corner columns at IIT in terms of what Rosalind Krauss calls the "baring of the device." This is not an attempt to make transparent the means by which things were made, nor is it an image of tectonic integrity, as Frampton would have us believe; rather, it is the expression of an ideological concern—for instance, with the use-value of objects. This idea was initially understood as a reaction to the nineteenth-century object, where surface acted to cover and conceal its internal workings. Futurism, de Stijl, and Constructivism stood in opposition to this tradition defining modern architecture through the baring of internal mechanism.

In either case, today such a baring no longer seems adequate to explain and define the conditions of structure, because the mechanical and tectonic condition of presence as an articulated necessity in Cartesian space no longer has the imperative it held a century ago. Equally, the question of presence as an underlying prop in the metaphysical system can no longer be reasonably sustained. Rather, the corner columns can be seen as the figuring of absence. In this context, the voided column in the collage of the Resor House prefigures IIT (fig. 13.5). Like the mirror and cruciform columns that become tears in the space of the Barcelona Pavilion, the white absence simultaneously suggests another attitude toward figuration: it is both the absence of figure and revelation of a ground that appears as figure.

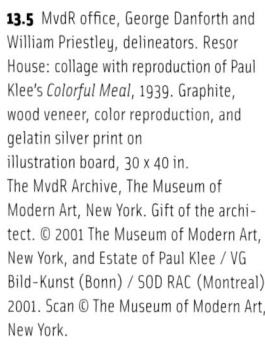

13.5 MvdR office, George Danforth and William Priestley, delineators. Resor House: collage with reproduction of Paul Klee's *Colorful Meal*, 1939. Graphite, wood veneer, color reproduction, and gelatin silver print on illustration board, 30 x 40 in.
The MvdR Archive, The Museum of Modern Art, New York. Gift of the architect. © 2001 The Museum of Modern Art, New York, and Estate of Paul Klee / VG Bild-Kunst (Bonn) / SOD RAC (Montreal) 2001. Scan © The Museum of Modern Art, New York.

Mies introduced figural expression into his work early, at the beginning of his career in Europe, first in the Glass Skyscraper project of 1921/22, which was a figural extrusion, and later, in America, in the Resor House project of the late 1930s. In both cases, the figural expression is different. While the Glass Skyscraper is pure expressionist figuration, in the project for the Resor House, figure is introduced in the form of an enlarged Klee painting and the photographed collage of a landscape that plays between the real and the abstract. In many ways the attempt at the figural in the Resor House is like Giacometti's framing of the human figure in his small boxlike sculpture of 1950 called *Woman Walking between Two Houses* (fig. 13.6). Here the figure and ground remain articulated, suspended from one another in their ideal state. This suspension of figure and frame becomes blurred in Serra's sculptural intervention at Mies's New National Gallery in Berlin. While sculpture is traditionally framed by architecture, in the steel block embedded in Mies's Berlin podium, Serra insists that sculpture can intervene critically in architecture to recover architecture as the lost origin of sculpture. It is in this sense that the ground plinth becomes a figural element.

13.6 Alberto Giacometti, *Woman Walking between Two Houses*, 1950. Bronze, glass, paint, 12 x 21¼ x 3¾ in.

At IIT, the absent columns at the corners of the object-buildings present the nonpresence of Mies's grid as a continuum of virtual building which, in its dissipation, locates a conflict internal to the traditional figure/ground relationships. Here, architecture that seems able to sustain an ideal figural or framing condition turns instead to the possibility of figuring the voided ground. Mies confronted the problematic of abstraction and materiality head on: in this sense the virtual was privileged over the material. The voided L of the corner column cannot be read as an attempt at dematerialization, but rather is a virtual grid literally present in its absence. Thus, architecture does not simply feature its processes of making merely because its tectonic has been the dominant mode of its legitimization. For architecture to become critical it must rethink the tectonic, but not through its objects or their processes, which will always both represent and exist in structure. Rather, architectural processes can invade structure with the figural and reframe structure with the ground.

The difference between the autonomy of Mies's grid of horizontals and verticals and an ideal grid is important. Mies's idea of the autonomy of structure as independent of its tectonic implications becomes a critique of structure itself. In this way, Mies turned away from the dialectic by figuring the ground, the void between the object-presence of his buildings. In figuring the ground, Mies challenges both the pedestal and the unified object, and in so doing restores to his objects a new dignity freed from idealist history. Any rethinking of Mies today, therefore, cannot take place solely within or between the idealist and the materialist impulses, but rather must demonstrate the improbability of these categorical dialects. It is in this improbability that his solitude lies.

CHAPTER 14

BLURRED ZONES

Author's Note: Since I first conceived of the term *blurring* in architecture and the concept for a book called *Blurred Zones* some thirteen years ago, the term has become quite popular—so much so that my editors argued for changing the title of the book. Architects such as Toyo Ito and Diller + Scofidio now use the term, but in an entirely different manner from that used here. For example, Diller + Scofidio use the term quite literally, as in their Blur Building. I continue to use blurring in the context of the work in *Blurred Zones* because the idea of blurring has not been argued in the conceptual sense that it is presented here.

According to the French thinker Michel Foucault, everything exists as between the visible and the articulate. This condition of between assumes that the two poles—the visible and the articulate—are more or less stable. In the mediated world of today, however, even the visible is becoming articulate. As a consequence, there is an excess of articulation. When the articulate is increasingly compressed into shorter and shorter time spans, like twenty-second sound bites, the visual becomes more and more a question of image rather than substance. Another consequence of our mediated age is the loss of the immediate relation between the visible and the body, that is, the tactile and the affective. Architecture can provide affect—a form of articulation that appeals to both the somatic and the articulate: to the body, the mind, and the eye at the same time. This is something that other media do not do.

Blurring, or the blurred zones that characterize the work my office produced in the 1990s, deals with the world of affect rather than effect, as presenting a strategy for a different mind/body relationship in architecture. Affect is concerned with the way particular forms of architectural effects, tropes, rhetoric, can displace our conventional or expected experience of space. If, as Walter Benjamin said, architecture is viewed in a state of distraction, then such affects might provoke a different awareness of a space/time experience. For example, figure/ground is an effect that concentrates on the aesthetic materiality of form; shape produces a clarity of affects. Blurring reduces the affect of these effects, producing a need for different effects. It must be understood that blurring in this context is never literal; one never sees blurring.

Affect operates from the way the upright body moves in and around space; it recalibrates the subject's somatic experience of both presence and information, as well as one's fundamental desire for these experiences. This desire generates an unconscious, somatic expectancy on the part of the subject. For example, when one goes down an unfamiliar set of stairs in the pitch dark, say a flight of steps to a basement, a somatic expectancy occurs vis-à-vis each next step. Hence at the last stair at the bottom, the body automatically takes another step. When the foot comes down unexpectedly on the floor, one often feels as if one has lost one's balance. This is a somatic expectancy, a desire on the part of the body to repeat what it has learned to anticipate. Benjamin calls this reaction a matter of habit. Habits are rooted in desire, and desire is often motivated by habit. For example, we often take the same route to destinations we repeatedly return to. Most architecture is a concretization of habit. There are primitive and unconscious motivations that become conscious in architecture: the desire for ground or to be rooted; the desire for shelter; the desire for meaning. These desires, more than the objects of their desire, seem to motivate a more or less status quo in architecture. If architecture can begin to dislocate this motivation, then the desire manifested in the habitual or somatic expectancy can perhaps be reoriented.

The word *architecture* conjures up an enormous range of meanings that embraces everything from home to building, symbol to function. But while it includes these things, it also assumes certain conditions beyond the bounds of what is necessary and sufficient to define architecture's particular discourse. In turn, these assumptions repress other possibilities. Blurring fundamentally involves the question of becoming unmotivated of three conditions: the becoming unmotivated of presence, of the sign, and of the subject. The key concept in the process of blurring is *becoming*. For example, there can never be a total lack of motivation in presence. Presence itself is a motivated condition. The *becoming* unmotivated is a movement from the fullness of motivation to something less motivated—a between condition.

Blurring is one strategy for unmotivating not desire itself but the specific desires for such things as presence, ground, and meaning. Blurring is a conceptual activity. This is because it is literally impossible to blur an architectural element such as a column or a wall. A blurring action begins to displace categories such as the visible and the articulate by detaching form from a one-to-one relationship with function and meaning. Blurring seeks to undermine the conceptual as well as the physical clarity of elements such as figure and ground.

In Woody Allen's film *Deconstructing Harry*, a character who has little psychological awareness of himself often appears visibly out of focus. This initially has a disturbing visual effect on the audience, but over the time of the film it becomes a one-liner because nothing more is made of it; very little relates this blurring to the psychological condition of the character. In a sense, it is an effect without substance, and therefore with very little affect.

When we go to the movies, we not only want to be entertained, we also have a desire to understand what the movie is about. The most popular movies are the ones that are the most easy to understand because they satisfy our desire to know. The difference between a movie and what one calls "film" is that film attempts to unmotivate the viewer's desire to know and to be entertained in order to present the being of film itself—its rhetoric and its tropes.

Architecture, unlike film, is more often than not an everyday occurrence. While it is not meant to entertain, it is equally not meant to call attention to its own rhetoric, which is seen as a response to a desire for place, a desire for ground, for containment, representation, and so forth. Whether conscious or not, one of the basic desires of humankind is to make things real, tangible, secure, and comfortable. Architecture is a major locus of such desires, as they involve not only presence, an actual enclosure, but also the metaphysical idea of comfort and security. In post-1968 France, the question of presence is both active and fundamental; architecture cannot be thought without presence. The presence of walls, floors, and ceilings is a real materiality. Today, however, the idea of a virtual space foregrounds the question of presence. Since one cannot get rid of actual presence, what is the blurring that occurs? Unmotivating does not do away with issues of comfort and security. Rather it attempts to problematize their use as legitimating factors in architecture.

The idea of conceptual blurring raises the issue of contemporary media. Does architecture still function symbolically the way it did before print and broadcast media became so dominant? Do we look to architecture for narratives or the kinds of information that are now being provided in other media? It would seem that the public today no longer looks to architecture to provide information in the way it once did. Blurring in architecture is not to suggest a movement from a symbolic environment to one in which there is no meaning. Rather it is to suggest a condition where architecture is neither dependent on its former narratives nor devoid of meaning but resides between the two, where other forms of meaning, and meaningful situations, can occur.

These situations lead to the becoming unmotivated of the sign. The becoming unmotivated is a process of blurring between the clarity of meaning and no meaning. Architecture can never become totally unmotivated, that is, have no meaning. For example, signs like the ground, the enclosure, the façade, which have dominated architectural discourse since the sixteenth century, are what might be called "motivated conditions." Because these motivated conditions have been taken for granted, over time they have taken on qualities of the natural, when in fact they are only conventions. Take, for example, the term *façade*, which is used as a catchall term for elevation, vertical plane, etc. Façade is an example of a loaded, or motivated, term that is assumed to be natural and thus aesthetically neutral. But literally *façade* means face, to have a face; most exterior vertical planes are legitimated as façades by having a face. A face is composed; it has an aesthetic and, from that aesthetic, both an iconic and symbolic meaning. A façade creates difference and hierarchy between in and out; public and private; sacred and profane. Blurring attempts to erase that hierarchy and the conditions that previously legitimated such concerns, but without losing the enclosing condition of the vertical plane. Rather than legitimating enclosure (while being enclosure), blurring allows the vertical plane to be something else.

If it is possible to blur and displace traditional presence—to conceptually dislocate the stability of place—and if the sign can become less motivated and move toward an indexical condition, this then leaves the condition of the subject. This concerns the attempt to move from a motivated, desiring subject to one who is less motivated, that is, to a situation of more pure desire. The human subject will always be a desiring one. This cannot be changed. But in architecture that desire can be expanded beyond the usual motivations of shelter, enclosure, stability, ground, etc., by opening up the realm of the unconscious, where desire operates. This suggests that architecture can move from the conscious world of presence and motivated signs toward a world that opens up to unconscious phenomena. In this way, architecture can think of space and time as motivated by concerns other than traditional ones of a desiring and motivated subject.

How does one change the motivation of the subject-user or the subject-architect who inhabits or makes architecture? In other words, if architecture is viewed as something that is known and understood, can one change architecture to something that can present the unexpected within the expected? Throughout the history of architecture, when a break or displacement of the known has occurred, architecture has taken the new and incorporated it into a new normal, or typical, condition. Architecture has traditionally moved forward by transforming the present and thereby upsetting the normative situation. Blurring, on the other hand, displaces the idea of one's time, rather than conforming to time in the present, in order to open the past to another future. If one assumes the past as known will always lead to the present, nothing will change. If the present is displaced by looking to the past in order to blur the present to suggest a previously unknown future, it is possible to change the desires and expectations of the subjects.

Blurring takes many different definitions—the between, the interstitial—and many different forms in the work that is presented here. Basically, the process of blurring introduces a third phase into the process of design. The first phase of any design process considers site, program, and function, which are the reality of what is required. Each of these can be seen as textual material constituting the most immediate information on which any specific design is based. The second kind of textual material comes from the interiority and anteriority of architecture. The interiority of architecture defines the discipline, what it is that makes architecture singular; anteriority is the sedimented history of architecture, which has defined architecture at any given historical moment.

The texts of function, site, and program and the texts of the interiority and anteriority of architecture together define a traditional practice. Architects always define what they do in relation to these texts because it is impossible to do architecture without recalling its anteriority, its interiority, or its singular condition of sign and signified as functioning things.

The attempts to create a blurring require the introduction of other, third texts. These texts initially appear to be unmotivated by the traditional concepts of program, site, context, interiority, or anteriority. In one sense, these texts are both arbitrary and contingent, in that they both relate to and have the ability to alter the conditions of the traditional texts. While there is no such thing as the purely arbitrary, the introduction of an arbitrary condition into the relationship with the other two texts begins to blur the previous one-to-one relationship between the forms one produces and their functions or meanings. Thus these supposedly arbitrary texts in many cases are contingent on their capacity to blur. In a sense they are selected to produce architectural effects that will displace traditional ones. When one looks at resultant forms, they no longer appear to be motivated by site, function, program, interiority, or anteriority. Rather, they appear to be "out of focus," blurred by the superposition of the texts of function and site with other texts. It is difficult to tell if the resultant forms come about through functional requirements or from a desire to produce meaning; neither seems to explain them. This produces what will be called a diagram, a blurred condition between form and content, between site and program, where signs no longer read as fully motivated. The interference pattern of the diagram prevents a recourse to the former relationship of form and function, form and content.

The projects presented in *Blurred Zones* in one way or another represent a movement toward becoming unmotivated of the former texts of architecture, which together constituted a hegemony and acceptance of the metaphysics of presence. This project of the becoming unmotivated requires one important caveat: it requires that I also unmotivate myself toward the things that I like and desire, even toward my own theories and designs. Because I have likes and desires, it is sometimes difficult when someone says that a project does or does not conform to the theory of displacement. I often say, damn the theory, the thing looks terrible; we cannot have anything like this. And sometimes the reply is that I am going against my own theory because theory can only take one so far. In the end, I have to trust my own intuition, no matter how flawed it may be, because intuition comes from the unconscious fire of one's own history, and may open up what was previously repressed both in oneself and, for me, in architecture.

CHAPTER 15

L'ORA CHE È STATA

It was Alberti who first said that painting's most important task was to establish a *storia*, a history that would allow painting to develop. This history required there to be a subject, and from that, a relationship between the subject and the object—how the subject views the object. At this point the object becomes more than just a thing. Because it now has a history, it begins to have a form, a representation, and a meaning, and thus a metaphysic beyond its being, which reads into being, into form. The entire enterprise of metaphysics in the arts and architecture can be said to be lodged within this "invention" of history, and thus of meaning, by an unsuspecting subject.

The history of any discipline brings us to the point where we are prepared to understand the discipline as it exists, but it does not prepare us for anything new that might come from within the discipline. This internal newness is composed of the singular projects that produce irreducible effects autonomous to any discipline. These projects not only change the discipline from within but also change its existence within a general cultural project. This difference between the discipline as it exists and the idea of an originary project which alters that discipline begins to define the subject of this essay: the difference between the metaphysics of presence in architecture and the presence of a metaphysics in painting.

What has been variously called deconstruction or poststructuralism in current philosophy and comparative literature can be said to have two primary points: the critique of idealist philosophy, or, more specifically, its dialectic, and what for lack of a better term can be called a critique of the metaphysics of presence. Philosophy in particular projects architecture as the locus of the metaphysics of presence, since it seems at first glance to be lodged in both objective reality and its representations. Whether philosophy's interest in architecture is useful or not, and whether the assumption that architecture is the locus of the metaphysics of presence is true or merely an unquestioned hypothesis that is part of architecture's mythology is certainly at issue today in architecture.

Since the consciousness of the subject was proposed in texts like Alberti's proposal of a *storia* in the early fifteenth century, the metaphysics of presence has become a foundational myth, an architectural theology. With the introduction of the subject, the object became both an object and its own mediation (which was formerly thought to be mediated by God). That is, it was an object and its own representation, perspective, history, and their representations. When representation entered, two what could be called "look likes" emerged: the thing itself and the representation of some other thing. Architecture always clearly looked like architecture, but so did the column look like a tree, and many modern houses looked like ships. The idea of representation of a form in being instantiated the concept of metaphysics. When this happened, representation was no longer thought to be a convention in architecture; rather, it was thought to be a natural truth.

It is also noted in other disciplines. For example, the philosopher Jacques Derrida has said, "Architecture will always mean," and the art historian Rosalind Krauss has written, "Architecture will always have four walls." These two important cultural critics are not known for necessarily stating the obvious, so there must be a reason why they made these statements. From a historical perspective, from a lay point of view, their statements merely reflect what has always been believed about architecture: that architecture reflects some form of natural truth. For example, a building with four walls presumes that there is a corner, and a classical colonnade, while perhaps no longer retaining its original meaning, nevertheless still means something today. However, in fact a corner is not simply a corner; it is both a thing and an idea, a cause and an effect. The way a corner is solved, that is, as an effect, is the result of a cause, of the need to enclose space, to have an inside and an outside.

The corner is one example of an uncritical historical assumption that simply because it has existed in architecture for as long as anyone can remember presumes that it will always exist in the same way to produce an effect. When statements about meaning and walls are made by serious intellectuals, the basic problem is obscured: all architecture does not necessarily have to mean, and architecture does not necessarily have four walls. Derrida's and Krauss's comments are lodged within the historical context that licenses what is called the metaphysics of presence. What makes these statements more problematic for architecture is that both Derrida and Krauss in their own work in philosophy and painting and sculpture have argued precisely against the very same metaphysics.

Thus, it is clear that the metaphysics of presence is a very elusive concept. Its current history can be traced back to Martin Heidegger's critique of metaphysics and the idea of presence as a historical matter, which ironically reinscribes his own critique in a metaphysical context. Then Emmanuel Levinas and Edmund Husserl each in his own way attempts to critique Heidegger's problem. Levinas suggests that there is something that preexists presence. It is a violence that appears in both writing and the law. Derrida follows by suggesting that anything can be known only by how it is different from some other thing or, alternatively, from some absence. For Derrida, to have presence means to give something form beyond merely its appearance privileged by seeing, that is, what I see is what I know to be and to be truthful. Thus for Derrida, presence, and ultimately its metaphysics, is an illusory and uncritical assumption of sight. Derrida would further argue that this ur-presence, this form, emanates from a system of concepts, and thus from a language and ultimately from a writing, which is an irreducible effect of language. Clearly, since both painting and architecture seem to rely on and privilege sight, it would follow for Derrida and others that the metaphysics of presence lies in these disciplines, that in fact architecture, if not painting, is the primary locus of such a condition. It is just such an unexamined truth that leads to the problem, which presumes meanings, walls, and thus corners.

To be a natural and even autonomous effect of architecture, the resolution of a corner is only seen to be so because of the operation of something called the metaphysics of presence, which presumes a corner to be both necessary and natural to architecture. Once metaphysics is questioned, then such things as the architectural resolution of a corner is not necessarily an irreducible or autonomous effect. For example, there are no corners in Buckminster Fuller's domes or Greg Lynn's blobs. But corners are not the only manifestation of the operations of the metaphysics of presence in architecture. For example, how a building meets the ground has traditionally been a condition which is made thematic in architecture, that is, are all the columns the same size and length? do they meet the ground at the same elevation? and so forth. These are just some of the questions that enter into a discussion of building and ground, a discussion that quickly elides with the pictorial concerns of figure and ground in painting. The ground in both architecture and painting become implicated in pictorial concerns such as datum, picture plane, and the like. If both disciplines are to produce effects, then the ground and the canvas are clearly a cause; they are not going to go away.

While generally considered to be flat, the ground in architecture plays a different role than the ground, or canvas, in painting. First, the ground in architecture is horizontal and thus has a different relationship to the subject than the usually vertical ground of the painted surface. Whatever attempts to the contrary, the literal figure/ground relationship in architecture —a building standing on a site—will clearly challenge any attempt to reduce such a literal volumetric presence. In painting, there is a literal canvas as a ground. There have been many attempts to thematize the surface of the canvas in painting, that is, to make it other than literally flat. One of these is to thematize this flatness by making the ground more flat, that is, more conceptually flat, as was the case in collage. This collage is done by using known pictorial effects, but collage also creates new effects (which later become categorized as pictorial) in the denial of metaphysics and in a movement to pure presence. In architecture the ground is rarely made more groundlike—that is, just ground or pure ground —because it is rarely thought to be anything other than real ground. A more likely scenario would be not to thematize the ground as a conceptual datum, but to suggest in the modeling of the horizontal surface a ground with multiple data.

Derrida first presents his critique of the metaphysics of presence in *Of Grammatology*, in which he writes that the metaphysics of presence is an uncritical, historically determined concept. From this it is obvious that metaphysical painting and the metaphysics of presence are concepts of a different order. While the metaphysics of a church may produce an affect of spirituality in a viewer, it says little about the metaphysics of presence in church architecture. Likewise, metaphysical painting is not about the status of metaphysics in painting. Rather, it concerns the creation of a metaphysical or otherworldly affect in the viewer, as Giorgio de Chirico did, often by using architectural imagery to create such an affect. There is, however, a difference between metaphysics as a style in painting or architecture, which produces an affect, and the critique of the metaphysics of presence that opens up new originary effects in architecture.

De Chirico's paintings are laconic, restricted, and concise to the point of being mysterious. They are representations of a sublime abstraction, similar to an abstraction seen in the drawings of Aldo Rossi, which became saturated with memory, a terse, minimal, distant reality. In architecture, when the stark reality of metaphysical painting appears in the buildings of Giuseppe Terragni, Luigi Moretti, and Rossi, are they so different from de Chirico's drawings? In fact, if Rossi's buildings create any metaphysical affect of unease, these affects were first suggested in his own paintings. And are not Terragni's Casa del Fascio and Moretti's Accademia della Scherma, as well as the haunting arches of the tower of Italian civilization in the Esposizione Universale di Roma, indebted in some way to the uncanny sense of de Chirico's work? The difference between the intention of these buildings as haunted abstractions and the questioning of the metaphysics of presence in architecture is the point in question. Rossi's work may produce an affect of the uncanny, but neither his work in architecture nor de Chirico's in painting addresses the question of the metaphysics of presence. Even though metaphysical painting and abstracted architecture may at first seem to look alike, there is a further similarity. Both Rossi's and de Chirico's work make thematic one of the convergences of metaphysics in architecture and in painting: and that is in the unquestioned use of pictorial codes. These conventions—figure/ground, picture plane, edge stress, flattening of image, deep and shallow space—are part of what continues a metaphysic (if not a metaphysical look) in both the painting of de Chirico (and of Rossi, for that matter) and the architecture of Rossi. Because these are long-held conventions, it has been difficult to open them up to new internal effects.

The difference between flatness in painting and flatness in architecture is also useful to consider in this context. There is an important difference between flat space, which is literal spatial depth, albeit shallow, and flatness, which is a conceptual quality of both deep and shallow space. Flatness is clearly one of the essential pictorial possibilities of the picture plane in painting, because the canvas is literally a flat surface. To overcome this, to produce the illusion of deep space in the perspective paintings of architecture, say, in the paintings of Piero della Francesca, an illusion or a representation of deep space was projected.

At the same time, Bramante, who worked with Piero, was making his architectural speculations on a flat surface. There is an important difference between the painter Piero, painting architectures, and Bramante, also a painter, working out architectural ideas in painting. Bramante first outlined his architectural spatial program in the famous Prevedari etching, in which a concatenation of deep and shallow spaces prefigure his work at St. Peter's. Then, in his church of San Satiro in Milan, Bramante produced a false perspective of an apse, simulating deep space in flat space. While originally imported from the idea of flatness in painting, this idea of flatness was to become a conceptual device in architecture as an effect, as a way of denying the literalness of real architectural space.

Flatness is clearly a cause in painting that produces effects. Edge stress, picture plane, frontality are other such causes, but flatness is unique because of its relationship to architecture. While it is a cause in painting, flatness becomes an effect in architecture. More important, in both cases it produces what can be considered pictorial results, whether as a cause or an effect, and thus continues a metaphysical condition.

When flatness is an effect of architecture, it is not so much literal flatness but a simulated or conceptualized flatness that is at work. That the ideas of flatness, frontality, edge stress, etc., may originate in painting is not the issue. Rather, it is how these concepts are dealt with differently to produce potentially autonomous effects, whether in painting or architecture. For example, Brunelleschi introduces different uses of perspectival effects in his churches of San Lorenzo and Santo Spirito in Florence. The confirmation of the subject occurs in both churches through his insistence on monocular vision. In San Lorenzo, the effect is to make literal deep space conceptually deeper, while at Santo Spirito the opposite effect is achieved by layering deep space to create a sense of flatness across and perpendicular to the central nave axis.

Collage is another example of how a pictorial flatness was layered on to a literal one. Clement Greenberg claims that the intentions of both Braque and Picasso were to overcome the increasingly dominating effect of literal flatness produced by the smaller and smaller divisions of analytical cubism on the canvas. Placing large areas of real material on the canvas was not so much an attempt to overcome metaphysics with pure presence as it was to bring flatness from its literal condition to a conceptual and pictorial one.

One would have thought that since presence is obviously a different form of reality in architecture than in painting—that is, real three dimensions versus a simulated third dimension—that the problematic of the metaphysics of presence would not be as critical an issue in painting as it is in architecture. However, if anything, the reverse is true. While the metaphysics of presence is generally accepted in architecture (hence the problematic which first must overcome this complacency) it has been the basis of much of painting from the late 1960s to the present.

For example, in the 1970s, the reduction of the metaphysics of presence in art, that is, of the pictorial and illusionistic conventions, was important to produce in art what Krauss called an index. The idea of the index was to reduce the metaphysics of presence to pure presence. An index is a mark, trace, or imprint—like footprints left in the sand—of a former event or presence. When Gordon Matta-Clark cut a house in half, he left a trace of the act while reducing the metaphysic of the idea of the "home," shelter, enclosure, etc., to pure presence. Matta-Clark also illustrates one of the differences between the metaphysics of presence in painting and in architecture. While through this cutting Matta-Clark can attempt to produce pure presence, in so doing he not only reduces the metaphysics of presence in architecture, he reduces architecture. Now a formerly habitable house is no longer habitable, or even a house. In its reduction, it is no more architecture than a Piero painting.

The problem with pure presence is that it returns phenomenology to an essential condition. While phenomenological concerns are always initially present in most art forms and architecture, they ultimately reverse themselves and instantiate metaphysics. As Derrida has shown, phenomenology must be overturned in order to open up metaphysics to its own singular, autonomous, and irreducible disciplinary effects.

The difference between the affects of the look of metaphysics and the critique of the metaphysics of presence is a critical point. This difference basically concerns effects which are unique to any discipline. A perspectival painting of a building is different from a building seen in perspective. The effects in such a painting by de Chirico do not accrue to perspective but rather the saturation of color and the harsh, cold light he is able to depict are painterly effects which can never be replicated in architecture.

In this context it is useful to compare a de Chirico and, say, a work by Bernini, with a Francis Bacon and a Borromini. Bernini was the first architect to import theatrical effects from other disciplines, which as a spectacle of effects created subjective affects and a more passive observer. De Chirico creates the affect of unease in his paintings with effects such as those that are proper to other disciplines, such as architecture. On the other hand, both Borromini and Bacon create unease through an internal production of new effects, internal to the act of architecture and painting.

Michael Fried, in his seminal essay "Art and Objecthood," describes the difference between minimalist sculpture and minimalist painting as one of theatricality. He goes on to say that minimalist sculpture by nature was theatrical, that its effects were borrowed from other disciplines, staged, as it were; whereas minimalism in painting was an intrinsic effect, an originary discovery made in painting. A unique or irreducible effect does not necessarily reinscribe a metaphysics of presence. As Jeffrey Kipnis has said, Jackson Pollock did not paint ideas; instead, his painting indicated an idea about process, event, and ultimately existentialism. The difference between one Pollock and another is the ideas they contain about painting beyond the visual.

Thus the issue is not theatricality versus the not-theatrical; rather, it is the fact that the theatrical leaves the world intact. In this sense, metaphysical painting does not necessarily change existence, while opening up the metaphysics of presence to a critical context possibly does. Such a critical context allows for originary effects that are no longer from within the history that created the illusion of the metaphysics of presence as an originary truth. The essence of the discipline is no longer consolidated in history, because both Bacon and Borromini produced effects which were outside of the history of their disciplines.

The metaphysics of any presence evolves as a historical phenomenon, becoming a history of new effects, like collage and perspective, which at one time had a critical capacity, but today have lost that. For example, collage and perspective have become part of an established phenomenology of a discipline. The uncritical assumptions propagated by the metaphysics of presence inhibit the development of new effects. But these alone would not be sufficient in themselves to produce a level of criticality. In order to produce such a context, as new states of knowledge about a discipline, these must be articulated not in terms of history but rather from history, from the interiority of any discipline.

CHAPTER 16

A MATRIX IN THE JUNGLE

Several years ago, Fredric Jameson said that the computer would be capable of giving us a new nature; not an unnatural nature but a nature derived directly from computerized algorithms and processes. Such a thought means it would no longer be necessary to look at nature with the same eyes through which Le Corbusier observed the natural shapes of D'Arcy Thompson. (It was precisely from the latter's immense body of work that Le Corbusier deduced most of the plastic, spiraled shapes and complex proportional relationships that produced his "Modulor" system.)

Architecture has traditionally been founded on several supposedly clear relationships to nature, with the idea that these be pleasant to sight, hearing, and touch. Computer technologies may now force us to rethink the quality of these relationships, and therefore what was once considered to be natural in architecture.

These new natures, which are found and manipulated only through the use of architectural algorithms, already exist. But how are they to be evaluated? What is needed is a critical matrix concerning these new natures, one that will help determine in turn the characteristics of what could be called "critical value." This task is presently difficult because there is no longer an in-place dialectic, itself a critical matrix that made value easy to determine.

This creates a double problem with these new natures. First is this lack of a dominant dialectic culture, and second, the loss of a distinction between original and copy. In the digital world the origin of the original can no longer be traced. Its use value and its own materiality have, in a certain sense, vaporized. At the same time, computation has made the more general question of value problematic, proposing values through electronic works themselves.

How can the value of such work be recognized? How can we know whether or not what we are evaluating is a finished product or a work that is still evolving? This is not an era of simple alternatives, when things are either black or white, good or bad, old or new, rich or poor; when, for example, one could say, "That's a good thing." Depending on the situation, values in the past may have been related to the functional use of objects, or codes that only took into account the esthetic or metaphorical aspect of their function. In such a context, a work could be easily judged good or bad, because the performance criteria were already established. There was no intrinsic value in objects; rather, this was thought to reside in the relationship of the object to the critical context.

When the awareness of architecture as a discipline first evolved in the late fourteenth and fifteenth centuries in Italy, it was necessary to define architecture as a relationship between a subject (in time) and its object (in space); between what was man-made and what was natural. Before this moment, the relationship of man and nature was mediated by an idea of God, through which everything maintained a value. In the shift from theocentrism to anthropocentrism, God no longer appeared as mediator (that is, the one who gave value), and the subject itself was called upon to determine value.

Brunelleschi was the first to turn to science in search of a foundation for architecture. Since that time, architects have suffered from what could be defined as "science envy." (In fact, one might well ask if computation is another form of science envy in order to relieve us of the problem of value.) Brunelleschi used perspective, which was derived directly from mathematics and science, to redefine the subject through new spatial and temporal relationships.

This monocular view saw the world in a completely new way, reified through the perspectival canvas. The monocular subject not only created its own dimensions but also attributed a dimension to vision itself. This type of vision continues to define the subject's spatial condition in architecture to the present day.

Thus the first system of architectural values was supplied by an awareness of the subject, received through the viewing of an external object.

The subsequent conditions of value came immediately from Alberti, who wrote in *Della Pittura* that the most important condition for art was its history. From the moment that art needed to establish a relationship with its past, a history had to be fabricated to explain the newly found condition of the subject.

In *De Re Aedificatoria*, a book similar to Vitruvius's *Ten Books*, Alberti presented a categorical treatise outlining the relationships between place, value, and use.

This was elaborated as a temporal evolution throughout the history of architecture, from the Greeks and Romans to the then-contemporary situation in Italy. His arguments immediately became part of architecture's value system as new forms of representation, not so much from nature or from God, but rather from antiquity, now understood as the new history of the subject.

Again referring to Vitruvius, Alberti maintained that a column must not simply be structural but must also appear structural; that is, *firmitas* must constitute the representation of the structure at the same time that it is the structure itself. With this thought, Alberti gave architecture a new type of sign, one that both is and at the same time expresses reflexively the condition of the thing itself.

These conditions of a sign are unique to an architecture conceived within a metaphysics of presence. It is of little consequence that things evolve from one style to another, from the Renaissance to mannerism, from baroque to Victorian, and so on, up to the indefinable position of today. In these representations of the subject-object relationship, the relationships of subject to object, of man to nature, of sign to physical presence have remained essentially unaltered. And, while certain borders may be out-of-focus, the central architectural material remains intact.

In the light of this history and our present condition of supposed change, questions must be asked about today's algorithms. The algorithms imported from the aerospace industry, automobile production, and special effects in film may actually lead to the modification, transformation, and transgression of architecture's nature in a way that questions and makes untenable that nature. Until algorithms are written by architects for architects, there will always be unanswered questions of this kind. Programs such as Alias, Maya, 3D Studio, FormZ, and Autocad all presume certain architectural values.

They contain latent styles and ideologies that powerfully condition each object constructed with them. These styles and ideologies do not necessarily modify or transform the discipline of architecture because they have little knowledge of such an idea. For example, my work on what I call a *Virtual Palladio* discovered the inability of existing software to formally model Palladian rhetoric and principles. Today's softwares make the same mistake as all of nineteenth-centry historiography did: framing and modeling Palladian typology with an ideal spatial structure, which takes such a study further away from what Palladio might have been. Furthermore, to analyze Palladio today is necessarily different from how another author might have worked fifty years ago simply because new conceptual tools are available. Poststructuralism, born out of the search for an *episteme* embracing the analog and digital in information technology and biotechnology, suggested new ways of looking at Palladio.

Therefore, such a study of Palladio today must of necessity be different from that of someone like Rudolf Wittkower. The same problem occurs with contemporary projects.

Most of the architectural CAD programs in use today perform the same operation on any architecture. They take the typological elements of a James Stirling, an Aldo Rossi, a Richard Meier, or a Frank Gehry and reduce them to their simulacrum without articulating the difference between a copy and an original. But this is just one of the conceptual difficulties with today's algorithms. When there are algorithms sensitive to the fact that they are transgressing the existing natures and codes of past architectures, transforming the dynamic between subject and object, the question of value inexorably arises. Then the issue becomes, what in these circumstances gives value to any work?

To address this question, the productions of computer-based techniques need to be located within a critical matrix. Until there is such a matrix, how can we know if the computer is aware of the algorithms we use? How do we know whether we are working on an illustration of architecture or architecture itself? How is it possible to maintain control of our work, and thus a critical consciousness (lacking specifically architecture-based algorithms), faced with the techniques of representation and animation presented by these new media?

Are these new natures truly radical, or is the critical consciousness we bring to these works merely a prejudice based on what we know and like? In other words, are judgments still based on conventional ideas of beauty and classical ideas of frontality, and do virtual matrices really have nothing to do with classical conventions?

Virtuality is one part of an evolving architectural value system, and on this point I am in agreement with Derrick de Kerckhove. Modernism is a past in relation to these new architectural values created by the virtual. In this context, the investigation of the virtual and its theorization become important.

For example, what will it mean to be "lost in space"? Although one can literally lose oneself in the space generated by the computer, I do not have the same sensation of loss in a room with walls. Real space has never been a space of losing one's self, while feeling lost is a potential condition of the virtual world. One of the more interesting questions posed by the virtual is, how is it possible to transfer the sensation of losing oneself from the virtual to real space and time?

Recently I found myself facing the work of a paperless studio at Columbia University with two of my favorite colleagues, Greg Lynn and Jeffrey Kipnis. The studio project proposed a spatial theory that moved the virtual world closer to something that resembles a "jungle." Not a jungle in the literal sense of the word, but a spatial jungle as a basic concept of virtual space. They asked me, as a "classical" architect, to evaluate their ideas. At first I thought, "On what basis can I say something?" Finally I realized that using the jungle as a spatial concept of reference for the virtual seemed a useful metaphor. The students thought they were dealing with a benevolent jungle and were completely enthusiastic about it, but they had not considered the jungle in terms of a type or a set of principles. They did not attempt to define a virtual jungle; they never questioned the value of their concept, what might have created it, and how this new jungle might be organized.

I pointed out that one way to consider the jungle might be as a substitute for a classical labyrinth, only a search for a more complex matrix of evaluation. But in the labyrinth, there is an objective; if we take the wrong direction, we find ourselves in the wrong place. In the labyrinth there is a dialectical relationship between space, time, and goals, and thus values. However, in the jungle there is no dialectic; there is no plane of reference. We cannot distinguish the land from the air, the water, or the depth of limitless space.

Thus the jungle represents a metaphor for the conditions of virtual space. We must understand what kinds of human behavior will exist in the jungle, as opposed to the human in the labyrinth. This means that new rationalities must be formulated, adapted to the type of time-space relationships experienced in the jungle. We must not limit ourselves simply to producing new spatial relationships and images for them.

We must also find a way to theorize work that does not simply lie within the existing algorithms of the computer. Thus the development of such specifically architecturally based algorithms becomes of critical importance.

When the theory of general relativity was formulated, it became clear that time was the fourth dimension of space. Transparency as an architectural paradigm, mentioned by Nino Saggio in regard to the Bauhaus, would not have been possible without such a theory. Later, however, weak points were seen in this theory, and a new theory appeared, developed around quantum mechanics. Quantum mechanics began the postmodern idea of time and space.

In turn, quantum mechanics was replaced by an even more miniaturized morphology, like that of string theory. Today there are computer programs capable of modeling string theory, just as the theories of general relativity and quantum mechanics were modeled.

Since the Renaissance, architecture has confronted scientific and theoretical concepts of time and space, both physical and biological. This is because architecture defined itself with respect to the natural.

When, in the seventeenth century, scientific concepts changed, so did architecture. Today, architecture must again confront another condition of change: a new biology and fluid mechanics. The truth is, none of us, as architects, can examine with any expertise the effects of such scientific concepts when they are imported into architecture.

We use science analogically. Therefore, care must be taken that we are not simply illustrating scientific research in formal terms. Rather, the attempt should be to understand the epistemological problems generated by these changes, from general relativity to quantum and fluid mechanics. In this way it might be possible to understand how to model changes in space and time.

The example of the Guggenheim Bilbao by Frank Gehry is useful in this context. It was partly designed on programs in a CATIA system. There is no question that the work has had an enormous impact on contemporary architecture. But at the same time, one can ask what the time-space differential might be between Bilbao and Borromini. Is there any distance, any transformation? Perhaps Bilbao deals only with the illusion of a change, instead of with real change.

Today we are not looking so much for answers as learning to ask the right questions. Scholars in various disciplines are developing algorithms that deal with new concepts of space-time. While this research may be valuable for architects with respect to solid modeling and animation programs, it only furnishes us with productive stimuli to help us confront our own problems, nothing more.

Equally, movement, say from static to fluid mechanics, has yet to constitute a change in our perspectival system. The new complexities have always existed, repressed within pre-existing conventions. At the same time, the present potentialities provided by the computer also simultaneously repress and hide other operative possibilities. It becomes our task as architects to construct new tools and new algorithms capable of producing the complex environments necessary to our present conditions. Perhaps these are the matrices in the jungle.

CHAPTER 17

TERRAGNI AND THE IDEA OF A CRITICAL TEXT

Written over the course of more than forty years, *Giuseppe Terragni: Transformations, Decompositions, Critiques* is not the book that I would write today. It presents an evolving view of its subject, an amalgam of ideas rather than a consistent point of view. It is also the work of two architects, neither of whom can be called an architectural historian or critic. But the work of both is situated as an attempt to displace their respective architectures from particular historical references and precedents. This displacement raises the idea of the term *critical* in an architectural context. And it is in the context of this term that the distinction between architect and historian is crucial.

17.1 Giuseppe Terragni, Casa Giuliani-Frigerio, Como, Italy, 1939–40. Northwest corner.

The book presents two buildings through parallel and complementary sets of texts. Giuseppe Terragni's architecture may be seen as one, architectural, text, analytical with regard to its antecedents, while my approach is more conventionally analytical. This critique will attempt to examine, briefly, the direction these parallel texts have taken and to address the deviations that have occurred from the anticipated direction. It was originally thought that the conclusions of the analysis of the Casa del Fascio would be reinforced by the analysis of the Casa Giuliani-Frigerio. But the Casa Giuliani-Frigerio resisted the application of the premises of the previous analysis, raising questions about the applicability, in a generalized form, of the analytical process through which the Casa del Fascio was read. As such, differences between the two buildings took on greater significance than their similarities.

In one sense, the Casa Giuliani-Frigerio can be said to represent an inversion of several of the strategies at work in the Casa del Fascio. The essentially frontal aspect of the Casa del Fascio's façades, with their repetitive images and mostly solid corners, is not present in the Casa Giuliani-Frigerio, with its ambiguous and eroded surface fragments that sometimes appear as planar, sometimes as solid, and sometimes as the residue of an initial gridding. Sometimes these readings are best conceptualized from oblique points of view; sometimes the oblique view confounds them. Similarly, the complex but conceptually symmetrical bay organization in the Casa del Fascio—a tripartite system played against a bipartite one—has no direct parallel in the Casa Giuliani-Frigerio, where there is no cohesive, easily discernible formal strategy, even though formal readings are present. The Casa Giuliani-Frigerio

17.2 Giuseppe Terragni, Casa del Fascio, Como, Italy, 1933–36. Southwest facade.

resists simple interpretation and integration; its elements can often be seen as separate, although interdependent, entities. The nature of the Casa Giuliani-Frigerio's façades—the sliding screens, tab ends, and cardboard cutouts—suggests a space made through additive processes rather than something that has been hollowed out and eroded from an original solid. But the fact that its façades mask the interior space rather than reveal its disposition indicates that it is not space that is at issue in this building. Buildings always literally contain space, yet the space in the Casa Giuliani-Frigerio, and to some extent that in the Casa del Fascio, remains strangely unmarked by the buildings' notational systems.

But the Casa Giuliani-Frigerio has to be seen as more than a simple inversion of several of the strategies at work in the Casa del Fascio, for it is not just an inversion that is the significant difference between these two buildings; rather, the consequences of the inversion are important. Compared to the Casa del Fascio, the Casa Giuliani-Frigerio cannot be read in a linear, sequential manner. Its views do not add up to a recognizable series of transformations from some a priori geometry. While traditional architecture tends to be understood sequentially and as an accumulation of perceptions intentionally ordered by an architect, the Casa Giuliani-Frigerio raises the possibility of a different kind of perception, a perception of accretions contingent—as with other buildings—on the physical traversal in and around the building but, significantly, the traversal of a path that is never unique or hierarchical. At the same time, what is perceived in the Casa Giuliani-Frigerio through accretion is not a pragmatic spatiality. Because the architecture itself no longer comprises a coherent image but rather a series of incohering fragments that initially appear to adhere to formal, structural, or compositional logics only to erode at the seeming point of reading, the experience of the viewing sensate subject is no longer the end result of a single—or even multiple—directed reading. In this sense, the Casa Giuliani-Frigerio comes closer to providing a disjunctive, disorienting, and possibly more active cognitive relationship between building and viewer —object and subject—than previous architectures.

As indicated above, the Casa Giuliani-Frigerio can be said to be basically additive, just as the Casa del Fascio is primarily subtractive. But paradoxically, in the sense of its composition, or decomposition, the Casa Giuliani-Frigerio can be read as a subtractive building, an agglomeration of the parts of a complex form, whereas the Casa del Fascio, the compositional strategy of which is essentially subtractive, is linear in its conception and thus could be read as additive. Therefore the Casa del Fascio is subtractive in a physical sense and additive in a conceptual sense, and the Casa Giuliani-Frigerio is physically additive and conceptually subtractive. As analyzed earlier, this oscillation between additive and subtractive is another aspect of the critical nature of the latter building in that no single stable reading results, in that the readings can no longer be traced back to, or derive their meaning from, a single origin. This relates to the post-Kantian idea that the critical involves the uncovering of unconscious repressions always present in some idea of a transcendental origin. In this case, this very lack of stability is seen as being critical in that it posits a less naturalized viewing subject, and a less naturalized object. In this sense, these buildings do not fit comfortably into the category of modernist architecture—they do not adhere to a liberating, utopian discourse. Quite the contrary, they play elaborate games with many modernist precepts and can be seen as offering a different response to the historical conditions surrounding modernist architecture.

In particular, the Casa Giuliani-Frigerio can be seen as both conceptually complex and comprising a distilled collection of disjunctive investigations. These two aspects, the initial state of complexity and a reduction to simplicity, are played out in the architecture as a contradiction that is never resolved. It is an agitated, fractured condition that can never be reduced to a neutral or "zero" condition of origin. It is this quality of indeterminacy that prevents the work of Terragni from being read as nostalgia for a "simpler" past, in the context of the complexities and demands of "modernity." The positionings created for the contemporaneous inhabitant, spectator, or passerby, as well as for political and social institutions in an oblique sense, allow for neither a regression nor an unfettered or naïve progressivism.

The idea—present in both buildings—of a façade masking the interior structure of a building, of the façade and interior space not being interdependently identified, is a major break with the functionalist and cubist traditions that were widely seen in architecture between 1920 and 1940. At that time, with respect to the relationship of outside to inside, the functionalist tradition was concerned on a quasi-moral level with the union of form and function, while the cubist tradition was concerned with the spatial implications of tipping the plan upright, much as in a Paul Cézanne canvas, into an elevational view. These concerns were linked in the work of Le Corbusier and Pierre Jeanneret, particularly in the early houses at Garches and Poissy. The façades of the Casa Giuliani-Frigerio, however, with their ingeniously deceptive references to the interior plans, can be seen as an inversion of the Corbusian synthesis. The façade can be said to have become its own plan. This is different from Le Corbusier's tipping of the plan into the façade of Garches, allowing for a reading of the entire volume and the other three façades from a single viewing. The façades of the Casa Giuliani-Frigerio are plans in the sense that they demand both a reading of their integer relationships as signs and the visual experience of the actual phenomena. When it is no longer possible to link façade articulation with an internal order in a symbolic, iconic, or functional relationship, or with external order with respect to the contextual orientation of other buildings, it can be postulated that these markings have some other value. The effect is to oblige the viewer to read the façades of the building as an index or text of critical, rather than purely functional or formal, notations, which produce not only a challenge to established architectural vocabularies but also suggest the possibility of new ones. It is this challenge that takes the work out of the category of the conventionally formal and places it in the domain of the critical, a domain that is inextricably tied to social, and not purely architectural, references.

The drawings and texts in the book attempt to define the differences between the work of Giuseppe Terragni and other architects of the same historical period, such as Le Corbusier and Mies van der Rohe, in other than stylistic terms. In analyzing the differences within the work of Terragni, this book distinguishes itself from other similar analytical and critical work by such people as Rudolf Wittkower and Colin Rowe. These differences, of which I had been only partly aware when I began my doctoral dissertation in 1961, became a central focus of this book. It was this aspect of the work that led to an inquiry into what is typically understood as formal analysis and formal design, and from there to a general rereading of the formal in architecture. A linguistic analogy, and in particular the idea of a critical text, was engaged to expand the accepted boundaries of the definition of the formal.

While an initial definition of the term *critical* situates the possibility of knowledge as opposed to knowledge itself, an idea put forward in Immanuel Kant's *Critique of Judgment*, it is elaborated upon here not only as the possibility of articulating "in being" that which lies under the appearance of things but also as an internal criticism of architecture itself. This internal critique comes out of an understanding of the unconscious repressions that exist in any of the internal mechanisms of a discourse, particularly in reference to an idea of origins. A critical text therefore makes the subject aware of the unconscious forms of repression that determine consciousness. In this sense, a critical architecture is not merely one that is a manifestation of being or meaning but rather a manifestation of the unconscious relationships that determine being and meaning.

As stated earlier, the Casa del Fascio and the Casa Giuliani-Frigerio can be called examples of critical architectural texts in that the meanings of their façades, plans, and sections can be read as displacements from an architecture of origin, hierarchy, unity, sequence, progression, and continuity to one of fragmentation, disjunction, contingency, alternation, slippage, and oscillation. In this sense the Casa del Fascio and the Casa Giuliani-Frigerio raise questions about their historical status as Fascist architecture, which is in part dependent on an identification, by some historians, with such criteria as classical ordination, monumentality, scale, and other rhetorical devices. The Casa Giuliani-Frigerio is an architecture that communicates ideas, but not primarily by the traditional method of elaborating a simple configuration into a more complex one, or by decorating an enclosure with architectural "warping and woofing." It is not an architecture that is the end product of a process that begins with a simple geometric object. Rather, the Casa Giuliani-Frigerio may be described as the "decomposition" of a hypothetically prior, more complex entity. Its unstable, asymmetric conditions testify to this: an element is registered in relation to a particular configuration in one view, only to be registered to a second and perhaps completely different configuration in another. When an observer attempts to coordinate the second reading with the first, the first falls away, and vice versa. This sets up a condition of oscillating readings as opposed to the alternating readings that were dominant in the Casa del Fascio. The difference between these two types of reading is crucial. In the Casa del Fascio, there are stable readings that alternate from one to the other. In the Casa Giuliani-Frigerio, the constant oscillation between readings never allows for stable readings to fully cohere.

The language of architecture has historically shifted from the culturally contingent to the conventional to the natural. When the language of architecture is understood as natural, the question of the possible is removed, and cultural shifts in architecture are limited. Formal displacements, articulations, and experimentation can be posited as critical in this regard, in that they do not assume that the condition of an architectural language is objectively given but rather that it constitutes a series of unarticulated repressions. Dominant among these is the idea of historical precedent and stable and transcendent origins. The formal can be critical precisely because it operates on the borders of historical precedent. While all architecture engages formal components, the formal is potentially critical when it participates in the invention—or reinvention—of disciplinary languages not simply for the sake of invention alone but as an analytical commentary on disciplinary precedents. While it cannot be said that all formal manipulations are critical, this argument thus raises the question of whether an architecture can be critical without formal manipulations.

In this sense, the two buildings by Terragni would seem to challenge Manfredo Tafuri's assertion that the idea of the critical is always embedded in the concept of history. Establishing an inherent connection between the critical and the historical assumes that architectural language is given or can be fully known a priori. In this context, the potential development of a critical notation as opposed to the gestural—its possibilities—is restricted, since such a view of the historical assumes that the realm of possible repressions is already known. The difference between Tafuri's idea of the critical and the idea of the critical proposed here hangs on this issue.

It is in the context of questioning the assumed natural connection between history and the critical that the architecture of these two buildings in particular should be understood. The idea of the critical as analyzed in these buildings proposes neither a progressivist view of history, as for example was the case with modernism, which was seen to add to the history of architecture, nor a notion of a historical imperative, a view from the zeitgeist. Rather, it is more of a redefinition of the role of history in relation to the processes of design, approached through a strategy of distancing the work in question from any inherent relationship to social and political context while nonetheless highlighting the political and cultural dimension of formal invention.

In essence, then, the idea of critical in this text attempts to open up the question of the language of the formal, to reformulate it through the linguistic analogy of the "text," as a tissue of ever changing traces and interpretations. However, like the terminology of semiology itself—which, among other limitations, leaves out the phenomenal, the physical, and the affective dimensions of signs—my use of the term *text* also has both positive and negative implications. As already indicated, a linguistic analogy shifts architecture in general, and the architecture of Terragni in particular, out of the aesthetic and functional realm by allowing the traditional signs of architecture—columns, walls, windows—to be read as inscriptions, as textual notations, material open to more expanded analysis. At the same time, this work defines what the linguistic analogy of textuality excludes in relation to architecture. The "texts" of practice or analysis manifest the legible dimension of ideas and objects and attempt to link these with preexisting ideas and objects. They are descriptive instruments that share some of the qualities of established methods of using geometry or mathematics to describe architecture. And while the concept of the critical text can be utilized in a manner parallel to the architectural concepts of transposition and transformation that are the objects of its analysis, this methodology often reveals that which refuses to yield to the language of such analysis. The analytical metaphor is less one of enlightenment than one of the revelation of something trapped in a textual net. At best, the analytical work of identifying a critical textuality rescues a building's internal relationships from the mute isolation of a reductive formalism, not in the sense of exposing syntactical rules but by momentarily inscribing conventions, deviations, and reformulations.

What this book also demonstrates is the problem of attempting to articulate the consequences of objects that are also experienced in their physical displacements, the moving in and around of objects and spaces. It demonstrates that the thought processes that make up architecture are not fully transcribed in written or spoken text, and are interdependently displayed through such texts as well as through some forms of physical relationships or specifically architectural data such as drawings or models. This is not to support the resistance to interpretation all too common to the architectural profession. It is merely to suggest that the use of linguistic strategies as an isolated interpretive approach to the field of architecture has significant limitations.

Such limits are indicated by, for example, the movement of one window, the projecting window on the rear façade of the Casa del Fascio, which can be seen as a microcosm of a critical text. This window, which hinges open in a plane parallel to the vertical face of the building, is functionally and visually obscure. It exists both as a textual notation and as an indication of the elusiveness of such a concept to a purely linguistic interpretation. Its significance is accessible only partially through an analysis of the drawings in the context of a linguistic reading, and only partially through a visual and somatic reading. Without an analysis of the drawings, this window can only be read as a "dumb" compositional device. However, as was noted in the analysis of the Casa del Fascio, when the reading of the drawings is compared to the visual and somatic experiences—a somatic reading, as it were, of the building—additional readings accrue. In plan, the Casa del Fascio seems to be a square, and the initial casual experience of the building is as a square. However, an examination of the actual drawn dimensions of the plan reveals that the side façades are slightly shorter than the front and rear façades. And when the one window that does not pivot or rotate diagonally—the one window to puncture an exterior façade plane—is opened outward from the rear façade, the building becomes—at least conceptually—a dimensional square. This can be represented—in a lateral sense—in a drawn plan or section. But the experience of the open window that causes the building to be an actual square cannot be known from its representation on paper or screen. The window's eccentricity, its positioned view from below, the details of its mechanism, the gap that it leaves when it is activated depend on an experiential view. But such a view reveals little of Terragni's play on geometry. There is thus an oscillation between the knowledge offered by the drawing and that available through experience. Both conditions of interpretation are partial, and while they could be said to add up to one unified reading, the fact is that the window itself serves to indicate the difference between the two. It is almost like seeing the virtual points of a space in a mirror, which, while they can be seen and experienced, do not exist as such in "real" space. On the other hand, while the real space seen in the mirror can be measured and conventionally transcribed, the altering mediation of the mirror is not diminished. Terragni's Casa del Fascio and Casa Giuliani-Frigerio are "real" buildings, but they really exist in the mirrors of the many drawings that comprise this book as a work of architecture.

As was asked in the introduction, can it be said that certain types of architecture are more open than others to complex textual readings? Is this quality inherent in the architecture or in the methodology of reading? Unquestionably any building can be read textually through a privileging of, for example, its functional, structural, social, and aesthetic codes. Thus it can be said that all architecture can be read textually. It can also be said that no architecture is more inherently textual than any other. But the thesis posited here is that certain conditions of architecture are particularly open to textual readings that displace canonical interpretations through the use of a primarily formal discourse, defined within the parameters of a historical period. That is, certain buildings loosen the relationships between historical, aesthetic, and functional conventions and in doing so encourage readings that not only entail the internal recognition of such shifts but also displace the conventional notions of reading. Such displacements are here called *critical*.

CHAPTER 18

DIGITAL SCRAMBLER From Index to Codex

In her two essays "Notes on the Index: Seventies Art in America," first published in *October* 3 and 4 (spring and fall 1977), Rosalind Krauss articulated an idea for defining the diverse genres and styles of art in the 1970s. Rightly or wrongly, she defined this idea as an index. This placed art in a context first used by Charles Sanders Peirce to describe the difference between linguistic signs: between symbol, icon, and index. For Peirce, a symbol was an arbitrary and culturally based referent; an icon had a visual similitude to its object; and an index had a physical and temporal relationship to its referents. Like footprints left in the sand suggesting some prior physical presence, indices are physical marks, traces, imprints, or clues concerning some real event rather than a transcendental truth or signified. In this context the index is the trace of a former presence. The index could also be understood to operate like the clues given in a mystery or detective novel, which is the most modern of all literary discourses because it relies on the traces of something prior. The solution to the crime requires a tracing backward to an event and not to some a priori truth; whatever truth may be—that is, who committed the crime—is revealed only in the process of retracing an action or an event that occurred.

Underlying Krauss's invocation of the index was an attempt to explain away one of the major problematics of the poststructuralist era: the metaphysics of presence. That is, many of the formal and pictorial conventions that are sedimented in the arts constitute in most cases their metaphysics. The index then was one way, even if not stated as such, to problematize the metaphysics of presence by moving the art object toward a condition of pure presence.

Minimalism, earth art, and particularly photography were all attempts to empty representation and image of their latent pictorial codes. Presence became the emptier of the metaphysics of presence. For example, when Gordon Matta-Clark sawed a house in half so that it was no longer a functioning house, he attacked not only the metaphysical content of family, the traditions of occupation and function, but also, more important, the form of the house. For Krauss, these cuts are like linguistic "shifters" that empty the house of meaning, because in themselves the cuts have no meaning. The house is no longer a house, but rather an empty presence. No longer did Matta-Clark's house refer to a prior absolute truth or other presence. Rather, it was the site of a simple action, an event which caused such traces to appear.

In a striking difference from the work that preceded it, the art of the 1970s not only emptied out meaning—a relationship to some idea of a transcendental signified, of one object before all other objects—there was also an emptying out of residual pictorial codes, the latent formal manifestations in objects that carry aesthetic information. This emptying out of the pictorial codes is different from what occurred in the abstract expressionism of the 1960s. In this work there was still a pictorial necessity. For example, the picture plane was still active as a datum, as was the edge of the canvas. By the late 1970s, there was a further and important shift in the idea of the index in terms of the photograph. Since the photograph was seen to be a record, and therefore a trace, of some event, it became an operative art condition of the index.

Since then, and partly because of the introduction of digital manipulation in photography, the presence of a photograph as a truthful record of an event has been brought into question.

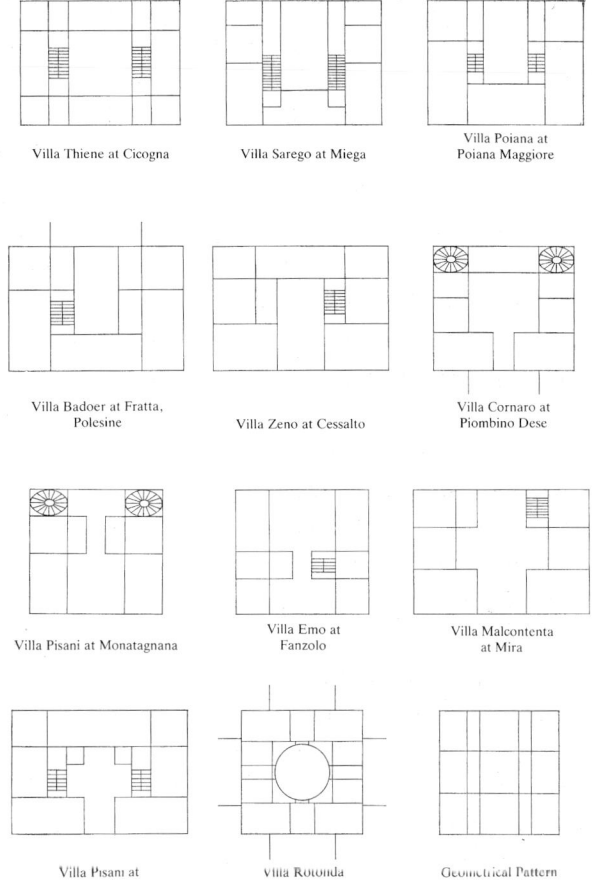

18.1 Rudolf Wittkower, Diagrams of Palladian villas, 1949.

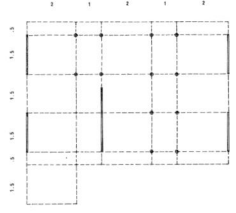

18.2 A Colin Rowe, Analysis of Le Corbusier's Villa Stein, 1947.

18.3 Giambattista Nolli, Map of Rome, 1748.

Previously, a photograph of a painting with a verified author's signature would certify that the photograph was the representation of the real painting. Today photographs can be doctored in such a way that a signature could be either erased or added without such an action being detected. Thus the photograph no longer stands for an index of presence. The photograph is once again an object being manipulated, and therefore no longer empty of value. It is now open to a more problematic internal manipulation. Just as the photograph is no longer necessarily an index to an objective truth, an uncoded message, the index is no longer a way of assuring a condition of pure presence. When a photograph can be digitally altered, the nature of the alteration returns a code (an internal mathematical logic) to the message. These codes depend on an internal logic that is autonomous from both a context and an event.

In architecture after the 1970s and 1980s other problems with the index surfaced. These concerned the nature of its representational or sign function. Architecture, like photography, is different from painting in that it is already an index. Its signs are traces of its own physicality. But architectural signs are also icons. For example, while a column is the sign of a column, its structuring function depends on it looking like a column for its representational function.

In one sense, architecture has always been about codes, whether literally, in building codes, or metaphorically, in classical codes—the rules of proportion and ordination in building systems. These classical codes often went unexamined because they became iconic and conventional. This was thought to be the natural condition of architectural signs, that is, that architecture as commonly understood will always look like architecture —like columns, pediments, bases, etc. In classical ordination, codes were basically a set of rules for the transmission and classification of particular signs, so that those signs could be repeated in different contexts. Proportional conventions were usually measurements of presence and palpable geometries. However, as a series of proportional conventions, classical codes were not generative material, they were proscriptive and still metaphysical.

Many times when an A-B-A or A-B-B-A relationship was used to denote proportional relationships in plans and sections, these notations did not recognize other relationships, such as those of position. Notation was defined by geometric lines rather than by spatial position or relationships. The thicknesses of divisions such as the inner and outer edges of walls were rarely considered. For example, Rudolf Wittkower's famous diagrams of Palladian villas (fig. 18.1) were line drawings that reduced the thickness of walls and their poché to a constituent geometry. In Wittkower's analysis, space was passive—a residual component. Colin Rowe's later analysis of Le Corbusier's Villa Stein at Garches (fig. 18.2) and subsequent urban plans for his book *Collage City* introduced the idea of space, but only as a solid-void, figure-ground, gestalt dialectic, and again not in any way as generative material. Through Rowe, Nolli's map of Rome (fig. 18.3) became a mantra for the New Urbanists' idea of figure-ground as the pictorial frame for a "good plan." However, in the late 1970s, architects questioning the convention of figure-ground began to open up other aspects of the coded conventions in architecture.

Geometry and classical proportions dominated the codes of architecture in the early

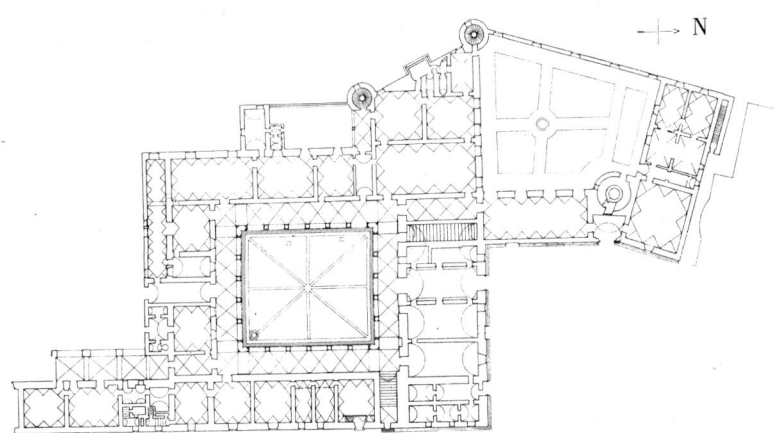

18.4 Luciano Laurana, Palazzo Ducale, Urbino, 1465. Plan.

18.5a–b Luciano Laurana, Palazzo Ducale, Urbino, 1465. Intersection of two columns at courtyard corner.

Renaissance, particularly in the work of Brunelleschi and Alberti. But Alberti began to focus on another problem, one apart from Brunelleschi's attempts to transform a Gothic columnar structure into Renaissance perspectival space. Alberti articulated the wall both as a constructional system and as a conceptual entity. Walls, unlike columns, had no agreed-upon conventions, and geometry replaced classical ordination as a guiding principle in wall building. But walls also have thickness, something Cartesian geometry does not necessarily take into account. For example, in Luciano Laurana's Palazzo Ducale in Urbino, the regular geometric grid that defines the courtyard has an extra dimensional layer (fig. 18.4). This layer, which is outside of the grid, allows for both the thickness of the column and the spatial interval between columns to remain constant. Each façade ends with a column, which in turn produces a third condition, the intersection of two columns at each corner

18.6 Donato Bramante, Santa Maria della Pace, Rome, 1501–04. Superposition of Tuscan and Ionic orders at courtyard.

18.7 Filippo Brunelleschi, Cloister courtyard, Pazzi Chapel, S. Croce, Florence, 1429–61.

18.8 Donato Bramante, Santa Maria della Pace, Rome, 1501–04. Courtyard corner.

of the courtyard (fig. 18.5a, 18.5b). This produces the need for a formal resolution but does not resolve the integration of space and geometry. To consider corners as material being in the fifteenth century also required some form of conceptual, or metaphysical, resolution.

Recognizing this metaphysical problem, Bramante looked at the corner differently than Laurana did at Urbino. He worked toward a certain organicism of presence, an active unity between geometry and space in which the geometric structural grid and the spatial volume had to be one and the same thing, without an extra layer to compensate for the thickness of the wall plane. In Bramante's schema, space is not the passive residue of a gridded courtyard geometry but something coactive as presence with it. There is no gridded band around the space to take up the thickness of the wall. According to classical ordination the spatial interval between columns needed to be maintained, that is, needed to be a datum of equal integers. At the courtyard of Santa Maria della Pace in Rome, Bramante superposed the existing proportions of two orders—the Tuscan and the Ionic—changing both their iconic condition and their conventionally coded relationships (fig. 18.6). This superposition first produced a kind of index from two formerly iconic signs. This was achieved in a modification at the base of the columns at the corner. The resulting corner, however, was neither iconic nor indexical. Rather, in spite of the classical restrictions, the superposition of the Ionic and the Tuscan codes led to something quite startling, something unpredictable, which exceeded both the accidental and the literal corner of the Pazzi Chapel in Florence (fig. 18.7) and the formal corner at the Palazzo Ducale.

The corner at Santa Maria della Pace suggests that the volume of the courtyard produces a vectoral force which is outside of any geometric order, compressing the corner into its resultant material being (fig. 18.8). In one sense, the result is an index of the space acting on the geometry. But since this was, at the time, a singular and unique event in architecture, there is no semiotic or prior historical condition from which to read the index. Rather the corner is the uncovering of an internal possibility of architecture, which, because there is no precedent, acts as a different form of index, that is, as something which could be provisionally called a generative or mutational code; a coded index as opposed to a conventional index.

Instead of referring back to the classical orders, or to a specific event, this unexpected outcome referred internally to its own logic. This logic produced a density that exceeded rather than reduced information, and in that excess produced an effect in the object. This effect produced a new autonomous architectural idea about corners, something between a code and a conventional index.

All architecture has the possibility to be both a code and an index. Because there is no universal iconic sign system in architecture, and since architecture is always a second language, all architectural representation is coded. This concept of a coded index differs from conventional ideas of a code or index of an event because it could be generative rather than regulatory or secretive. Coding as a form of index, upon inspection, reveals something that cannot be seen and thus understood at first sight. This seeing is different from that which is recognized by a formal or pictorial reading of a code. For example, the condition at the corner of the Palazzo Ducale courtyard tells us something about what we actually see: two sides of equal value are joined at the corner. This reading can lead to several interpretations. In the first, the plaza is formed in an additive way, with the side arcades tipped up to form the space. In this case the corner is not thematized but is simply the natural result of the intersection. In a second reading, the doubling of the columns at the corner can be read as thematizing the completion of each side, and thus as articulating the corner in a formal sense. When this is compared to the corner of the courtyard at the Pazzi Chapel, the idea of the formal becomes clear. The corner at Urbino suggests something beyond its literal self—a formal proposition—while the corner at the Pazzi Chapel is simply a literal intersection, nothing more. That the intersection at Santa Maria della Pace seems to suggest the collision or disappearance of matter through some sort of force is only a further instance of the manner in which this corner problematizes conceptions of the formal. In many respects, Urbino and Santa Maria della Pace are similar, but there is an important difference. What is at work at Santa Maria della Pace is neither a conventional code, nor a literal or formal presence. Whereas previous architectural codes dealt only with positive integers—columns, capitals, pediments, etc.—here coding also incorporates space as an active force, the presence, as it were, of an absence. Both the materiality of the arcaded wall and the spatial volume of the courtyard are engaged. The code is read not because of some previous external example but because of an internal superposition of the two orders, which creates a new effect.

The possibility of reading such indices and codes today was preceded by the transition from a purely formal reading to a semiotic one that occurred from the 1960s to the 1980s. Relationships of rectangles and squares were no longer sufficient to explain the complexities that architecture faced. The epistemology that related some stable condition of form to some progressive condition of an ideal universe, seen as some absolute condition, was questioned. Again, in order to overcome its metaphysical connotations, architecture began to be examined as a semiotic system, one without any pictorial or formal conventions. However, any reading of a Bramante or a Palladio that no longer searched for an ideal still had to contend with the aesthetic residue implied in any iconic or semiotic system, which were assumed to be fundamental to any architectural condition. Some historians even argued that the new semiotic systems did not take into account the affects that geometrical relationships and spatial being, that is, height, material, surface, etc., of buildings produce. Similarly, in the limitation of formal analysis, whether proportional or aesthetic, was a latent and perhaps unconscious desire to reduce conditions of complexity to simple geometries, like reducing architectural thickness to simple lines. Through the introduction of different geometries—topological, fractal, etc.—nature is no longer understood as a series of complex forms that can be reduced to simple forms. Rather, all forms can be seen as suspensions of more complex systems—as exemplified by earthquakes, landslides, and tsunamis—whose geometries, like fractals, are not even based on whole numbers. Neither static nor necessarily linear, and seemingly dislocated, they demand other interpretations. How these disturbances of form implicate space might propose what could be called a less motivated object. How such a space becomes coded to produce a less motivated object of space and geometry is a key issue, for it requires different ways of thinking and reading architecture.

As the reading of architecture moved from a formal system to a semiotic one, there was a concurrent movement in the general condition of culture from a technological and mechanical explanation of the world to one that is more biological, in which different conditions of the physical objective world as explanatory models are proposed. This also made it possible to suggest models of explanation other than mathematical, that is, geometric—Platonic and Cartesian or Euclidean—and other than general relativity theory, quantum mechanics, and so forth. For example, difference could be seen as dynamic, as in biological models with organizing principles that no longer required stable, static whole integers.

To open up ways of reading and making architecture is to propose another strategy of reading and another kind of "writing" other than the indexical, one that is no longer defined only by geometric ordering. It requires that semiotic and geometric systems become secondary to ways of producing objects that have more to do with spatial position, superposition, and misreading than with the geometry of the shape. This can also lead to a reevaluation of the work of an architect like Palladio and produce through other readings the revelation of a different writing of space and position.

Historically, Palladian villas have been read in several ways. One, proposed by Palladio himself, is a proportional analysis of the size of a room (fig. 18.9). Other readings look at the villas as variations from an ideal cube. These variations always work from an ideal square in plan. Usually they are read from in front of the steps of a portico to some exterior line in the back, but always within the limits of a square form in plan. Similarly, other readings of the same ideal square can begin at the back and extend to the front. But there are still other ways of reading Palladio that have no relation to the proportions of rooms or to the ideal geometry of a square. One such reading proposes a virtual and fluctuating condition of the volumes of space, as opposed to a literal reading of the lines of a static geometry. A virtual condition in Palladio begins from a symmetrical sequence of spaces, which, reading from front to back, can be coded A-B-C-B-A (fig. 18.10), denoting both positional and functional relationships but not ideal geometric relationships; these integers have no specific shape or proportion. While the volumes of such a virtual villa can be defined by conventional functional terms such as *portico*, *circulation*, and *main space* or proportional or letter distinctions in an attempt to displace the established means of reading, a different notational system or coding can be proposed. The idea of such a coding opens up the Palladian tropes to a notational reading strategy. In this sense, it is possible to look at a building such as the Palazzo Chiericati differently from previous analyses (fig. 18.11).

The Palazzo has two distinguishing characteristics. First, the loggia runs across the full façade and simultaneously acts as a portico. Second, unlike any other Palladian villa, it consists of a series of horizontal layers in plan, parallel to the picture plane. The key to understanding the mutations that occur, like the odd corner condition at Santa Maria della Pace, is the pairs of doubled columns that are compressed together at the center of the front loggia. These suggest a reading of a portico that also is compressed into the loggia, or body, of the building. This can be read as a coded as opposed to a formal relationship of position *A* of the portico and position *B* of the circulation space in a conceptual idea of a villa (fig. 18.12). At Chiericati, the missing portico *A* has been compressed into the transverse circulation space *B* (fig. 18.13). This space is usually between the portico *A* and the dominant major space *C*. The *C*, or main, space is compressed from an ideal centralized form, as if it had been placed in a vise and a pressure applied to it. In Palladio's vocabulary the major space *C* is articulated by a figural *poché* (fig. 18.14). The next layer is a rear circulation space *B*, and then an actual portico *A*. One way to understand Chiericati is to compare it to a mental idea of a villa consisting of a portico, circulation space, main central space, circulation, and rear portico. In a first reading of Chiericati one sees the absence of an actual portico, a loggia for a circulation space, and an implied portico in the rear. Thus any A-B-C-B-A comparison to a conceptual condition includes a virtual *A* at the front and rear. This reading

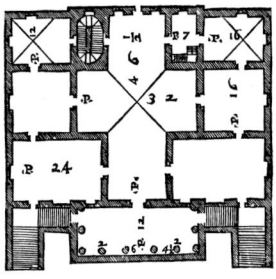

18.9 Andrea Palladio, Analysis of Palladian villa by proportional size of rooms, 1570.

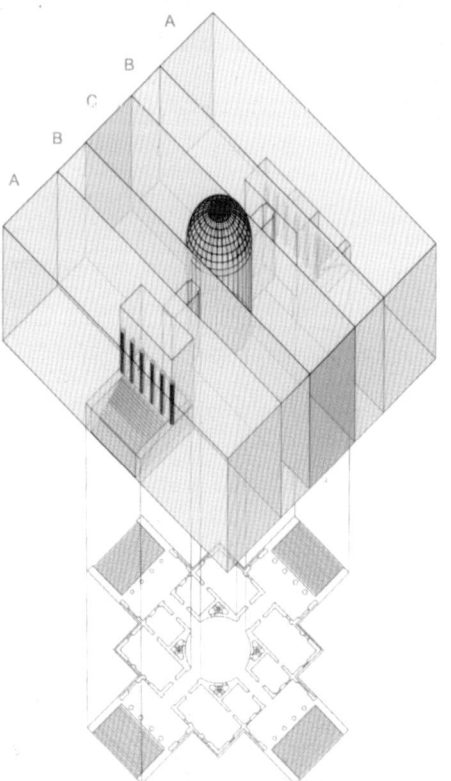

18.10 Peter Eisenman, Diagram of *A-B-C-B-A* analysis of Palladian "virtual villa," denoting positional and functional relationships both front to back and back to front.

DIGITAL SCRAMBLER

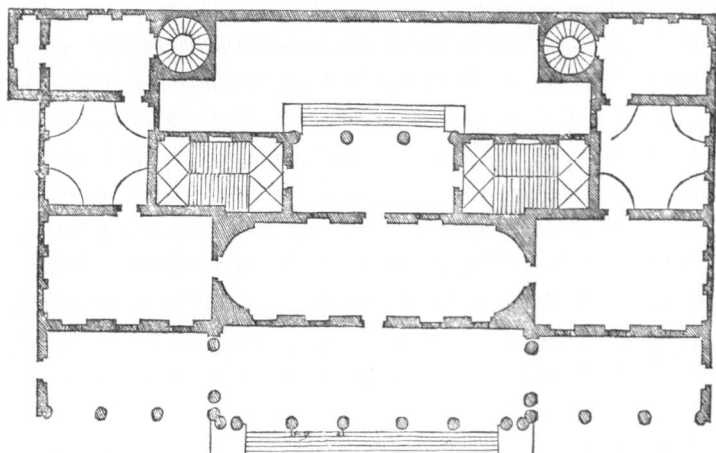

18.11 Andrea Palladio, Palazzo Chiericati, Vicenza, 1550. Plan.

of a hypothetical villa only approximates the real building. Another reading reveals two other virtual *A* conditions: a compression from front to back, and then from back to front. In the first, *A* is compressed over *B*, with the portico and its stairs and columns pressed into the loggia. In the second reading, the portico is pressed into the *B* circulation bay from the rear, leaving a void in the rear yard. This *A* over *B* condition, this compression, creates a conceptual spatial density, which is keyed by the pair of columns in the portico pressed into the second pair of columns. This compression of *A* into *B* results from a spatial force that produces a conceptual density in the condition of space *B*.

This particular coding contains three major characteristics. The first is the relation of the actual components to a conceptual or hypothetical villa. The second is the conceptual density that is then created by the mental superposition of the coded two components, that is, the portico space pressed into the loggia. The third reading is the compression of a hypothetical ideal villa type into a series of linear elements. No one reading is better than or to be preferred over another. Each merely contains different information. These readings fluctuate. If one is taken as a stable or dominant base, the other reading can no longer be sustained. If the second reading is taken as a base condition, the first is no longer possible. The only way to have both is to deny a base condition which problematizes any hierarchical or dialectical reading.

From Palladio's Palazzo Chiericati, it is possible to look at Schinkel's Altes Museum in Berlin, which resembles Chiericati in its overall massing and layering. Here another set of codes is operating, which break from the formal conventions of the neoclassical. A displacement of position creates a different kind of conceptual spatial density. This is initially caused by the unstable location of the dominant spaces, particularly the central rotunda in relation to the exterior enclosure.

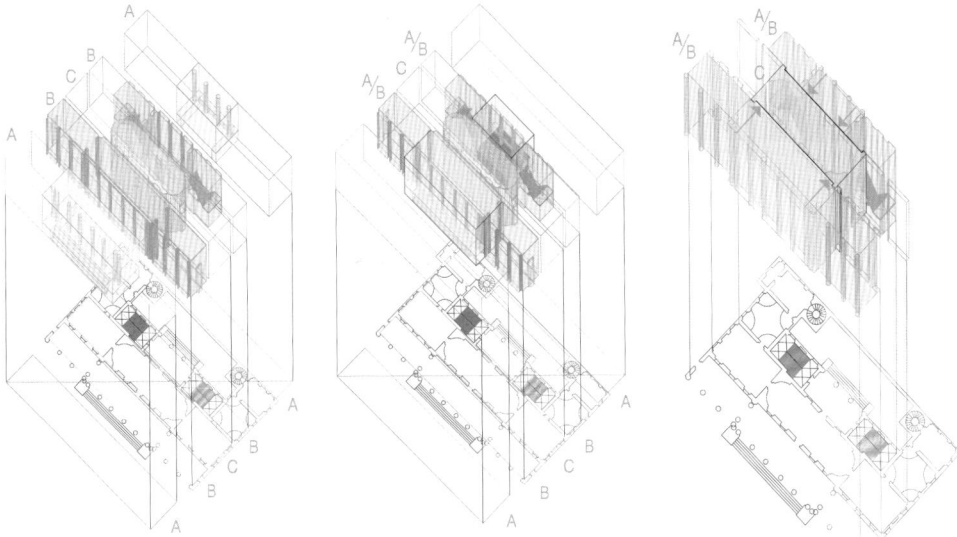

18.12–14 Peter Eisenman, Diagrams of Palladio's Palazzo Chiericati.

While both Chiericati and the Altes Museum have porticos and central ceremonial spaces, and both are layered from the front to the back, each is a misreading of different codes. Chiericati is a frontal, layered Renaissance building. The viewing subject is meant to be centered at the front. Schinkel's building is neoclassical; it is to be seen in a receding perspective from an oblique corner (fig. 18.15). Palladio's work is often seen as the deformation of a nine-square geometric grid; Schinkel's is not. However, by putting them in a similar textual context, it is possible to assign a similar A-B-C-B-A conceptual notation (positional as opposed to geometric, proportional, or dimensional) to both.

On first appearance, the Altes Museum is a cross between Palladio's Villa Rotunda and Chiericati, because Schinkel inserts a central drum into the parallel layers. The drum is bilaterally symmetrical from side to side, but not from front to back. This is the key to a series of internal displacements (fig. 18.16).

The strategies of reading and interpreting provoked by Schinkel's plans are similar to those of reading Palladio. When one condition is assumed to be stable, as in the exterior side façades, which are symmetrical front to back, the asymmetrical location of the major elements of the plan appear to have shifted inside the symmetrical shell. In the plan of the building, the three internal figural volumes—the central drum and two flanking courtyards—are seen as shifted off center from front to back. Alternatively, if these three volumes are seen as stable and centrally located, then the front stoa is seen as something added, as a frontispiece to the building volume. This latter reading confounds the initial reading of the side façades. In a final reading, the drum and the two horizontal bars are themselves seen as shifted to the rear with the addition of the layer of small rooms in the rear of the two courtyards. Notably, the conventions of the symmetry of the traditional neoclassical palazzo are disrupted in these new readings, which again introduce a new idea of coded relationships.

18.15 Karl Friedrich Schinkel, Altes Museum, Berlin, 1823–30.

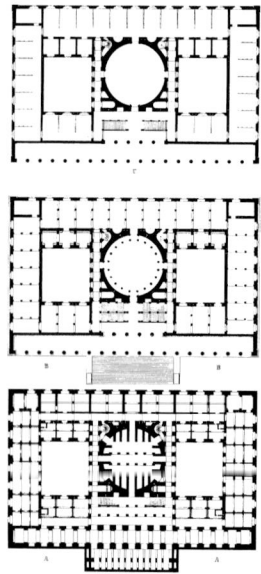
18.16 Karl Friedrich Schinkel, Altes Museum, Berlin, 1823–30. Plans.

The idea of coding as a notation of spatial force and position allows a rereading of the formal in terms of what can be called different textual conditions in Bramante, Palladio, and Schinkel. This kind of reading uncouples the traditional formal relationship of proportional ratio to functional use (both "form follows function" and "form defines function"). It is also possible to take the same idea as a reading and produce a project from it, a project that provokes a writing, that is, provokes the potential generative nature of a coded notation. This idea animated our project for the City of Culture of Galicia in Santiago de Compostela, Spain.

The idea of a *codex* is an important one to locate the theoretical strategy of our project in Santiago, because the word combines ideas of index and code. Originally a *codex* was a Christian manuscript written on leaves of parchment. The word stems from the Latin *caudex*, or wooden stump. Christian manuscripts were written on parchment because both sides of the page could be used, while a papyrus scroll, the traditional form of Hebrew scriptures, could be inscribed only on a single side. By the second century, Christian iconography depicted evangelists holding codices, while Hebrew prophets were shown with scrolls. The introduction of a codex or manual in the secular arts and sciences occurred in the fifteenth century. Among the most well known are the codices of Leonardo da Vinci. Many of Leonardo's codices are written backwards, from right to left, so they can be read only through a mirror, which reverses the text. Acting as a signal that one must read differently, this reversal displaces the established means of reading. This is precisely what a coded index requires, a way of reading differently. Coded indices disperse meaning in such a way that the display of language for itself is questioned.

While traditional codes can be seen as the basis of the pictorial conventions—frontality, edge stress, etc.—that operate in painting, these conventions are almost unknown to most ordinary viewers, although not to serious painters. When codes become conventions they only act on memory, on what has been known in the history of any discipline. Once these codes have become conventions they lose their strangeness. It is this strangeness that differentiates imagination, that is, the possibility of new effects, from memory. In this sense codes operate differently from ordinary language usage (excluding poetic and literary forms) because they have a different interiority, a different relationship of sign to signified. In common language, the sign-signified relationship is supposed to be transparent; in a

DIGITAL SCRAMBLER

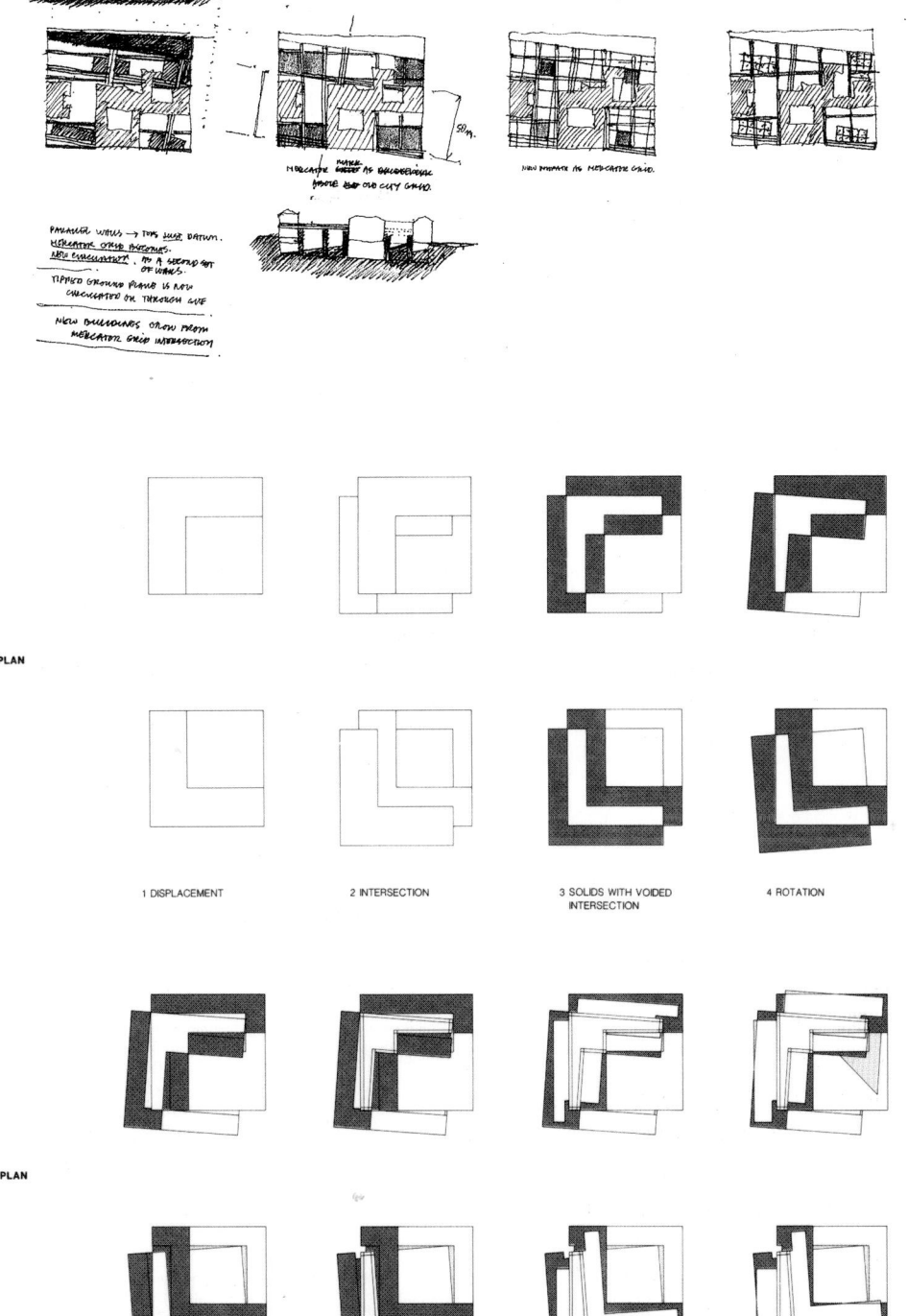

18.17 Eisenman Robertson Architects, IBA Social Housing, 1981–85. Sketch by Peter Eisenman showing superposition of historic Berlin maps.

18.18 Eisenman Architects, Guardiola House, 1988. Trace diagrams.

code like poetry and literature this relationship is more opaque, creating a strangeness in the object and thus questioning familiar conditions of reading.

The use of the word *codex* in the context of architecture and in the particular project at Santiago signals an important shift in our work, from traditional coded conventions to a form of coded index. Much of my own work in the 1970s and early 1980s was an attempt to reduce the classical pictorial conventions of a so-called good plan by also introducing the idea of the index. This work was characterized by ideas of trace, imprint, and superposition. (See *Cities of Artificial Excavation*, 1994.) Most of these projects dealt with two-dimensional traces in plan which, in order to achieve a third dimension, were extruded vertically (fig. 18.17). Only in the case of the Guardiola House (1988) were both imprints and traces attempted in section (fig. 18.18). But in every case this work was marked by the absence of a former

18.19 Eisenman Architects, City of Culture of Galicia, Santiago de Compostela, Spain, 1999–in progress. Site diagram showing layers of historical and topographical information used to generate three-dimensional forms.

presence, through some kind of imprinted geometry; like two halves of a plastic mold, these traces were never spatial in a volumetric sense.

While the project at Santiago begins as a series of plans overlaid as a palimpsest, an archetypal form of an index, these overlays are then extrapolated into a three-dimensional matrix. Whether as a palimpsest, a photograph, or a cut in a building, indices are precise records of former presences (fig. 18.19). At Santiago, the indices become scrambled by a series of deformation and flow lines extrapolated from the original tartan grid.

These lines represent the activity of a new digital—as opposed to analogic—code: a code that scrambles the prior notations. Neither geometric nor planimetric, they are analogous to the strands of the nucleotides of a molecule. As they change spatial position, they change notation. Here they are no longer indices of meaning but schemata of a three-dimensional matrix (fig. 18.20a-e). The generator of the forms is now a torquing digital vector, a scrambler of the superposed grids, which registers something other than an extrusion from the horizontal plane. The resultant matrix is no longer an index of this activity. Because of the scrambler it cannot be traced back to some origin. There is no longer a linear narrative or legibility in presence.

What is created by the force lines in the vertical (third) dimension was something other than a projection or morphing of geometry (fig. 18.21). Any mechanical warping, such

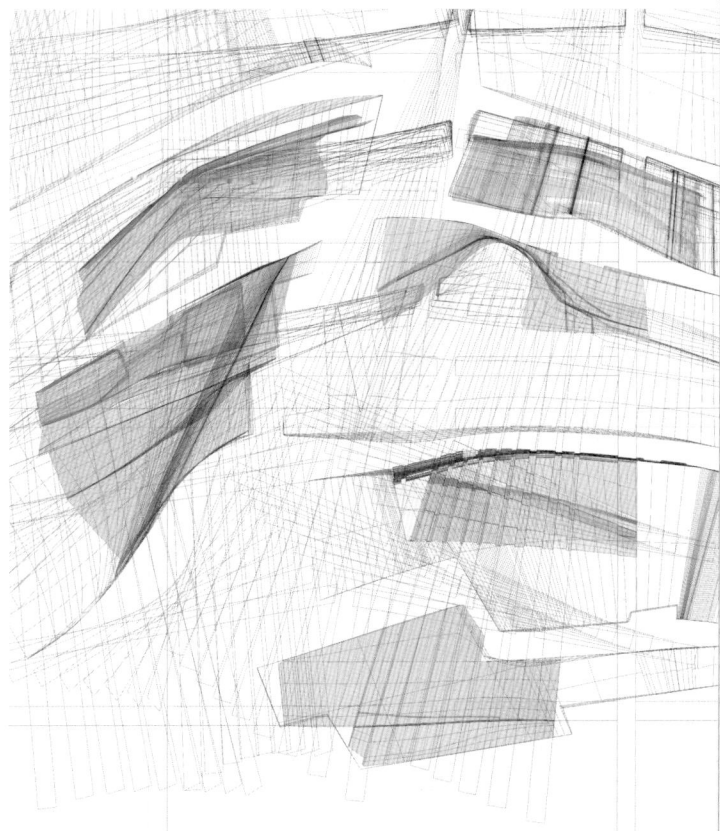

18.20a–20e Eisenman Architects, City of Culture of Galicia, Santiago de Compostela, Spain, 1999–in progress. Deformation diagrams showing how vector lines of force create new interior volumes within exterior forms.

DIGITAL SCRAMBLER

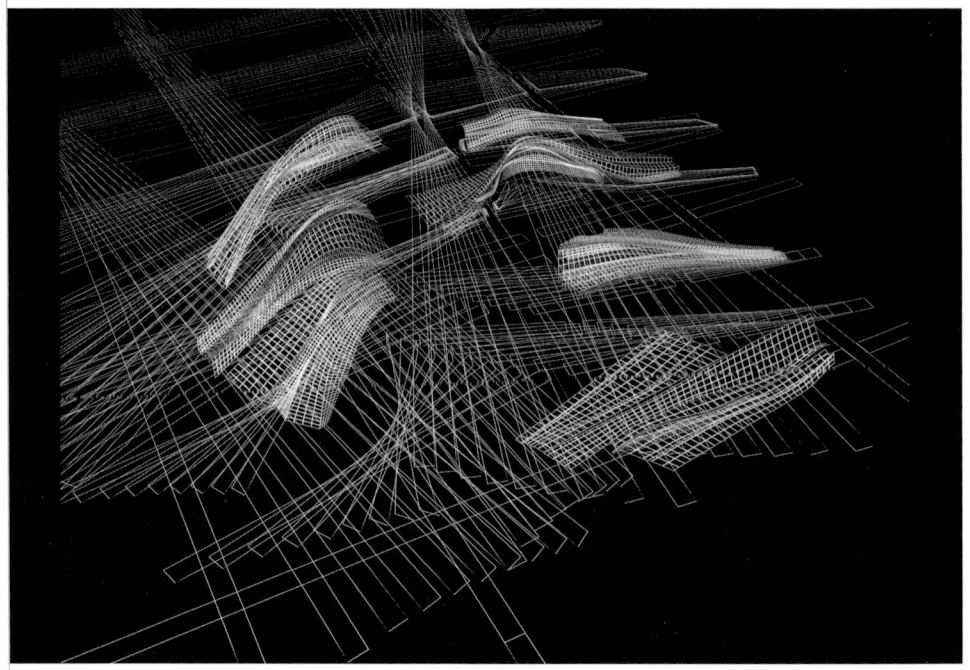

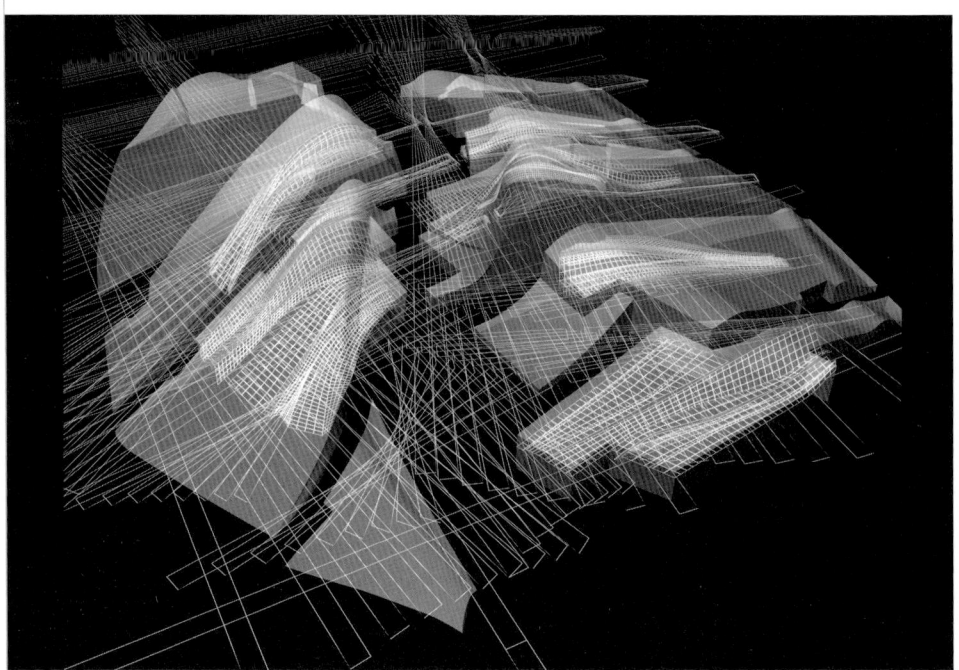

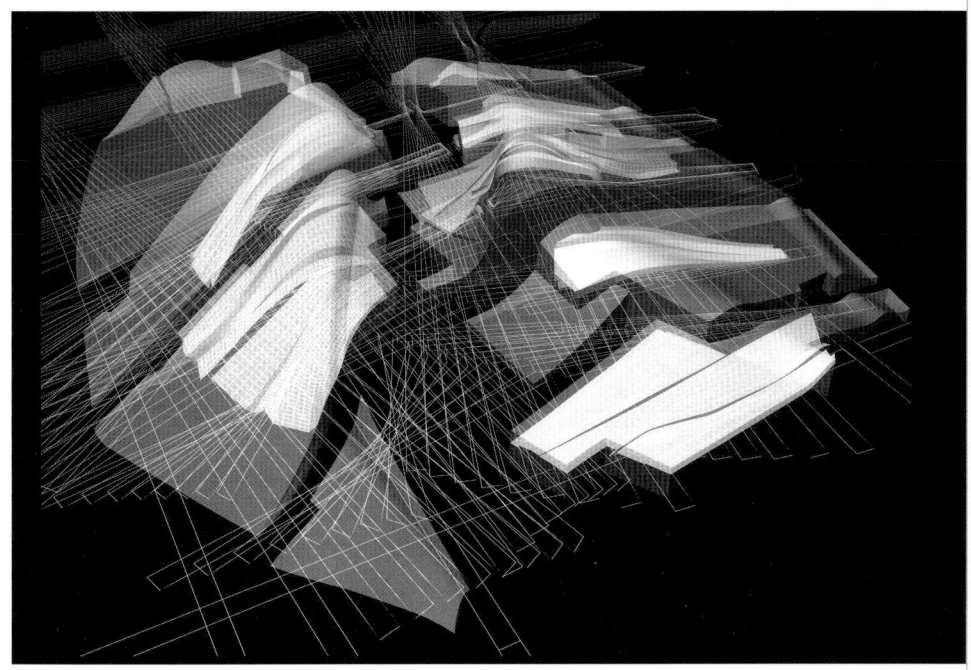
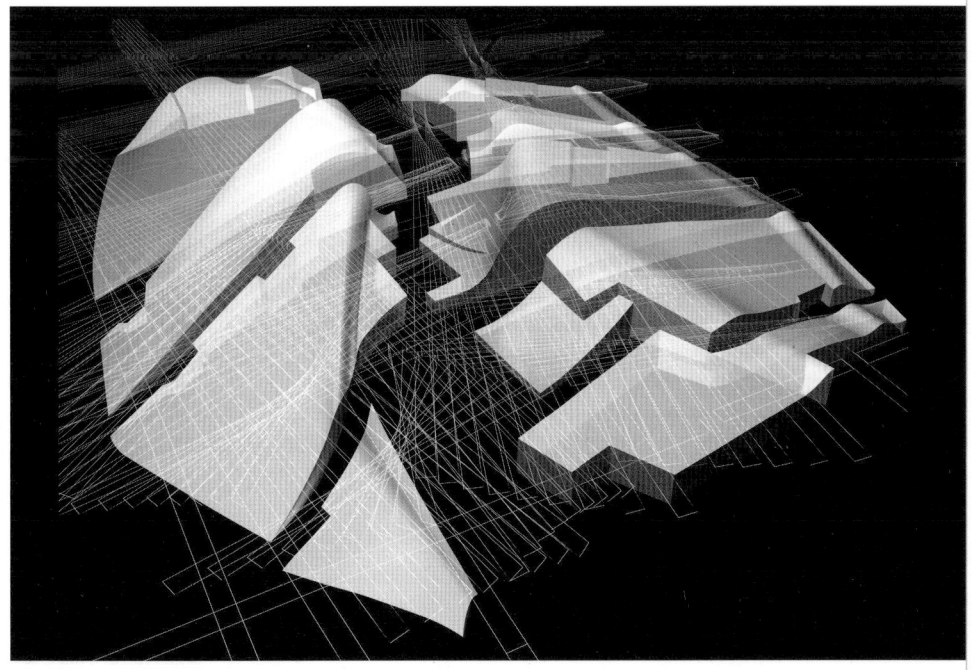

DIGITAL SCRAMBLER

18.21 Eisenman Architects, City of Culture of Galicia, Santiago de Compostela, Spain, 1999–in progress. Competition model, 1999.

as a vertical rotation of the lines, would be no different from a vertical extrusion. These actions, similar to the spatial vectoring of the cortile of Santa Maria della Pace, produced a result that no longer was the outcome of a mechanical process.

It must be understood that grids, endowed with a rationality since the Renaissance, and regulating lines, which have a more metaphysical dimension, are not the same thing. In the City of Culture, the two are combined to produce something that is no longer a geometric grid but is more akin to the organicism proposed by Bramante, in which a geometry of surfaces and spatial flows no longer distinguishes between points, lines, and planes.

In contrast to the proscriptive codes of classical architecture and the Cartesian geometry of modernism, the generative use of geometries today can be understood in the context of developments in our understanding of nature and biological systems. D'Arcy Thompson's *On the Growth of Forms in Nature* was a compendium of organic formal organizations that influenced an entire generation of architects, beginning with Le Corbusier in the 1920s, who saw in these known organizations a natural condition that could be mirrored in man-made forms. Our understanding of nature today no longer conforms to these easily recognizable patterns. Natural organizations such as avalanches and tectonic plates, clouds and coastlines are seen to have dynamic organizations that involve forms in a space-time continuum. These "new natures"—new coded systems that can now be modeled on a computer—form the basic energy behind our project at Santiago. They act both as a substrate for organizing the required elements of the building and, simultaneously, as a codex that requires a reverse reading to a nonexistent origin.

CHAPTER 19

THE WICKED CRITIC

All of us live life but very few have an idea about it.
—Goethe

In the prologue to Goethe's *Faust*, part 1, the Devil makes a bet with God that he can seduce any mortal away from his morality. In the first act the Devil then makes a second wager with the known-to-be-moral mortal, Dr. Faust. He offers Faust the opportunity to do anything he wants, to be the master, as it were, of the Devil himself; but in return, when Faust dies he will go to hell, where the Devil will become his master. Faust is intrigued by this proposal, for while he is a moral man, he is also a person who in life has been unable to act; he has only been able to think about action. Now, because of his bet with the Devil, he believes he can act. This allows him to fall in love with Margarite, a woman he has secretly desired from afar but never pursued. Later, in a garden where he and Margarite become involved, Faust suddenly hesitates; he is incapable of fulfilling his desire. Ultimately the Devil wins his bet not because he takes away Faust's morality but because he is able to lure Faust away from passion itself. The Devil tricks Faust, who assumes that by only thinking about passion he can remain moral. Faust fails to understand that only by being involved with passion itself, that is, living life itself, can the Devil be beaten.

Manfredo Tafuri also made a bet with the Devil. His attempt to beat the Devil lay in his belief that the writing of history, his passion, is also a moral act. To fulfill his passion, Tafuri attempts to define this writing of history as distinct from architecture itself. For Tafuri, if the autonomy of history is not possible, there is no possibility of a difference between the act of architecture itself, its making, and its thinking. Thus architecture becomes his own personal morality play, and history its stage. Tafuri's attempt to beat the Devil will be to define the terms of a history of architecture as distinct from the practice or the act of architecture; to make the history of architecture autonomous from the making of architecture. In this context, history was to become his action. In other words, the bet that Tafuri makes with the Devil concerns whether Tafuri can simultaneously think and act through history. The definition of this autonomy will become central to his passion.

As Faust becomes a surrogate for the Devil, G. B. Piranesi will become the surrogate for Tafuri. In his singular essay "'The Wicked Architect': G. B. Piranesi, Heterotopia, and the Voyage," Tafuri, through Piranesi's projects, outlines several procedures necessary for cutting history, as a separate discourse, from the context of architecture. He recognizes this cutting as double-edged, as having both positive and negative implications. It is thus necessary for Tafuri to introduce the Marquis de Sade into his argument. He cites Pierre Klossowski on Sade: "The worthy philosopher," Klossowski says, "is proud that the fact of thinking is the only valid activity of his being" (46).[1] On the other hand, "The wicked man who philosophizes does not grant to thought any value other than that of favoring the activity of the strongest passion, passion that in the eyes of the well-bred man is always a shortcoming. But if the greater evil lies in concealing the passion under the appearance of thought, the wicked one sees nothing in the thought of the honest man than the covering up of an impotent passion." The implicit suggestion here is that only through negation, as a form of action that might be considered wicked, can thinking as an activity not be deferred from experience but rather become thinking *as* experience. Here the negative as a moral act, as denying the distinction between good and evil, becomes the term of a morality play which for Tafuri frames the autonomous.

Because Tafuri's idea of an autonomous history must deal with writing, it ultimately must confront the question of language and the linguistic analogies in architecture, which for Tafuri, by 1968, had become problematic. Thus, again he cites Klossowski saying, "The traditional language, which Sade uses with impressive force, can easily admit everything that conforms to its logical structure: it undertakes to correct, censure, exclude, and omit anything that would destroy this structure, that is, non-sense. To describe the aberration is to set forth positively the *absence* of elements that make it possible for a thing, a condition, a being, not to be livable. And yet Sade accepts and keeps that logic without question; indeed, he develops it, he systematizes it to the point of violating it. And he violates it by conserving it only to make of it a dimension of the aberration" (47), that is, as the negative of difference. Thus, in order to initially define history as autonomous, Tafuri introduces the negative as a critical difference between writing and acting. The negative creates an initial division between history and discourse.

Sade would be of no importance to us if he had not written about the acts he committed. As an architect, Tafuri seemed incapable of actually making architecture, in physical, concrete terms, and therefore of engaging in the passion of that act. Instead, he deferred and sublimated that action into writing. Looking at Sade helps us, in this way, to explain Tafuri's insistence on the morality of the wicked. Tafuri, who was perhaps tormented by the difference between writing and action, or rather writing *as* action, as architecture, sees that difference as passion itself. For Tafuri, language becomes the possibility of action only when nonlanguage erupts into language, with the possibility of an active negative—that is, when passion and wickedness both enter the experience of language.

Tafuri writes, "In this perspective the wicked architect presents himself as *monstrously virtuous*; the eruption into writing of that which is external to it brings into discourse the category of aberration as an immanent reality" (47). What makes language itself become such a lived experience is the introduction into language of the negative, that is, as the impossibility of experiencing language without its negative other—nonlanguage. When writing introduces the negative into its discourse, it too becomes a condition of lived experience. Without the negative, for Tafuri writing is no longer the possibility of action but separate from it. Throughout history, lived experience was external to writing. The introduction of the negative makes language itself a living condition rather than a description of one. Thus the negative, as in the disjunction of the sign/signified relationship (Tafuri's "silence of the signs"), will be seen as an already existent possibility, an immanent condition within language. This immanence will in turn become a possibility of the autonomy of language itself. Tafuri asks, "How many problems will he encounter in his attempt to close up the difference between the written act and the committed act" (47)? When the written act becomes a committed act, when the committed act and the written act can be seen to exist within one another, rather than as dialectical opposites, a nonlinguistic phenomenon is introduced into language. Whereas writing and nonwriting were dialectical, when writing and action are enfolded within one another, nonlanguage becomes inherent within language, as an already given condition. This is the initial movement toward the development of history as an autonomous discipline.

Throughout his essay, Tafuri uses Piranesi, as is the case in much contemporary European thought, as both an autobiographical mirror/figure and as a way to introduce the possibility of the autonomy of history. He offers Piranesi as a wicked architect "who in the monstrousness of his contaminations, reveals the cracks guiltily repressed by a deviant rigor" (47). Piranesi also represents Tafuri's own attempt to cut history from architecture, specifically in his *Campo Marzio*. Tafuri cites the *Campo Marzio* as presenting an autonomous condition of history by also initially cutting architecture from its linguistic foundations.

Tafuri saw the demand for an unambiguous definition of language in Piranesi's *Campo Marzio* as a paradoxical revelation of its necessary absence. The negation and affirmation of language in Piranesi's work cannot be split apart, yet the *Campo Marzio* contains the impossibility of the synthesis of history and form making. Tafuri writes, "The 'great absentee' from the *Campo Marzio* is language" itself. Pure geometry, as language, confronts experience, the experience of the everyday. This confrontation causes language to be seen as an oscillation between autonomy, that is, the internal disruption of the sign and the signified, and the idea of the sign existing not as pure sign but as a heteronomy that exists within a space-time experience of the subject. Tafuri says that "Piranesi's heterotopia lies precisely in giving voice in an absolute and evident manner to a contradiction: . . . Reason is shown to be an instrument capable of anticipating . . . the monsters of the irrational" (46). In both conditions language is no longer dominant: "The ruthless authority of language is felt in an almost unbearable way by the person who discovers not only its arbitrariness but also its instability." Tafuri's discovery of the ruthless arbitrariness of language is one aspect of architecture's autonomy. In this sense, the *Campo Marzio* represents the absolute disintegration of formal order, of what remained of the humanist *Stimmung*, of its sacred and symbolic values" (38).

The *Campo Marzio* subverts the real dimensions of the buildings, "a truth beyond the real," Tafuri writes. In this sense, Piranesi produces a virtual Rome outside of real time and real space. This document, then, is a useful example for Tafuri for two principal reasons: first, in his montage of actual buildings, fantasy buildings, and buildings moved from their actual sites, Piranesi breaks from archaeology as narrative plan, in real time and space, to one which is disjuncted in space and time, where plan no longer represents a history; second, this disjunction reveals the impossibility of an unambiguous language. Unlike its Italian political associations of *autonomia* in the late 1960s, or Aldo Rossi's use of the term to suggest a typology of historical forms, Tafuri's attempted autonomy of history detaches from the object only those things which are traditionally associated with architecture's history and its nature, that is, the disassociation of those things thought to be understood as the discourse of architecture: function, place, structure, and meaning.

Thus the disarticulation that Tafuri sees in Piranesi presents the negative not as the complexity of a stable language but as an instability inherent in language, that is, as an internal, autonomous condition of language. It is this reading of autonomous, not as a formal autonomy, as in Russian linguistics or in traditional architectural formalism—as form without context and content—but as an attack on the very linguistic basis for architectural thought, that introduces Tafuri's concept of an autonomous history. For Tafuri, it is not form that is to be taken out of context, as was the case with collage and montage, but rather the sign of form that is to be cut from its signified.

Here, Piranesi acts as a sanction for the proposed divorce of architectural signs from their signifieds. This rupture constitutes one aspect of an autonomy, where the possibility of architectural signs to become unmotivated is proposed. In one sense, a zero degree of motivation is problematic in architecture because the internal structure of the sign is different from the linguistic sign. Since the column will always be both the column in itself and the sign of the column, this condition can only be represented as unmotivated. The becoming unmotivated of the architectural sign initially requires a separation between the column's structuring function and its sign function. But only in their becoming can both conditions remain in place and become problematized.

Tafuri reexamines the hermetic, cut-off fragmentation of the architectural order proposed by Piranesi as an example of "the isolation of the elements and their sudden breaking off just where they should confirm the organic connection of the whole" (27). Tafuri sees in this breaking off the moment when history and the nature of the architectural discourse can become detached. For example, Tafuri says that Piranesi no longer founds language on the authority of history but rather in its separation from history. When the sign becomes separated from one of its signifieds, when language is free from the authority of history, this separation imposes itself as an in-progress critique of language itself. It is this evolving internal critique that becomes an important condition of Tafuri's proposed autonomy of history.

Another aspect of the sign/signified rupture evolves from Tafuri's analysis of Piranesi's Collegio Romano. Tafuri says that Piranesi's critique of the sign/signified relationship begins in the Collegio Romano project as a critique of place. The Collegio appears as an organism, as an operating whole that looks like it is centrally and symmetrically organized. In other words, those things that define place—center, symmetry, containment—are all present. While the Collegio Romano has all of these, it signifies none of them. Rather, Piranesi inserts into this construct, which appears to have a centrality, conditions that make this sense of the whole impossible. The Collegio becomes a systematic critique of the concept of center, not in itself but, more important, as a critique of the sign of center. Tafuri suggests that the center of any circle is a sign that may refer to the idea of center, the signified center, or it may just be a literal circle. The Collegio is neither a literal circle nor something asymmetrical because asymmetry would not constitute a critique of the sign of center; it would merely be something that was not centered. Piranesi presents center in the Collegio as the sign of center. Since only the appearance of center is present, the negation of this appearance is the negation of the signified. For Tafuri, this negation leads then to the autonomy of the sign of center.

A further separation of history from discourse in the Collegio Romano is seen in the disruption of the traditional narrative form of architecture. The disruption of a linear or single concept of space and time, that is, a center, also means to disrupt its narrative condition, which in turn disrupts the sign/signified relationship. This is seen in the plan of the Collegio, which becomes distinct from its function simply because one cannot imagine how one could walk through and use the building in any conventional sense. The fact that the Collegio has a programmatic character, that it appears to be functional and thus seemingly tied to content, that is, that it has the illusion of a useful plan, is the sign of a form-content relationship. But if one attempts to reconstruct the Collegio as an operable plan, one finds stairs that lead nowhere and spaces that end abruptly in no exit or have no conceivable means of access; in other words, one cannot move narratively through the plan. The plan as a sign does not connect with its traditional signifieds, such as use or shelter. Thus the Collegio is neither the sign of center nor the sign of a narrative strategy, but in fact becomes the sign of itself, its own autonomous condition, which refers internally to the possibility of an architectural discourse separated from its previous, that is, historical, uses. To change the linear concepts of time and space—the linear meaning of a narrative—is, Tafuri says, to define a new power: "the 'power' . . . of the new techniques—unnamed but lying underneath" (30), that is, autonomous. For Tafuri, the Collegio reveals an interior condition of architectural discourse distinct from its history, an interiority separated from an anteriority, as it were, a separation that was formerly repressed by the traditional linguistic context of the form-meaning relationship. He says that what differentiates Piranesi's design from the abstract designs so customary in eighteenth-century competitions is that its form is abstracted out of context. In modernism, for example, autonomy came to be seen as a form of abstraction; for Tafuri the Collegio was not a collage, an abstract design, but rather a critique of abstraction. In this context, abstraction can be seen to repress the autonomy that lies within the conditions of being within a sign-signified relationship, dominated by a linguistic sign. In this sense the Collegio, rather than extracting sign from meaning, implodes into the sign itself. Implosion is no longer a question of a form taken out of context; rather, the relationship between context and form is obliterated so that form is no longer speaking but becomes, as it were, silent. It is this silence that, for Tafuri, operates metaphorically to signal the rupture with the signified. Tafuri describes this silence as an "excess of eloquence" (53). For Tafuri the question of the excessive does not lead to either a rampant organicism or personal expressionism but rather to an internal void, a void that separates history from the project of architecture.

A third example that Tafuri uses, the rear of the altar of Piranesi's Santa Maria del Priorato, "reveals completely the internal dialectic of Piranesi's virtuous wickedness" (49). Tafuri says, "What is given as *evident*, as an immediate visual stimulus from a *common* point of view," that is, from in front of the altar, "reappears purified, rendered pure intellectual structure, on the reverse side, on the *hidden* side" (49). In other words, the rear side of the altar in its stripped-down geometry appears as a pure sign, as a sign of the rupture of the sign-signified relationship. What the two different faces of the altar of San Basilio propose is the possibility of language being a revelation of its own negativity.

For Tafuri, the theoretical condition of the altar of Santa Maria del Priorato, "the destroyed organicity of space, makes room for the hermeticism of their object void." Space as void becomes an operative as much as form. The altar space becomes the void, the silence, that is, of things without their history. "The isolation of the architectural objects corresponds to the back of the altar of San Basilio. The hermetic muteness of things in themselves by the freezing of their geometric structures" (52).

While the front of the altar of San Basilio is the voluptuous and the excessive, the back is not its dialectical opposite but rather the negative as the void that can be presumed to exist within all presence. It is the autonomous negative preexisting within baroque excess, about which in 1968 Tafuri says, "The desert of the signified once more must be filtered and examined closely" (53). Architecture, unlike language, is not able to produce an autonomy of the sign, a reduction to zero of the symbolic, because the sign cannot be separated from its being. This is a lingering problem for Tafuri's project. Thus in any architectural presence, despite the possibility of the negative—the other of nonpresence—presence still contains a symbolic residue, which perhaps can signify only the announcement of a semantic void. The sign of the void is only the sign and not the fact of history's disengagement from the architectural project.

The year 1968 is often cited as pivotal. It was the year of student riots throughout Europe and the uprisings in American ghettoes. These manifestations represented a new phenomenon: rather than explosions outward against some external force, they were implosions inward, against something lying within. This implosive possibility had been prefigured by two cultural critics. In 1964 Marshall McLuhan had written in *Understanding Media* that because of media, the space and time of the components of systems as we had known them had contracted, causing an internal implosion. Guy Debord noticed a similar phenomenon in his 1967 book *The Society of the Spectacle*. He wrote, "All that once was directly lived has become mere representation."[2] Debord would say that society had become a "shadow reactivity" behind the image of structure—a negative autonomy where the visible negation of life has invented a form for itself.

While architecture has always been sustained by its own internal discourse, these in turn have been influenced by external conditions. Therefore, it is not surprising that at this time, after the publication of these texts, together with Jacques Derrida's *Of Grammatology*, three major architectural texts appeared: Robert Venturi's *Complexity and Contradiction in Architecture* (1966); Aldo Rossi's *The Architecture of the City* (1966); and Tafuri's first major book, *Theories and History of Architecture* (1968). These three books, which would sustain architectural thought almost to the present day, each in its own way reflected the change in the conditions of society and its culture. Each in one way or another reintroduced history as an active condition of the present. But only Tafuri reintroduced history as an agent of radical disjunction. Tafuri's idea of the autonomy of history was presented in the context of the demise of the promise of social utopia in the mechanical-industrial world, which had sustained modernist thought until 1939. By 1968 it was clear that what modernism had projected had not come to pass; that what was seen as radical behavior in the 1920s had in fact been consumed by the very forces and hierarchies of capital that modernism had sought to overcome.

Thus a possible autonomy of history represented, for Tafuri in 1968, a radical incision —into the then-present discourse of architecture. Through a series of contradictions, disjunctions, and disarticulations, it presented history's potential liberation from discourse. While these ideas seem to be similar to Venturi's, Venturi's contradictions were not negations. Rather, they were developed within a preexisting classical language in which contradiction was to be understood as enrichments of that language, as variations on a theme. This is distinct from Tafuri's idea of contradiction and autonomy, where language itself, no longer given as stable, problematizes the possibility of a synchronic discourse between history and the project. While Venturi presumes the stability of language and a continuity in that stability, Tafuri questions the stability of language per se, as a precondition for a bond between history and architecture. Rossi's own introduction of historical types only acted to reinforce continuity with the past rather than act as a rupture between discourse and history.

When Tafuri turned back into history, it was not as a continuing and active struggle with the then-present but rather as a struggle to free history from the internal discourse of architecture. Thus Tafuri uses Piranesi as a way of understanding not so much the eighteenth century as to understand the predicament that Tafuri was facing at the time. His invention of a radical version of Piranesi attempts to theorize the void that Tafuri proposes between history and architecture. What is interesting about Tafuri's invention of Piranesi is that Tafuri uses not a sociopolitical discourse to articulate the void, as might be expected from his political stance, but rather what could be considered a formalist investigation of Piranesi.

Traditionally, one aspect of the history of architecture has attempted to define the normal and the typical. The critical practice of architecture thus had in turn been forced to overcome the forms of what had been theorized and historicized to be normative or natural. Critical architecture has marked the history of architecture through this confrontation. This confrontation always radicalizes what was thought to be normative at any moment in time. Tafuri uses Piranesi not as he was but as an instrument for understanding the radical disjunction that Tafuri was proposing between history and architecture. The fact that this rupture proposed a different idea of architecture's relationship to the social order from what had previously been articulated could be considered a radical gesture. In the early 1970s, Tafuri was searching for a context of behavior not only for himself but also, given the absorption of dialectics and language by capital, for architecture itself. Given the absorptive power of media, a radical difference—the divergence of an accepted history from the nature of architecture—presented one course of action.

After 1968 it was possible to understand the hegemony, the overbearing conditions of both linguistic and visual phenomena, which in a sense repressed other potential autonomous conditions of being. For Tafuri, language became a labyrinth without exits, heterotopia and the voyage locked in a desperate embrace. The Piranesian heterotopia presented a problematic that could never be resolved within the context of a history internal to architecture. This unresolvability confronted architecture with the negative and history with its own autonomous potential. Autonomy was now posited as the unresolvability of that which is dialectical: the negative as an autonomous interiority, "the presence of contradiction as an absolute reality" (54). Tafuri recognized in Piranesi the inherence of the aberrant within the real. The dissolution of form and the void of the signifiers become the negative in itself. The construction of a utopia of dissolved form becomes the recuperation of the negative. In Piranesi's "discovery" of Tafuri, architecture is nothing more than a sign and an arbitrary construction.

In turn, Tafuri's discovery "of the absolute 'solitude' that engulfs the subject who recognizes the relativity of his own actions" (54) is one of the great anticipations of the future that can be identified with Tafuri's work; it is an autonomous history of that future, which is the card that Tafuri played to beat the Devil. A future as a constant becoming rather than being, not an avant-garde of the perpetually new but the becoming of the critical act of an art that "can only destroy itself, and which only by destroying itself can constantly renew itself" (54). Tafuri's autonomous history becomes both the critical, and the wicked, act.

Notes

1. Manfredo Tafuri, "'The Wicked Architect': G. B. Piranesi, Heterotopia, and the Voyage," in *The Sphere and the Labyrinth: Avant-Gardes and Architecture from Piranesi to the 1970s*, trans. Pellegrino d'Acierno and Robert Connolly (Cambridge: MIT Press, 1990), 46–47. All subsequent quotations are from this essay, which is the focus of this analysis. Specific page numbers are noted in the text.
2. Guy Debord, *The Society of the Spectacle*, trans. Donald Nicholson-Smith (New York: Zone Books, 1994), 12.

APPENDIX Letter from Jacques Derrida to Peter Eisenman

My dear Peter,

I am simultaneously sending this letter with the accompanying cassette to Hillis, who was supposed to join us during this seminar. Since he is also supposed to 'moderate' and lead it, but for other reasons as well, Hillis is therefore, along with you, "the first addressee" of these few questions. He is more comfortable in the labyrinth than anyone else, as we all know. For what I am going to say to you will probably reverberate in a sort of labyrinth. I am confiding in the "record" of the voice or of the letter, that which is not yet clear to me and which cannot yet guide my steps toward an exit and hardly towards an "issue." I am not even sure that what I am sending you "stands," that it holds up. But that is perhaps by design —and maybe of the type that I have heard you discuss. In any case, I greatly regret having to refrain from participating in this gathering with you, you both, all of you.

But now don't worry, I will not create a scene. And I am not going to take advantage of my absence, not even to tell you that you may believe in it—in absence—too much. This reference to absence is perhaps one of the things (for there are others) that has most troubled me in your discourse on architecture, and that were it my first question, you can perhaps benefit from my absence to discuss it: absence in general and the role that this word 'absence' could play in what you believed you could *say* if not *do* in your architecture. One could provide multiple examples of this, but I will limit myself to what you say regarding the "presence of absence" in *Moving Arrows, Eros and Other Errors* and regarding the castle of Romeo as "a palimpsest and a quarry." This discourse regarding absence or the "presence of absence" puzzles me, not only because it deploys so many ruses, complications, and traps that the philosopher, particularly if he is a bit of a dialectician, knows too well and fears finding you "caught up in," but also because it authorizes many religious interpretations— if not to say vaguely Judeo-transcendental ideologizations—of your work. I suspect you of having somewhat enjoyed and encouraged these interpretations, even as you discreetly denied it with a smile, ensuring that the misunderstanding remains more or less a misunderstanding. My question has to do not only with absence or the presence of absence but also with God. There—if I did not come, it was not only because I was tired and overworked, "held up in Paris," but precisely to have the opportunity to ask you directly a question regarding God, something which I would never have dared do in Irvine if I had been there in person, but I am glad that this question comes to you by way of this voice, that is to say, on tape. This same question brings up others, a whole group of closely related questions, for example, at the risk of shocking you, whether it concerns houses, museums, or university research labs, what distinguishes your architectural space from that of the temple or a synagogue (by this I mean a Greek word serving a Jewish concept)? Where would be the difference on this matter, if there is one, if there had been one, in your work and in the work of those architects with whom you feel to be in good company? I remain very perplexed by this topic, and if I had been there, I would have been a difficult interlocutor. If you build a religious space, Buddhist, for example, or a cathedral, a mosque, a synagogue (a hypothesis which you are not obligated to accept—but why wouldn't you), what would be your primary concern today? I will allude to the Libeskind project for the Jewish Museum in Berlin. We spoke of it the other morning in New York, but let us leave that aside for the moment.

Naturally, this question also concerns your interpretation of *chora* in "our" "work," if one can say this in quotations, our work "in common." I am not certain that you have de-theologized and de-ontologized the notion of *chora* as radically as I would have expected (*chora* is neither the void, as you sometimes suggest, nor absence, nor invisibility: nor certainly the contrary, which—and this is what interests me—has a large number of consequences). It is true that for me it was easier in a certain way, I did not have to "do" anything and would have been unable to do anything, I mean, for the city of Paris, for La Villette. You see what I mean (and it is perhaps the whole difference between us), but I would like you to say something about it to our friends in Irvine, while speaking to them about the difference in our respective relationships to discourse, on the one hand, and to the function of architecture and its realization on the other. Take advantage of my absence to speak freely. Well, don't just say anything, since everything today is "recorded," and memory, which is always the same, is no longer the same, I will know all that you will have said publicly. I had the feeling, and I think you mentioned it here or there, that you found me too reserved in our "choral work"—a little bit absent, in short, entrenched in discourse, without obliging you to change, to changing places—in sum, not disturbing you enough. This is no doubt true, and there would be much to say on this subject, which is complicated, because it is that of place (*chora*) and displacement at the same time. If I had come, I would perhaps have spoken of my own displacement in the course of the "choral work," but here it is you who should speak of it. So tell me, if, *after* Choral Work (as you yourself said at Irvine in the spring), your work effectively took a new direction, what indeed happened? What did this time mean for you? This history? How would you define or match it? When did we really begin to work together, if we ever did, on this Choral Work, which is not yet built but which we see and read about everywhere? When will we stop?

This brings me directly to the next question, which also concerns a certain absence. Not mine today at Irvine, where I would have so much enjoyed seeing you and other friends—especially as I was one of those who organized this gathering (and thus ask you to excuse my absence and to have the others also pardon me)—but absence like the shadowed sound of the voice—you see what I mean by this. What relationship (new or archi-ancient, different in any case) does architecture, yours in particular, maintain, or should maintain, with the voice, with the capacity of the voice, but also with the telephonic devices of all kinds which structure and transform our experience of space on a daily basis? It is a question of a phone call—almost immediate, of course, *virtually* immediate I would stress, but also the vocal recording, as in the case here, incorporating the gap in time which this presumes and establishes simultaneously. If one can imagine an entire labyrinthian history of architecture guided by the braided thread of this question, where would one—and you—stand today and tomorrow? This question of history, like the history of making space, like the spacing of time and the voice, cannot be separated from the history of visible (immediately mediated), that is to say, from the entire history of architecture; which is so great that I would not even dare to touch on it, but I will "address" this question, as you say in English, through economy and through metonymy in the form of a single world, glass (*glas, glass*).

And what is there of glass in your work? What would you say about it? What would you do with it? How does one talk about it? In terms of its optical or tactile qualities? (Speaking of tactility, it would be good if—to add to what we were discussing the other morning in New York—you spoke to our friends of the erotic ruses, the appeal to desire, or dare I say the "sex-appeal" of the architectural forms which you invent, with which you work, to which you submit. Whether these directions are new or not, is this seduction a supplement, into the bargain, like a "bonus of seduction" or a "bonus of pleasure"? Or is it essential? Is it rather that the bonus *itself* is essential? But then what is the bonus itself? A reward? What is, for the author of *Moving Arrows, Eros and Other Errors*, the relationship between the bonus and the rest, amidst the calculations and negotiations of the architect? Could you elaborate on that, as my American students sometimes ask me so disarmingly?) I return to my question after this long parenthesis regarding your desire, from which my question on glass may not be so far off. In what terms does one discuss glass? In terms of technology and materials? Economic terms? Urbanism? Social relations? In terms of transparency and immediacy, of love or supervision, of the potentially effaced boundary between public and private, etc.? And further, "glass" is an old word, and if I think that you are interested in glass, that you may in fact appreciate it, am I mistaken? Or is it only a matter of new materials which resemble glass but aren't glass any longer, etc.? Before letting you discuss glass, I would remind you of one of Benjamin's texts, *Erfahrung und Armut, Experience et pauvreté*, with which you are certainly familiar (it also concerns architecture and was published in 1933, which is not just any date in Germany or elsewhere). I will cite only that which our friends would certainly like you to comment on:

"But Scheerbart—to return to him—places the greatest importance to lodging these people, and following their model, their fellow citizens are lodged in apartments corresponding to their status: in glass houses, mobile and sliding, of the type that Loos and Le Corbusier have constructed. It is not an accident that glass is so hard and smooth a material that nothing can cling to it. It is also a cold and sober material. Things made of glass do not have an 'aura' (*Die Dinge aus Glas haben keine 'Aura'*). Glass is generally the enemy of secrecy; it is also the enemy of possession. The great poet André Gide once said, 'Everything which I want to possess becomes opaque to me.'"

(Here we return then to the question of desire and glass, the desire of glass; I had tried elsewhere to trace this experience of desire as the experience of glass in Blanchot, notably in *La Folie du Jour* and *L'Arret de mort*.)

"Do people like Scheerbart dream of glass buildings (*Glasbauten*) having recognized a certain new poverty (*Bekenner einer neuen Armut*)? But perhaps a comparison here will reveal more than the theory. When one enters a room from the eighties, and despite the 'comfortable intimacy' (*Gemütlichkeit*) which reigns therein, perhaps the strongest impression one has is: 'You have nothing to look for here.' You have nothing to look for here because there is no ground here upon which the inhabitant would not have already left a trace: by the knickknacks on the mantle, by the doilies on the upholstered armchair, by the sheer curtains at the window or even by the screen in front of the fireplace. A saying of Brecht's is useful here: 'Erase the traces!' (*Verwisch die Spuren!*), reads the refrain of the first poem of the *Anthologie pour les habitants des villes*... Scheerbart and his glass, and the Bauhaus and its steel have opened the way: they created spaces in which it is difficult to leave traces. 'After all that has been said,' declared Scheerbart twenty years later, 'We can surely speak of a "culture of glass" (*Glaskultur*). The new environment of glass will completely change man. And the only thing left to hope for now is that the new glass culture will not encounter too many opponents.'"

What do you think, Peter, of these propositions? Would you be an "opponent," a partisan, or, as I would suspect but am perhaps mistaken, neither one nor the other? In any case, could you say something about it and why?

This text of Benjamin's literally addresses, as you saw, a "new poverty" (homonym, if not a synonym, of a new expression, of a new French concept, designating an errant mass of poor, indeed of the "homeless," irreducible to categorization or classification and to long-standing marginality or of the social ladder: the low income, the proletarian class, the unemployed, etc.). And the new poverty of which Benjamin speaks, none other, should be "our" future, already our present. From this fascinating text, so politically ambiguous and which should not be fragmented further, I would extract this passage as well:

"Scheerbart is interested in the question of understanding what our telescopes, our airplanes and our rockets do to men of the past, in transforming them into entirely new creatures, worthy of being noticed and admired. Furthermore, these creatures already speak in an entirely new language. And what is Decisive (*das Entscheidende*) in this language, is the tendency towards an Arbitrary Construct (*zum willkürlichen Konstruktiven*); a tendency which opposes the organic. It is because of this tendency that the language of men, or rather, people like Scheerbart, cannot be mistaken for any other, for these men object to this principle of humanism that calls for interaction among men. Even in their very names. . . Poverty of experience (*Erfahrungsarmut*): one must not understand by this that these men desire a 'New Experience.' No, they want to be freed from experience, they desire a world in which they can recognize their poverty, externally and also internally, in a manner that is so pure and distinct that something fitting emerges. And they are not always ignorant and inexperienced. One could say the contrary: they have 'stuffed themselves' (*gefressen*) with all of that: 'culture' and 'mankind' to the point of being sated and tired. . . We have become impoverished. Of the heritage of humanity, we have abandoned one part after another, and we have pawned it at the mount of piety of one hundredth of its value, in order to receive as an advance a few coins of the 'Present' (*des Aktuellen*). In the door stands economic crisis, beyond that a shadow of approaching war. To hold on today has become the business of a small number of powerful people, and God knows if they are not more human than the majority, for the most part more barbarous, but not in the good sense (*nicht auf die gute Art*). Others, meanwhile, have to start over another time with Little. They relate it to the men who have created the Fundamentally New (*das von Grund auf Neue zu ihre Sache gemacht*), founded on understanding and renunciation. In its buildings (*Bauten*), its paintings, and its histories, humanity prepares itself to survive (*überleben*), if necessary, culture. And most important, humanity does this while laughing. Perhaps this laugh sounds barbarous. Good (*Gut*). Since he who is alone (*der Einzelne*) at times brings to this mass a humanity which, one day will be returned to him with interest." (trans. Ph. Beck et B. Stiegler).

What do you think of this text, Peter, in particular of poverty which should not allow another to be forgotten? What do you think of these two barbarities that must not be confused and, as much as it is possible—is it possible—not be allowed to contaminate each other? What do you think of what Benjamin calls here the "present" and of his "currency"? What, for you, would be the "good" barbarity in architecture and elsewhere? And the "present"? I know of a present which you do not want, but what ruptures most effectively (today? tomorrow?) with this present? And would you remove architecture from the measure of man, from his scale even, how do you understand this "destructive" in Benjamin's sense, discourse in the mouth of "these people [who] object to this principle of humanity that calls for [architecture's] correspondence with humanity. Even by their very names"?

Therefore, Peter, I would like, and your audience at Irvine, I imagine, would perhaps like to hear you speak about the shift in the relationship of architecture today and poverty, all poverties, that of which Benjamin speaks and the other, between architecture and capitalism (the equivalent today of the "economic crisis" of the 1930s "*in der Tür*," "in the doorway"), between architecture and war, today's equivalent to the "shadow" and of that which "comes" with it), the scandals of public housing, "housing" in general (without forgetting that which we discussed, you and I, and which is a little too complicated for a letter, of the habitable and the inhabitable in architecture), and the "homeless" and "homelessness" today in the United States and elsewhere.

This letter is already too long. I shall speed up a little to touch on other questions linked to what was written above. I cited these texts by Benjamin, among other reasons, to lead you to ruin and destruction. As you know, what he says regarding the "aura" destroyed by glass (and by technology in general) is articulated in a complex discourse on "destruction." On the other hand, in the *Trauerspiel* (and surely elsewhere but I have forgotten where), Benjamin speaks of ruin, notably of the "baroque cult of the ruin," "the most noble material of the Baroque." In the photocopied pages which I have enclosed, he declares that for the Baroque, "the antique heritage is comparable, in each of its components, to the elements from which they concoct a new totality. No, they *build* it, for the complete vision of this new thing is this: the ruin . . . the work affirms itself as a ruin. In the allegorical edifice of the *Trauerspiel*, these ruined forms of the salvaged work of art clearly have already come unfastened." I will not comment on the Benjaminian concept of the ruin, which is also the concept of a certain mourning in affirmation, indeed the salvation of the work of art, but I will use it as a pretext to ask you this:

First, is there a relationship between your writing on the palimpsest, your architectural experience of memory (for example, in Choral Work but also elsewhere) and "something" like the ruin which is no longer one thing? And what would you say—and would you even say it—is your calculation, reckoning of memory not Baroque in this Benjaminian sense, despite certain appearances? Second, if all architecture is finished, if it carries within itself, each time in an original style, the traces of its future destruction, the future anterior of its ruin, if architecture is haunted, that is to say, marked by the spectral silhouette of this ruin, at work even in its base of stone, in its metal or glass, what brings the architecture of "these times" (just yesterday, today, tomorrow: use whatever words you may, modern, postmodern, post-postmodern or a-modern, etc.) back to the ruin, to the experience of "its own" ruin? In the past, the major architectural achievements incorporated their essential destructability, even their fragility, even as a resistance to destruction or like a monumentalization of the ruin itself (the Baroque, according to Benjamin). A new image of ruin has come to trace itself in the design of architecture which we would like to recognize as that of our present day, of our future, if one can still say that, in the design of your architecture, in the future anterior of its memory just as it is designed or calculated already, just as it leaves its future trace in your projects. Considering what we said above regarding Man (and of God), will we be able to speak of the "memory of man," as we say in French, for this architecture? In relation to the ruin, fragility, destructibility, and therefore to the future, could you return to what we were discussing the other morning in New York regarding excess and "weakness"? Each time that excess presents itself (but it never presents itself except in the context of ontological oppositions), I myself hesitate to employ words of force or weakness. But it is certainly inevitable once this has presented itself. This is nothing more than a pretext for you to discuss this, you and Hillis.

Finally, from fragility I would turn to ashes, the other name for me of the essence (not the essential) of the step, of the trace or of writing, the nonplaced place of deconstruction. That is where it is written. (In *"Feu la Cendre,"* forgive this reference from almost twenty years ago—this conception of ashes, like the trace itself, was notably destined or rather submitted to the "total fire" and to the "holocaust." To retrace our steps, and to hear once again the fragile words "fragility," "ashes," "absence, "invisibility," of "Jewish" or not "Jewish" architectural space, what do you think of the "Berlin Museum Competition," which we also discussed the other morning in New York? In particular, what do you think of the words of Libeskind, the "winner" of the "competition" as printed in a recently published interview with him in the journal of Columbia's architecture school? I will just cite it here:

"And in turn, the void materializes itself in the space outside as something that has been ruined, or rather as the solid remainder of an independent structure, which is a voided void. Then there is a fragmentation and a splintering, marking the lack of coherence of the museum as a whole, showing that it has come undone, in order to become accessible, functionally and intellectually. . . It's conceived as a museum for all Berliners, for all citizens. Not only those of the present, but those of the future and the past who find their heritage and hope in this particular form, which is to transcend passive involvement and become participation. With its special emphasis on housing the Jewish Museum, it is an attempt to give voice to a common fate—to the contradictions of the ordered and the disordered, the chosen and the not chosen, the vocal and the silent. In that sense, the particular urban location of Lindenstrasse, of this area of the city, becomes the spiritual site, the nexus, where Berlin's precarious destiny is mirrored. It is fractured and displaced, but also transformed and transgressed. The past fatality of the German Jewish cultural relation to Berlin is enacted now in the realm of the invisible. It is this invisibility which I have tried to bring to visibility. So the new extension is conceived as an emblem, where the invisible, the void, makes itself apparent as such. . . . It's not a collage or a collision or a dialectic simply, but a new type of organization which is really organized around a void, around what is not visible.

And what is not visible is the collection of this Jewish Museum, which is reducible to archival material, since the physicality of it has disappeared. The problem of the Jewish Museum is taken as the problem of Jewish culture itself—let's put it this way, as the problem of an avant-garde of humanity, an avant-garde that has been incinerated in its own history, in the Holocaust. In this sense, I believe this scheme joins architecture to questions that are now relevant to all humanity. What I've tried to say is that the Jewish history of Berlin is not separable from the history of modernity, from the destiny of this incineration of history; they are bound together. But bound not through any obvious forms, but rather through a negativity; through an absence of meaning and an absence of artifacts. Absence, therefore, serves as a way of binding in depth, and in a totally different manner, the shared hopes of people. It is a conception that is absolutely opposed to reducing the museum to a detached memorial."

Once again the void, absence, negativity, in Libeskind as in your own work. I will let you figure this out by yourself, dear Peter, dear Hillis, I will tell you what I think some other time, but I suggested what I think at the beginning. I have again spoken too much, and naturally, I take advantage of my absence, I'll admit it, as a sign of affection. Excuse me, Hillis and you, and ask our friends, your audience, to excuse me for not being there to speak with them and to listen to you.

With affection, Jacques

P.S.1. This cassette was recorded and transcribed when I read, at the conclusion of an interview (in the special edition of the Spanish journal *Arquitectura* [270] on "Deconstruction" — that is the title of the introduction) these lines of yours which already anticipated my questions: "I never talk about deconstruction. Other people use that word because they are not architects. It is very difficult to talk about architecture in terms of Deconstruction, because we are not talking about ruins or fragments. The term is too metaphorical and too literal for architecture. Deconstruction is dealing with architecture as a metaphor and we are dealing with architecture as a reality. . . . I believe Post-Structuralism is basically what I mean by Post-Modernism. In other words, Post-Modernism is Post-Structuralism in the widest sense of the word." I think that I do not believe any of these statements, any of these 7 phrases, not 1, not 2, not 3, not 4, not 5, not 6, not 7. But I cannot explain that here and I, really, I never talk much *about* Deconstruction. Not spontaneously. If you wish, you can demonstrate 1, 2, 3, 4, 5, 6, 7 in front of your audience, try to convince them in refuting contrary propositions, or just let this postscriptum drop.

P.S.2. I forgot the fundamental question, of course. In other words, that of the foundation, of what you do at the foundation of the foundation, or at the foundations of your architectural design. Let's talk about the center of the earth even. I questioned you directly on God and Man. I'm thinking here of the Sky and the Earth. What is architecture, and first of all your own, supposed to see and do with *experience*, that is to say, with the voyage opening well beyond the earth? If we do not renounce architecture, and I believe that we do not

APPENDIX

renounce it here, what are its effects on the very "design" of terrestrial architecture, today, of this possibility? Of this definite possibility from now on of leaving the terrestrial soil? What would we say of the architecture of a rocket and that of aeronautics in general (already touched on by literature, well before becoming "effective") that it dispenses with the idea of foundations and therefore of "standing," "of the "standing up," of "standing up," of the vertical stance of man or building in general? Or do these architectures recalculate foundations and does the calculation remain a terrestrial difference—which I doubt somewhat? What would be an architecture which, without standing and without holding up, in a vertical fashion, does not yet fall into ruins? How are all of these possibilities and even these questions (those of holding up, holding together, standing—or not) registered if you think that they can be? What traces are already left in what you are currently building on the earth, in Spain or in Japan, in Ohio, in Berlin, in Paris, and tomorrow, I hope, in Irvine?

SELECTED BIBLIOGRAPHY Writings of Peter Eisenman, 1990–2004

1990

"Post/El Cards: A Reply to Jacques Derrida." *Assemblage* 12 (August): 14–17.

"The City as Repressed Text." *Tefchos*, no. 4: 60–63 (Greek and English).

1991

"Strong Form, Weak Form." In *Architecture in Transition: Between Deconstruction and New Modernism* (Munich: Prestel), 33–45 (German and English).

"The Author's Affect: Passion and the Moment of Architecture." In *Anyone*, edited by Cynthia Davidson (New York: Rizzoli International), 200–11.

"Unfolding Events: Frankfurt Rebstockpark and the Possibility of a New Urbanism." In *Unfolding Frankfurt* (Berlin: Ernst and Sohn), 8–17 (German and English).

"Viel/Faltig/Field/Feld." In *Frankfurt Rebstock Competition, Architecture and Urbanism (A+U)*, no. 252, September, 16–18 (Japanese and English).

1992

"K Nowhere To Fold." In *Anywhere*, edited by Cynthia Davidson (New York: Rizzoli International), 218–27.

"Oltre Lo Sguardo: L'Architettura nell'Epoca dei Media Elettronici [Visions' Unfolding: Architecture in the Age of Electronic Media]." *Domus* 734, January: 17–24 (Italian and English).

"The Affects of Singularity." *Architectural Design* 62 (November/December): 51.

1993

"Folding in Time: The Singularity of Rebstock." *Folding in Architecture: Architectural Design Profile* 102: 22–25.

"People Who Live in Glass Houses Should Not Throw Stones." In *Color of an Architect: Peter Eisenman, Haus Immendorff* (Hamburg: Artfound Print Co. and Hamburg: Galerie für Architektur Renate Kammer und Angelika Hinrichs), 2–11.

1994

"Confronting the Double Zeitgeist." *Architecture* 83, no. 10 (October): 51, 53, 55.

"Not the Last Word: The Intellectual Sheik [Colin Rowe]." *Any* 7–8: 66–69.

1995

"Critical Architecture in the Geopolitical World." In *Architecture Beyond Architecture*, edited by Cynthia Davidson (London: The Academy Group Ltd.), 78–82.

"Figuring the Ground." *Newsline* 8, no. 2 (November/December): 5, Cover.

"M Emory Games." in *M Emory Games: Emory Center for the Arts* (New York: Rizzoli International and Harvard University Graduate School of Design), 58–59.

"Presentness and the Being-Only-Once of Architecture." In *Deconstruction is/in America*, edited by Anselm Haverkamp (New York and London: New York University Press), 134–48.

1996

"Architecture in a Mediated Environment." In *The Idea of the City*, edited by Robin Middleton (London: Architectural Association), 56–63.

"Estrategias del signo: Giuseppe Terragni y la idea de un texto crítico [Terragni and the Idea of a Critical Text]." *Arquitectura Viva* 48 (May/June): 66–69 (Spanish and English).

"Formar lo poscrítico: arquitectura, función y significado [Forming the Postcritical]." *Arquitectura Viva* 50 (September/October): 17–18 (Spanish and English).

1997

"Autonomy and the Avant-Garde: The Necessity of an Architectural Avant-Garde in America." In *Autonomy and Ideology: Positioning an Avant-Garde in America*, edited by Robert E. Somol (New York: Monacelli Press), 68–79.

"Processes of the Interstitial: Notes on Zaera-Polo's Idea of the Machinic." *El Croquis: Peter Eisenman 1990–1997*, no. 83: 21–35 (Spanish and English).

"Separate Tricks." In *Chora L Works*, edited by Jeffrey Kipnis and Thomas Leeser (New York: Monacelli Press), 132–36.

"Written Into the Void." Manuscript, distributed at the MAK, Vienna, during the exhibition "Peter Eisenman: Barefoot on White-hot Walls," December 2004–March 2005.

"Zones of Undecidability: The Interstitial Figure." In *Anybody*, edited by Cynthia Davidson (New York: Anyone Corporation and Cambridge: MIT Press), 240–47.

1998

"Diagram: An Original Scene of Writing." *Any*, no. 23, 27–29.

"Zones of Undecidability: The Processes of the Interstitial." In *Anyhow*, edited by Cynthia Davidson (New York: Anyone Corporation and Cambridge: MIT Press), 28–35.

1999

"Diagrams of Anteriority." In *Diagram Diaries* (New York: Universe Publishing), 36–43.

"Diagrams of Interiority." In *Diagram Diaries* (New York: Universe Publishing), 44–93.

"Diagrams of Exteriority." In *Diagram Diaries* (New York: Universe Publishing), 164–209.

"The Diagram and the Becoming Unmotivated of the Sign." In *Diagram Diaries* (New York: Universe Publishing), 210–15.

"Time Warps: The Monument." In *Anytime*, edited by Cynthia Davidson (New York: Anyone Corporation and Cambridge: MIT Press), 250–57.

2000

"Autonomy and the Will to the Critical." *Chien chu*, no. 42 (November): 58–63.

"The Specter of the Spectacle: Ghosts of the Real." In *Anymore*, edited by Cynthia Davidson (New York: Anyone Corporation and Cambridge: MIT Press), 174–80.

"The Wicked Critic." *Any* 25–26: 66–70.

2001

"Mies and the Figuring of Absence." In *Mies in America*, edited by Phyllis Lambert (New York: Harry N. Abrams Inc.) 706–715.

2003

"A Matrix in the Jungle." In *The Charter of Zurich*, edited by Furio Barzon et al. (Basel: Birkhäuser), 28–37.

"Blurred Zones." In *Blurred Zones: Investigations of the Interstitial, Eisenman Architects 1988–1998* (New York: Monacelli Press), 6–9.

"L'ora che è stata." In *Metafisica*, edited by Ester Coen (Milan: Electa), 98–104 (Italian).

"Terragni and the Idea of a Critical Text." In *Giuseppe Terragni: Transformations, Decompositions, Critiques* (New York: Monacelli Press), 295–301.

2004

"Coded Rewritings: The Processes of Santiago." In *CodeX: The City of Culture of Galicia*, edited by Cynthia Davidson (New York: Monacelli Press), 27–35.

"Digital Scrambler: From Index to Codex." *Perspecta* 35: 40–53.

SOURCES

SOURCES

Ch. 1: "Post/El Cards: A Reply to Jacques Derrida," *Assemblage* 12 (August 1990): 14–17.

Ch. 2: "The Author's Affect: Passion and the Moment of Architecture," in *Anyone*, ed. Cynthia Davidson (New York: Rizzoli, 1991), 200–11.

Ch. 3: "Unfolding Events: Frankfurt Rebstockpark and the Possibility of a New Urbanism," in *Unfolding Frankfurt* (Berlin: Ernst and Sohn, 1991), 8–17.

Ch. 4: "The Affects of Singularity," *Architectural Design* 62 (November/December 1992): 42–45.

Ch. 5: "Folding in Time: The Singularity of Rebstock," *Columbia Documents of Architecture and Theory: D* 2 (1993): 99–111. (Reprint of "Folding in Time: The Singularity of Rebstock," in *Folding in Architecture: Architectural Design Profile* 102, ed. Greg Lynn [London: Academy Group, Ltd., 1993], 22–25).

Ch. 6: "Vision's Unfolding: Architecture in the Age of Electronic Media," in *The Invisible in Architecture*, ed. Ole Bouman and Roemer van Toorn (London: Academy Editions and Ernst and Sohn, 1994), 144–49. (Reprint of "Oltre Lo Sguardo: L'Architettura nell'Epoca dei Media Elettronici" [Vision's Unfolding: Architecture in the Age of Electronic Media], *Domus* 734 [January 1992]: 17–24).

Ch. 7: "Presentness and the Being-Only-Once of Architecture," in *Deconstruction is/in America*, ed. Anselm Haverkamp (New York and London: New York University Press, 1995), 134–48.

Ch. 8: "Processes of the Interstitial: Notes on Zaera-Polo's Idea of the Machinic," *El Croquis: Peter Eisenman 1990–1997* 83 (1997): 21–35.

Ch. 9: "Separate Tricks," in *Chora L Works*, ed. Jeffrey Kipnis and Thomas Leeser (New York: Monacelli Press, 1997), 132–36.

Ch. 10: "Written into the Void," Manuscript written in 1997 and distributed at the MAK, Vienna, during the exhibition "Peter Eisenman: Barefoot on White-hot Walls," December 2004–March 2005.

Ch. 11: "Diagram: An Original Scene of Writing," in *Diagram Diaries* (New York: Universe, 1999), 26–35.

Ch. 12: "Autonomy and the Will to the Critical," *Assemblage* 41 (2001): 90–91. (Reprint from *Chien chu*, no. 42 [November 2000]: 58–63).

Ch. 13: "Mies and the Figuring of Absence," in *Mies in America*, ed. Phyllis Lambert (New York: Harry. N. Abrams, 2001), 706–715.

Ch. 14: "Blurred Zones," in *Blurred Zones: Investigations of the Interstitial, Eisenman Architects 1988–1998* (New York: Monacelli Press, 2003), 6–9.

Ch. 15: "L'ora che è stata," in *Metafisica*, ed. Ester Coen (Milan: Electa, 2003), 98–104.

Ch. 16: "A Matrix in the Jungle," in *The Charter of Zurich*, ed. Furio Barzon et al. (Basel: Birkhäuser, 2003), 28–37.

Ch. 17: "Terragni and the Idea of a Critical Text," in *Giuseppe Terragni: Transformations, Decompositions, Critiques* (New York: Monacelli Press, 2003), 295–301.

Ch. 18: "Digital Scrambler: From Index to Codex," *Perspecta* 35 (2004): 40–53.

Ch. 19: "The Wicked Critic," *Any* 25–26 (2000): 66–70.

Appendix: Jacques Derrida, Letter to Peter Eisenman [October 12, 1989]. Trans. Sarah Whiting. *Assemblage* 12 (August 1990): 7–13 (Translation revised in 2006 by Ariane de la Belleissue Lourie.)

INDEX

INDEX

Adami, Valerio, 5
Adorno, Theodor, 101
Alberti, Leon Battista, xi, 114, 122, 137
Allen, Woody, 110

Bacon, Francis, 118–119
Benjamin, Walter, 21, 28, 43–44, 98, 101, 109, 163–166
Bergson, Henri, 81
Bernini, Gian Lorenzo, 118
Blanchot, Maurice, 7, 10, 41, 163
Bramante, Donato, xiii, xxii, 104, 105, 117, 138–139, 144, 150
Braque, Georges, 117
Brunelleschi, Filippo, 36, 117, 121, 137–138
Bryson, Norman, 36

Cacciari, Massimo, 101–102
Cézanne, Paul, 129
Chomsky, Noam, xi
Cohen, Jean-Louis, 78

de Chirico, Giorgio, 116–118
de Kerckhove, Derrick, 123
Debord, Guy, 157
Deleuze, Gilles, 13, 15–16, 28–29, 37–38, 41, 51, 56–57, 61–62, 69, 70, 81, 90
Derrida, Jacques ix, xii–xiv, xviii, xxvii, 1–5, 43–47, 68–69, 72, 75, 78, 80, 82–83, 85, 91–94, 97, 114–116, 118, 157, 160, 167

Eisenman, Peter, vii–xv, xvii–xxiii, xxv, xxvii, 5, 48–49, 51, 72, 141, 143, 145–147, 150, 160–161, 164–165

Forster, Kurt, 88–89
Foster, Hal, 101, 106
Foucault, Michel, 89, 91, 109
Frampton, Kenneth, 105–106
Freud, Sigmund, xvi–xvii, xx, xxiii–xxiv, xxvii, 76, 80, 92, 94
Fried, Michael, 46, 118
Fuller, Buckminster, 115

Gasché, Rudolph, 82, 84–85
Gehry, Frank, 123–124
Giacometti, Alberto, 107

Goethe, Johann Wolfgang, 152
Greenberg, Clement, xv, xvi, 117
Grimm, Jacob, 80
Guattari, Félix, 51, 56–57, 59, 62, 66–67, 69–70

Heidegger, Martin, 68, 83, 101, 115
Heizer, Michael, 37
Hoffmann, Josef, 80
Honnecourt, Villard de, 89
Husserl, Edmund, 115

Jameson, Fredric, 121
Jay, Martin, 36
Jeanneret, Pierre, 129
Jung, Carl, xx, 78

Kant, Immanuel, xvi, 93, 96, 129
Karatani, Kojin, 23
Kipnis, Jeffrey, 96–97, 119, 123
Klee, Paul, 106–107
Klossowski, Pierre, 152–153
Kraus, Karl, 80
Krauss, Rosalind, xi, xiii–xvii, 43, 46, 97, 106, 114–115, 118, 134

Lacan, Jacques, xvi, xxiii, xxvii, 36
Laurana, Luciano, xiii, 105, 137–138
Le Corbusier, xxii, xxv–xxvii, 26, 48, 66, 77, 89, 102–105, 121, 129, 135–136, 150, 163
Leibniz, Gottfried, 15–16, 28–29, 36
Leonardo da Vinci, 144
Levinas, Emmanuel, 115
Libeskind, Daniel, 45, 161, 166–167
Loos, Adolf, 66, 80, 101, 163
Lynn, Greg, 115, 123
Lyotard, Jean-François, 80, 84

McLuhan, Marshall, 157
Massumi, Brian, 56
Matta-Clark, Gordon, 118, 134
May, Ernst, 14
Meier, Richard, 123
Melville, Herman, 82, 84, 86
Michelangelo, 47
Mies van der Rohe, Ludwig, 9, 100–107, 129
Moretti, Luigi, 116
Morris, Robert, 37

Nietzsche, Friedrich, 13
Nolli, Giambattista, 135–136

Palladio, Andrea, 45, 88, 122–123, 139–144
Peirce, Charles Sanders, 134
Picasso, Pablo, 117
Piero della Francesca, 117–118
Piranesi, Giambattista, 36, 45, 81, 84, 152, 154–156, 158–159
Plato, x, 75
Poe, Edgar Allan, 73
Pollock, Jackson, xiii–xv, xvii, 43, 119
Proust, Marcel, 81, 84, 86

Rembrandt, xxv–xxvi, 45
Rossi, Aldo, x, 98, 116–117, 123, 154, 157–158
Rowe, Colin, 77, 105, 129, 135–136

Sade, Marquis de, 152–153
Saggio, Nino, 124
Sartre, Jean-Paul, 36
Schinkel, Karl Friedrich, 142–144
Serlio, Sebastiano, 88
Serra, Richard, xv, 101, 107
Smithson, Robert, 37
Somol, Robert, 90–92, 96
Stirling, James, 123

Tafuri, Manfredo, 80, 98, 101–102, 130, 152–159
Terragni, Giuseppe, viii–ix, xv, 116, 126–132
Thom, René, 14–17, 40
Thompson, D'Arcy, 121, 150
Tschumi, Bernard, xiii, 77

Venturi, Robert, x, xxvii, 157–158
Vitruvius, 43, 122

Wittgenstein, Ludwig, 80
Wittkower, Rudolf, 88, 123, 129, 135–136
Wolfflin, Heinrich, 61

Zaera-Polo, Alejandro, 50–51, 62, 70
Zevi, Bruno, 101–102